International Business English

Communication in English for business purposes

D0120836

Student's Book

Leo Jones
Richard Alexander

Ernst Klett Verlag für Wissen und Bildung
Stuttgart · Dresden

Cambridge University Press

Published by the Press Syndicate of the University of Cambridge
The Pitt Building, Trumpington Street, Cambridge CB2 1RP
40 West 20th Street, New York, NY 10011, USA
10 Stamford Road, Oakleigh, Melbourne 3166, Australia

© Cambridge University Press 1989

First published 1989
Fourth printing 1992

Printed in Great Britain at
the University Press, Cambridge

Werkübersicht	
ISBN 3–12–502750–0	Student's Book
ISBN 3–12–502770–5	Workbook
ISBN 3–12–502760–8	Teacher's Book
ISBN 3–12–502780–2	Set of 3 class cassettes
ISBN 3–12–502790–X	Set of 2 self-study cassettes
ISBN 3–12–502751–9	Video VHS PAL
ISBN 3–12–502752–7	Teacher's Guide (to the Video)

Beratende Mitwirkung an diesem Werk und Wortschatzbearbeitung:
Peter Kirchhoff, Fachbereichsleiter Fremdsprachen an der Volkshochschule
Wuppertal, Landesprüfungsbeauftragter für das Volkshochschul-Zertifikat
English for Business Purposes in Nordrhein-Westfalen

2. Auflage   2 7 6 5 4 | 1995 94 93 92

Alle Drucke dieser Auflage können im Unterricht nebeneinander benutzt werden,
sie sind untereinander unverändert. Die letzte Zahl bezeichnet das Jahr dieses
Druckes.
© dieser Ausgabe: Ernst Klett Verlag für Wissen und Bildung GmbH, Stuttgart 1990.
Alle Rechte vorbehalten.
ISBN 3-12-502750-0

Contents

Thanks

In preparing this book we've had generous help and advice from a large number of teachers and business people: our thanks to all of them.

In particular, we'd like to thank the following for their assistance during the research for this book, for using and evaluating the pilot edition and for contributing detailed comments and suggestions:

Sue Gosling
Lesley Stéphan in Lyon
Sandra Bennett-Hartnagel at Hewlett Packard in Böblingen
Pauline Bramall-Stephany at Braun AG in Karlsruhe
the British School of Monza
Business English Programmes in San Sebastian
CAVILAM in Vichy, France
the staff of Calor S.A. in Lyon, France
the English School of Osaka
Christine Frank at Sennheiser in Hanover
Eileen Fryer
Stephen Hagen at Newcastle Polytechnic
International House Executive Courses in London
ITCS 'Dell'Acqua' in Legnano, Milan
ITCS PACLE 'G.Maggiolini' in Parabiago, Milan
Christine Johnson
Peter Kirchhoff
Des O'Sullivan
PERKS Enseñanza de Idiomas in Barcelona
Francis Pithon of SETARAM in Lyon
Nic Underhill
the VHS Language Centre in Nuremberg.

RA would also like to thank Gerlinde for her support and sustenance while the book was being written.

Last but not least, special thanks to Peter Donovan, Peter Taylor and Avril Price-Budgen for their patience, good humour and expertise whilst *International Business English* was being planned, written, recorded and edited – and to Derrick Jenkins who brought us together, and encouraged and helped us throughout the project.

Vorwort

International Business English ist ein Lehrwerk für Lernende, die im Wirtschaftsleben tätig sind und Englisch im Beruf verwenden müssen. Ebenso eignet es sich für erwachsene Lernende, die am Ende ihrer Ausbildung in Wirtschaft und Handel tätig sein werden.

Der Begriff *Business English*

- Obgleich man einen bestimmten Teil des englischen Wortschatzes als *Business-* oder Wirtschaftsvokabular bezeichnen kann, ist dennoch ein großer Teil dessen, was man als Wirtschaftsenglisch bezeichnet, nichts weiter als 'normales' Englisch, das in wirtschaftlichen Zusammenhängen angewendet wird. Wirtschaftsenglisch ist also keine Spezialsprache. Das Lehrwerk bietet eine Fülle von Geschäftsanlässen und Situationen als Grundlage für gezielte Übung. Sie erweitern Ihre Englischkenntnisse, gewinnen mehr Selbstvertrauen und können sich letztlich flüssiger und präziser ausdrücken.

Aufbau und Inhalt des *Student's Book*

- In den *Units* 1–4 werden Grundkenntnisse des Wirtschaftsenglisch vermittelt. Diese Kenntnisse werden in den nachfolgenden *Units* gefestigt und erweitert. Lernende, die im Beruf schon Englisch verwenden, werden wahrscheinlich eine kürzere Bearbeitungszeit für die ersten *Units* benötigen als Lernende, die noch keine Erfahrung auf diesem Gebiet haben.
- Hauptbestandteil der *Units* 5–14 sind integrierte Aktivitäten. Diese bauen auf den Grundkenntnissen auf, die in den ersten vier *Units* vermittelt wurden. Jede *Unit* behandelt ein zentrales Thema. Dazu werden eine Fülle weiterer wirtschaftsbezogener Fertigkeiten eingeführt und geübt.
- In *Unit* 15 werden Fertigkeiten und Kenntnisse wiederholt und gefestigt, die in den vorausgegangenen *Units* behandelt wurden. Den Rahmen hierfür liefert ein detailliert angelegtes Planspiel mit realistischen Aufgabenstellungen in den Bereichen Lesen, Hören und Schreiben sowie Besprechungen/Konferenzen und Entscheidungsfindung.
- Am Ende des Buches (Seite 195) befinden sich die sogenannten *Files*. In einigen Aufgabenstellungen des *Student's Book* wird auf eine bestimmte *File* verwiesen. Dort erhält der Lernende eine Information über die Rolle, die er zu spielen hat. Der jeweilige Partner wird auf eine andere *File* verwiesen, so daß beide unterschiedliche Informationen haben und somit eine realistische Informationslücke besteht. Und wie in einer realistischen Geschäftssituation müssen beide Partner spontan auf das reagieren, was sie als Information erhalten haben, bzw. auf das antworten, was der Partner sagt.

1

Aufbau und Inhalt der *Units*

- Zu den Aktivitäten der *Units* gehören Aufgabenstellungen in den Bereichen Lesen, Hören und Schreiben. Außerdem gehören dazu: Diskussionen, Problemlösungen und Rollenspiele. Die Rollenspiele (Symbol: [💃]) sind ein wesentlicher Bestandteil dieses Lehrwerkes, ebenso das Üben und Durchspielen von Telefongesprächen (Symbol: [☎]). Die meisten Aktivitäten sind für Partnerarbeit oder Arbeit in Kleingruppen gedacht, damit jeder Lernende möglichst häufig teilnehmen kann.

- Die wichtigsten Begriffe der englischen Wirtschaftssprache werden immer im Kontext (durch Texte, Anweisungen und Übungen) eingeführt. Im *Workbook* wird dieses Vokabular zusätzlich wiederholt.

- Das spezialisierte Wirtschaftsvokabular wird durch Wortschatzübungen eingeführt. Hierbei ist zu beachten, daß jeder Industriezweig (manchmal sogar jeder einzelne Betrieb oder jede einzelne Abteilung) über eine eigene Fachsprache verfügt. Diese sehr speziellen Fachsprachen werden nicht durch den Wortschatz des Lehrwerkes abgedeckt.

- Die wichtigsten Problembereiche der englischen Grammatik werden in einem Grammatikteil behandelt. Alle entsprechenden Übungen hierzu haben einen wirtschaftlichen Hintergrund.

- Im Teil *Functions* werden Sprechintentionen vermittelt, die für die Bewältigung sprachlicher Wirtschaftssituationen erforderlich sind. In einigen *Units* wird dieser Teil durch einen *Reading Aloud*-Teil ersetzt. Hier soll durch lautes Lesen Aussprache und Betonung geschult werden.

- Übungen zur Verbesserung des Leseverständnisses sind in die jeweiligen Aktivitäten integriert. Zusätzlich befindet sich in einigen *Units* noch ein besonderer Abschnitt, der in der Regel auf eine Diskussion hinzielt.

- Übungen zur Festigung des Hörverständnisses (Symbol: [▭]) sind ebenfalls in die Aktivitäten integriert. Dazu gehören häufig die Annahme eines Telefongespräches sowie auch die Aufnahme und Wiedergabe einer telefonisch übermittelten Nachricht.

- In jeder *Unit* ergeben sich ganz natürliche Diskussionen als Folge von Übungen und Aktivitäten. Als Ergänzung findet man in einigen *Units* jedoch noch einen besonderen Diskussionsteil für Gruppendiskussionen.

Abschließend noch ein Hinweis für die Arbeit mit dem *Student's Book*. Grundsätzlich sollten Sie immer auf Ihr persönliches Wissen und Ihre Berufserfahrung zurückgreifen. Ihr Sprachlehrer wird Ihnen zwar helfen, Ihre Sprachkenntnisse zu verbessern. Der Wirtschaftsexperte jedoch sind Sie letztlich selbst.

Wir wünschen Ihnen viel Freude beim Englischlernen mit *International Business English*!

1 Face to face

*An introduction to the skills and techniques
required when talking to people in business
situations. Meeting and greeting people.
Asking questions. Countries and nationalities.
Developing relationships.*

1.1 First impressions . . .

A 🔲 Listen to the recording. You'll hear some visitors to an
office being greeted and welcomed.

Which of the visitors are greeted in the most friendly and efficient way?
Which of the visitors are made to feel most welcome?

B Work in small groups. Ask your partners these questions:

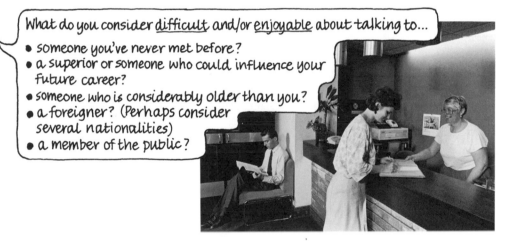

What do you consider **difficult** and/or **enjoyable** about talking to...
• someone you've never met before?
• a superior or someone who could influence your future career?
• someone who is considerably older than you?
• a foreigner? (Perhaps consider several nationalities)
• a member of the public?

C What impression do *you* try to give to the people you deal with in
business? What impression do you try *not* to give?
Add some more adjectives to these lists:

I try to be: *pleasant, sincere, efficient* . . . .
I try **not** to be: *unfriendly, shy, aggressive* . . . .

D Find out from your partners *why* they think it's important to give
a good first impression when greeting and meeting someone.

What should a receptionist (or the first person a visitor meets) in an
office say when they greet a visitor?

1.2 Asking questions

A Work in pairs. Decide what the *questions* were that led to each of these answers and write them down. Here's an example:

Answer: I'm a receptionist.
Question: *What do you do?*

1. Yes, thanks. I had a very good flight.
2. I'd like to see Mr Perez, if he's in the office.
3. On my last visit I spoke to Ms Meier.
4. It was Mr Grün who recommended this hotel to me.
5. I think I'd like to see round the factory after lunch.
6. No, my husband is travelling with me. I'm meeting him later.
7. We'll probably be staying till Friday morning.
8. No, this is his first visit – he's never been here before.

B Imagine that you're having dinner with Mr Singh, a client from India who you get on with very well. He is visiting your country for the first time. Work in pairs and write down *ten* questions you could ask (about his country, firm, impressions of your country, etc). Begin each question differently, like this:

> Did...? Are...? Is...? Do...? Does...?
> Have...? Has...? Who...? When...?
> Where...? What...? What kind of ...?
> How many...? How much...? How long...?
> Why...?

'Question tags' are often used to check whether we're right or not, as in these examples:

*India is very different from Europe, **isn't it**?*
*You haven't been round our works, **have you**?*
*You met Mr Grey yesterday, **didn't you**?*

C Complete these sentences, using question tags:

1. You've met Mr Suzuki, ... ?
2. It would be best to send them a reminder, ... ?
3. They don't normally pay up immediately, ... ?
4. You're waiting to see Miss Weber, ... ?
5. Mrs de Souza isn't arriving till tomorrow, ... ?
6. Your new receptionist doesn't speak English, ... ?
7. It must be quite difficult to sound efficient and friendly towards the end of a long hard day, ... ?

■ If you find it hard to use 'question tags' accurately, here are some expressions that are easier to use:

I expect India is very different from Europe?
I don't think you've been round our works?
I think you spoke to Mr Grey on the phone. **Is that right?**

D Complete these sentences with information from sentences 1–7:

 8. I believe .... Mr Suzuki?
 9. Do you think .... a reminder?
10. I don't think .... Is that right ?
11. You .... – that's right, isn't it ?
12. As far as I know, Mrs de Souza ....
13. Am I right in saying that .... ?
14. It ...., don't you think?

1.3 Do you enjoy your work?

You'll hear four people talking about their work:

1. Listen to each speaker and just answer these questions:
   What is the speaker's job?
   Where does he or she work?

2. Listen to each speaker again and note down your answers to these questions about their work:
   What does each speaker enjoy or find rewarding?
   What does each speaker find annoying or frustrating?

3. Compare your notes with a partner.

4. Ask your partner these questions:
   Which of the jobs that you have heard about would you most like to do yourself? Why?
   Which would you least like to do? Why?

5. Find out more about your partner's career. Ask about his or her:
   Present job – its rewards and frustrations
   Work experience – previous jobs (or educational courses, if your partner hasn't worked. But do find out about any temporary or part-time jobs your partner has done.)
   Education and training
   Ambitions and prospects for the future

6. When you have both finished, join another pair and tell them what you have discovered about each other.

1.4 Have you met . . .?

Listen to the three conversations. You'll hear some people meeting and being introduced to each other.

Here are some useful expressions you can use in such situations:

The class is divided into two teams: if you're in the A team, look at File 1 at the back of the book on page 195. If you're in the B team, look at File 7 on page 197.

1.5 Around the world

Vocabulary

A What do you call someone who comes from each of these countries? The first two are done for you as examples:

Someone from Scotland is *a Scotsman or Scotswoman*
Someone from Italy is *an Italian*
Someone from Wales is ...... *W.E.L.S.H. MAN / WOMAN*
Someone from ....

Australia	Canada	the USA	India
Pakistan	Sweden	Norway	Saudi Arabia
France	New Zealand	Japan	Holland

B Work in pairs. Make a list of the following:

5 Latin American nations
5 countries in the Middle East
5 countries in the European Community (EEC)
5 countries in Eastern Europe

5 African states
5 Asian countries

C When you're ready, join another pair. Ask them to tell you what they would call *a person* from each of the countries on your list. And do they know what *languages* are spoken in each country?

D People often have stereotyped ideas about foreigners – and even about people from other regions of their own country . . .
Ask the others in your group to describe 'a typical American', 'a typical English person', and other 'typical' nationalities from the lists you made.
To what extent are such stereotypes helpful and/or dangerous?

1.6 Developing relationships

A Work in groups and ask each other these questions:

- In your own workplace or place of study, who do you call by their first names, and who by their surnames?
- Who do you address at work using the familiar or polite forms of *you* in your language (*du/Sie, tu/vous, tu/lei, tu/Usted*, etc)?
- Are there people who use your first name but who *you* are expected to call by their surnames?
- Would this be any different with British or American people you work with? Or with other nationalities than your own?
- Who do you talk to at work about your family and after-work activities? Who do you meet socially outside work?

B You'll hear five short conversations between people who work in the same firm. Note down your answers to these questions about each conversation:

1. What is the relationship between the speakers?
2. What are their jobs?
3. What are they talking about?

■ A cool, formal relationship often becomes warmer and more friendly as people get to know each other better.

C Imagine that you and the others in the class are taking part in **a management training course.** You meet on Monday mornings. Your teacher will play the role of 'tutor'.

1. This is your first meeting. Introduce yourself to some of the other trainees. Stop talking when the 'tutor' arrives.
2. A week has passed. Talk to the person next to you until the 'tutor' arrives.
3. Now a month has passed. During this time you have got to know the other trainees much better. Talk to the person next to you until the 'tutor' arrives.
4. Now another month has passed and it's the last week of the course. Talk to the person next to you until the 'tutor' arrives.

D As you get to know someone you do business with (e.g. a client or supplier), it's useful to find out what your common interests are. Then you can have a social conversation as well as 'talking shop' (talking about business).

1. Work in pairs. Make a list of some general or more personal topics that you can talk about as you get to know someone better. These topics may vary according to the age, sex and importance and nationality of your companion – and your own interests.
2. Discuss your list with another pair.

3.  Form a pair with someone from a different group. Role play a meeting between a client and supplier. Imagine that you only meet twice a year, but you've established a good relationship.

Here are some useful expressions you can use at the beginning and end of your meeting:

A

Good morning, nice to see you again! How are you?
Hello again! How are you getting on?

Fine thanks, how are you?
Very well thanks, how about you?

B

Goodbye! It was very nice to have met you! Have a good journey/lunch/evening!
Give my regards to...
See you next week/month.
Goodbye and thanks for everything.

Thanks, and the same to you. You're welcome. I'm so glad we were able to meet.

4. Role-play another meeting with a different companion.

1.7 It's not just what you say . . .   *Discussion*

A   Try this quiz with a partner.

1. Which is the best definition of a good conversationalist?
   a Someone who always has plenty to say.
   b Someone who has plenty of amusing stories to tell.
   c Someone who will listen carefully to what you have to say.
   d None of these (*give your own definition*).

2. If someone just says 'What?' after you've carefully explained something, do you . . .
   a go through the explanation again using different words?
   b feel that you have been wasting your time?
   c feel that you have not been believed?
   d None of these (*give your own definition*).

3. If someone always looks you straight in the eye, this means that they are
   a honest   b rude   c trying to frighten you   d being friendly

≫→

4. If someone smiles while you're explaining something, this means they are . . .
   a not sincere   b happy   c not listening   d crazy

5. If someone frowns whilst you're explaining something, this means they . . .
   a are angry   b don't understand   c are concentrating
   d have a headache

6. If someone sighs while you're explaining something, this means that they are:
   a bored   b impatient   c unhappy   d suffering from indigestion

7. If a man wearing jeans and no tie comes into your office, do you think he . . .
   a isn't correctly dressed?   b can't be important?   c is quite normal?
   d is someone who has come to fix the electricity or something?

8. If someone shakes your hand very hard and long, this means . . .
   a they are very pleased to see you
   b they are trying to show you that they are sincere
   c they are waiting for you to say something
   d they are reliable and friendly

9. If a Canadian businessman keeps stepping backwards while he's talking to a
   Mexican businessman, this means . . .
   a he doesn't like Mexicans
   b the Mexican is trying to be too friendly
   c Northern people don't feel comfortable standing as close to another person
     as Southern people normally do
   d Canadians are less friendly than Mexicans.

10. If you are receiving a business card from a Japanese person, it is more polite
    to take it with . . .
    a your left hand   b your right hand   c both hands
    d one hand and present your own card with the other

11. If you are meeting an Arab client it is polite to . . .
    a get straight down to business
    b wait until *he* raises the topic of business
    c stick to small talk for the first few minutes
    d ask him to close the door of his office to prevent interruptions.

B   Now form a larger group and discuss how the impression you
may give, especially to a foreigner, can be affected by:

— Your expression (smiling, blinking, frowning, looking someone
  straight in the eye, looking down, etc)
— The noises you make (sighs, yawns, knocking loudly or softly at a
  door, clicking a ballpoint pen, etc)
— Body contact (shaking hands, touching, etc)
— Body language (crossing your arms, sitting up straight, etc)
— Your clothes and appearance (hair, make-up, suit, tie, etc)
— What you talk about (politics, business, sport, family, etc)
— Your tone of voice (sounding cool, friendly, familiar, serious, etc)

2 Letters, telexes and memos

How to lay out a business letter and envelope.
Some 'golden rules' for writing letters, memos,
telexes etc. Practice in planning and writing
letters, telexes and memos. Joining sentences.
Reading names and addresses aloud.

2.1 Speaking and writing

Discussion

A First, read this memo:

MEMORANDUM	Date: 24/4/–

From: H.G.W.   To: Department managers
Subject: In-service English classes

1. From Monday 8 May English classes will he held in the
   Training Centre (room 3.17). There will be 2 groups:
   advanced level (10.30–12.00) and intermediate level (8.30–
   10.00). Please encourage your staff to attend one of the
   sessions. All teaching materials will be provided but
   students will be expected to do homework and preparation
   outside working hours.
2. Please send me the names of all interested staff by noon on
   Wednesday 26 May. They will be given an informal oral test
   during the first week in May so that we can decide which of
   the classes is best for them.
3. The size of each class will be limited to 12 participants.

B 🔲 You will hear a conversation on the same subject. What
were the differences between the memo and the conversation?

C Work in small groups. Ask your partners these questions and
make notes on their answers:

1. What are the advantages of communicating with someone in a face-to-face
   meeting?
2. And what are the disadvantages of this?
3. What are the advantages of communicating with someone in writing?
4. And what are the disadvantages of this?
5. What does the term 'business English' mean to you?

2.2 The right address

A How is the layout of these addresses different from the way addresses are laid out in your country?

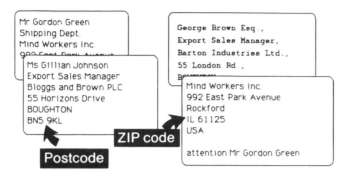

B 📼 Listen to the recording and address each 'envelope' correctly. (Later, you can check your answers in File 77.)

C Work in pairs. One of you should look at File 3, the other at 10. Dictate the addresses there to one another: you should spell out the difficult words. Dictate your own address, too.
(📼 Later you can hear them read aloud on the tape.)

2.3 Abbreviations

Complete these sentences by explaining what the abbreviations printed in bold type mean. Use a dictionary if necessary.

1. **Rd., St.** and **Sq.** are short for ....
2. **#24** in the USA and **No. 24** in Britain both mean ....
3. On an envelope the abbreviations **c/o, Attn.** and **P.O.B.** mean ....
4. You may see these in a report or textbook: **e.g.** or **eg**, **i.e.** or **ie**, **etc.** or **etc** and **P.T.O.** They stand for ....
    And you may also find these: **cf.** (compare), **do.** (ditto) and **viz.** (namely).
5. A British firm's name may be followed by **plc** or **PLC**, **Ltd**, **Bros** or **& Co.** These are short for ....
6. An American firm's name may be followed by **Corp.** or **Inc.**, meaning ....
7. In a printed text you may see these abbreviations: **@ ¥ 3000** each, **© 1989**, **Apple®** and **Macintosh™**. They mean ....
8. At the end of an informal letter, you might add a **P.S.**, in other words a ....
9. At the end of a formal business letter it's common to use the abbreviations **c.c.** and **enc.** or **encl.**, which stand for ....
10. But you'd only see these in *very* old-fashioned correspondence: ult. (last month), **inst.** (.................... month) and **prox.** (.................... month)!

2.4 The layout of letters

A This is the top part of a business letter, showing the styles and layouts that are used in British and in American correspondence.

- Which are British and which are American?
- When would you write to Mr James Green as *Dear Jim* or as *Dear Mr Green*?

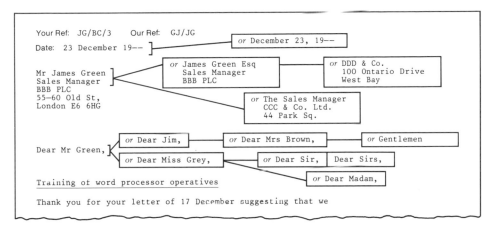

- How is a business letter in your country (or in your company's 'house style') laid out differently?
- Are there fixed rules about this in your country?

B Look at the four endings of business letters below.
Notice the useful phrases that are used in these letters.

- Which are in the British and which are in the American style?
- When would you use the different styles?
- If you've begun a letter *Dear Jim*, how would you end it?

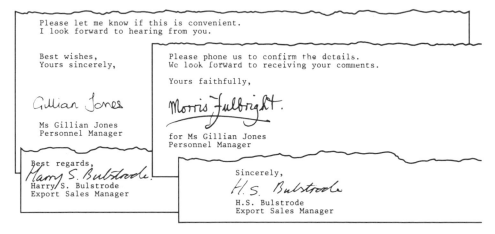

C   Work in small groups. If you receive a business letter, what impression do you get from these features:

- Lots of very short paragraphs
- `A letter typed on an old manual typewriter`
- Very long paragraphs without much white space between
- Numbered paragraphs
- **Large Print**
- *Decorative or unusual Print*
- The style of the company's letterhead and the company's logo

D   Work in pairs. Imagine that you are setting up your own business. Design your own letterhead and logo.

2.5   Joining sentences   *Grammar*

Ideas in writing can be connected in three different ways:

1. By using a *conjunction*:
   TIME: **and, before, after, while, when**
   REASON, CAUSE OR CONSEQUENCE: **and, because, so that, so . . . that, such a . . . that**
   CONTRAST: **but, although**

   I called her back **so that** I could confirm one or two details.
   The consignment was delivered **while** we were very busy.
   The goods were repacked **so** quickly **that** we had no time to inspect them.

2. By using a linking *adverbial phrase* (often starting a new sentence):
   TIME: **Before that, After that, And then, During this time**
   REASON, CAUSE OR CONSEQUENCE: **Because of this, This is why, As a result, Consequently**
   CONTRAST: **Nevertheless, However**

   I wanted to confirm one or two details. **That is why** I called her back.
   The consignment was delivered on Friday. **During this time** we were very busy.
   The goods were repacked at once. **Consequently** there was no time to inspect them.

3. By using a *preposition*:
   TIME: **before, after, during**
   REASON, CAUSE OR CONSEQUENCE: **because of, due to**
   CONTRAST: **in spite of**

   I called her back **because of** the need to confirm one or two details.
   The consignment was delivered **during** a very busy time.
   Due to our prompt repacking procedure, the goods were not inspected.

■ To show PURPOSE, an *infinitive clause* can also be used:
Billing has been computerized **in order to** save time and money.

A   Join the two halves of these sentences so that they make good
sense. The first is done for you as an example.

I never sign a letter	**although** a phone call is quicker.
I often prefer to write	**after** I have checked our stock position.
I usually telephone	**before** I have read it through.
Please check my in-tray	**in order to** save time.
I shall be able to confirm this	**because** we do not have sufficient stocks.
I shall be able to confirm this	**until** we have checked our stock position.
We cannot confirm the order	**while** I am away at the conference.
Please reply at once	**so that** we can order the supplies we need.
Please reply as soon as possible	**when** I have consulted our works manager.

B   Use a *prepositional phrase* instead of the conjunctions in these
sentences. Rewrite each sentence using the phrase on the right.

1. Who is dealing with your correspondence while you are away?   **during**
    Who is dealing with your correspondence during your absence?
2. I went to see the factory after I had looked round the offices.   **after**
3. I'll have to see the shipping manager before I confirm the order.   **before**
4. There was a delay because we had some technical problems.   **because of**
5. It was completed on time although some of the staff were ill.   **in spite of**
6. The visitors arrived while you were having your lunch break.   **during**
7. As the number of orders had fallen, the works closed down.   **Due to**
8. He is on holiday now. Then he will be in touch with you.   **After**

C   Rewrite each of these newspaper headlines as one or two
complete sentences. The first is done for you as an example.

Dollar rises – interest rates to fall?
Interest rates may fall because the dollar has gone up in value.

President visits Europe. Address to European Parliament.

Far East imports rise, US introduces quotas.

Acme Industries' profits fall. Chairman sacked.

Takeover bid rejected. "Offer still open" says Murdoch.

Talks in Brussels. Tariffs to change.

D   Short sentences are often clearer than long, complicated ones.
Look at the long sentences on the next page. Work in pairs and rewrite
each as two or three shorter sentences, beginning as suggested: ⋙→

As requested, I enclose our new catalogue and feel sure that you will find within many items to interest you, particularly our new range of colours that will brighten up your office and keep your staff feeling happy.

I am sending...

Working in an export department requires a great deal of specialist knowledge, including a mastery of the complex documentation, an awareness of the various methods of payment that are available and the ability to correspond with customers in a distant country.

If you work in...

One of the most difficult aspects of corresponding with people you have not met face-to-face is establishing a personal relationship with them in order to show them that you are not just a letter-writing machine but a real person.

Writing to people...

2.6   It's in the mail

Vocabulary

Fill the gaps in these sentences with words from the list.

carbon copy   courier   duplicate
general delivery (US) / poste restante (GB)
photocopy   postage and packing   mail (US) / post (GB)
printed matter   registered   return mail (US) / return of post (GB)
RSVP   separate cover   stationery

1. A package can be delivered by the mailman (US) or the postman (GB) or by a private .... service.
2. Purchases usually carry an extra charge for .... if they're sent by ....
3. An important or valuable document is best sent by .... mail.
4. It shows that you are efficient if you reply to a letter by ....
5. If you want people to reply to an invitation, put .... at the bottom.
6. If you send some documents in a separate envelope from your letter, these documents are sent under ....
7. If you're sending someone a letter, you should keep a .... or a ...., so that you can keep a .... for your files.
8. It is often cheaper (though less quick) to send catalogues through the mail as .... instead of by letter post.
9. Envelopes, ballpoints, felt tips and paper clips are all items of ....
10. A letter can be collected from a post office if it's addressed to '........................'.

2.7 Better letters

A Work in small groups. Look at the two letters on this and the next page.
Which would you prefer to have received yourself?
What are the differences in style between the two letters?

SUNSHINE FLAVOURS LTD.

44 Emerald Drive, Shannon Technology Park,
Cork CO6 9TS, Republic of Ireland.

Mme Susanne Dufrais,
Les Gourmets du Poitou S.A.,
33 rue Mirabeau,
44000 Poitiers,
France

18 January 19--

Dear Madam,
    As requested, we enclose for your attention our 19-- price
list and catalogue. I should like to draw your attention to
the fact that all our products are made from completely natural
ingredients and that we do not utilize any artificial additives.
    There are 213 different items in the catalogue and our
prices are reasonable and our quality is good. This is the first
time that we have included Scratch 'n' Sniff samples of our ten
most popular aromas.
    Should you require further information, please do not
hesitate to contact us. If the undersigned is unavailable, the
Sales Manager's personal assistant will be delighted to assist
you.
    We look forward to receiving your esteemed order in due
course.
    Yours faithfully,
    p.p. Sunshine Flavours Ltd

J. G. O'Reilly

    J.G. O'Reilly
    Sales manager

Sunshine Flavours Ltd

Mme Susanne Dufrais
Les Gourmets du Poitou S.A.
33 rue Mirabeau
44000 Poitiers
France

**44 Emerald Drive, Shannon Technology Park,
Cork CO6 9TS, Republic of Ireland**

18 January 19—

Dear Madame Dufrais,

You asked us to send you our price list and catalogue for the
19— season. I am sure you will find plenty to interest you in
it. You will notice that all our products are made from 100%
natural ingredients — we do not use any artificial additives.

≫→

17

This year, for the first time, we have included Scratch 'n' Sniff™ samples of our ten most popular aromas. I think you will agree that our range of well over 200 natural flavours and aromas is second to none and is outstanding value for money.

If you need more information, do please get in touch with me. If you are telephoning, please ask to speak to me personally or to my assistant, Ms Hannah Rosser, and we will be very pleased to help you.

I look forward to hearing from you.

Yours sincerely,

Jim O'Reilly

James O'Reilly
Sales manager

enc: catalogue, price lists, order form

Telex: 449801
Telephone: 021 23 459
Cables: SUNSHINE, CORK

B Find out what your partners think about these 'Golden Rules'. (Even if your partners normally only dictate letters, they still need to check them through before signing them.)

"GOLDEN RULES" for writing letters and memos

1 Give your letter *a heading* if it will help the reader to see at glance what you're writing about.
2 Decide what you are going to say before you start to write or dictate: if you don't do this, the sentences are likely to go on and on until you can think of a good way to finish. In other words, always try to plan a-head.
3 Use short sentences.
4 Put each separate idea in a separate paragraph. Numbering each paragraph may help the reader to understand better.
5 Use short words that everyone can understand.
6 Think about your reader. Your reader . . .
   . . . must be able to see exactly what you mean:
      your letters should be C L E A R
   . . . must be given all the necessary information:
      your letters should be C O M P L E T E
   . . . is likely to be a busy person with no time to waste:
      your letters should be C O N C I S E
   . . . must be addressed in a sincere, polite tone:
      your letters should be C O U R T E O U S
   . . . may get a bad impression if there are mistakes in grammar, punctuation and spelling:
      your letters should be C O R R E C T.

2.8 To plan or not to plan?

A We asked some business people this question:
'How do you plan writing a difficult letter, memo or telex?'
Listen to their answers. Which methods do your partners use before
writing a letter in their *own* language?

B As writing in English is much harder than writing in your own
language, careful planning is essential. Look at these ideas and find
out your partners' views:

Planning a Business Letter: 7 Steps

1. Write down your AIM: why are you writing this letter?
2. ASSEMBLE all the relevant information and documents: copies of previous
    correspondence, reports, figures etc.
3. ARRANGE the points in order of importance. Decide which points are irrelevant
    and can be left out. Make rough notes.
4. Write an OUTLINE in note form. Check it through, considering these questions:
    Have you left any important points out?
    Can the order of presentation be made clearer?
    Have you included anything that is not relevant?
5. Write a FIRST DRAFT, leaving space for additions, changes and revisions.
6. REVISE your first draft by considering these questions:
    INFORMATION: Does it cover all the essential points?
       Is the information relevant, correct and complete?
    ENGLISH: Are the grammar, spelling and punctuation correct?
    STYLE: Does it look attractive?
       Does it sound natural and sincere?
       Is it the kind of letter you would like to receive yourself?
       Is it clear, concise and courteous?
       Will it give the right impression?
7. Write, type or dictate your
    FINAL VERSION.

"Goodnight, Miss Travis,
I've finished my coffee
but I've left my biscuit.
Put it in my in-tray
and I'll deal with it tomorrow."

2.9 Writing memos

A memo (a letter sent to someone in the same firm) can be a brief note for the files or a reminder to someone. A longer memo to an English-speaking member of staff may need almost as much care as a letter to a client.

A Work in pairs. Design your own internal English-language memo pad. What size will it be? What information will it call for:

Name of sender, name of recipient(s), date, subject, 'copies to. . .', space for reply, 'reply to. . .', 'reply by. . .' etc?

B 1. Look at the memo below and decide how it can be improved.
2. Rewrite it in your own words.
3. When you've done this, compare your rewritten memo with the model in File 97.

MEMORANDUM

To: All members of staff, Northern Branch.
From K.L.J.
Date: 5 December 19—

As you know, one of the reasons for the introduction of PCs in Northern Branch was to provide us with feedback before we decide whether to install PCs in other departments. The Board has asked me to submit a report on your experiences by the end of this week. I talked to some of you informally about this last month. During my brief visit I noticed a junior member of staff playing some kind of computer game in the lunch hour, and a senior manager told me that he used his for writing letters — a job for a secretary, surely? So that I can compile a full report, I would like everyone to let me know what they personally use the PC for, what software they use and how long per day they spend actually using it. It would also be useful to find out how their PC has not come up to expectations, and any unanticipated uses they have found for their PC, so that others can benefit from your experience.

K.L.J

2.10 Writing telexes (and email)

As the average typed business letter costs £10 to produce, a telex can be much cheaper, and of course it will arrive quickly and can be answered by return.

Telexes are normally shorter than letters, but if they are too brief they may be hard to understand. The extra cost of a few more words may be better than spending time and money to put right a misunderstanding.

Work in pairs. Imagine that you are arranging a business trip to Vancouver, Canada, for yourself and two colleagues. You would like rooms at the Harbour Hotel, so you have telexed them for information. You have just received their reply:

```
+++
674935   FRANCOJ   I
HARHOT   VAN

TO: FRED MEIER
FROM: JACQUELINE LARUE - HARBOUR HOTEL VANCOUVER

YES, WE DO HAVE ROOMS AVAILABLE ON JUN 12,13,14
RATE FOR A ROOM ON OUR EXECUTIVE FLOOR IS 139.00 CANADIAN
DOLLARS PER NIGHT PLUS TAX. THIS INCLUDES BUFFET BREAKFAST IN
EXECUTIVE LOUNGE AND COMPLEMENTARY PICK-UP SERVICE BY LIMOUSINE
AT THE AIRPORT.
STANDARD NON-EXECUTIVE RATES ARE 95.00 DOLLARS OR 115 DOLLARS
WITH OCEAN VIEW. THESE RATES DO NOT INCLUDE BREAKFAST.
YES, YOU MAY GUARANTEE ROOMS FOR LATE ARRIVAL WITH YOUR DINER'S
CLUB CARD. PLEASE TELEX BACK ROOM RATES YOU WOULD LIKE FOR THREE
GUESTS. PLEASE INCLUDE YOUR COMPLETE MAILING ADDRESS, AND NUMBER
AND EXPIRY DATE OF CREDIT CARD IF YOU WISH TO GUARANTEE ROOMS
FOR LATE ARRIVAL. ALSO GIVE FLIGHT NUMBER AND ARRIVAL TIME IF
PICK-UP BY LIMOUSINE REQUIRED AT THE AIRPORT. WILL THE GUESTS
BE CHECKING OUT ON JUN 15?
PLEASE SEND TELEX TO MY ATTENTION
THANK YOU FOR YOUR ENQUIRY
JACQUELINE LARUE, ASSISTANT MANAGER, HARBOUR HOTEL
++
```

1. Draft a telex in answer to the one above, booking the rooms you require.
2. Look at File 108 to compare your telex with the version there.

■ Special **abbreviations** are sometimes used in telexes to save time and money. Unless you're quite certain that your reader will understand exactly what you mean, it's best to use normal English.

■ The kind of language that's used in a telex is also used in electronic mail (email) – messages sent from one computer to another.

2.11 Sending messages

Work in pairs. Imagine that *you* want to send these messages.

1. Decide how each message would best be transmitted – by letter, by telex, by fax, by phone or in a face-to-face meeting.
2. Plan and then draft the letters or telexes.
3. Work with another pair.
   Role play the phone calls or visits.
4. Another pair will be assigned to receive each message and evaluate it according to the 'Golden Rules' in 2.7.

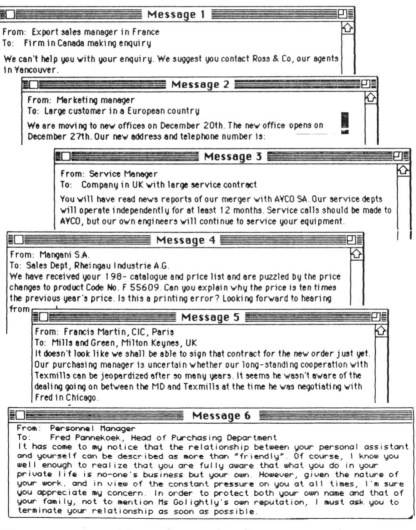

Message 1

From: Export sales manager in France
To: Firm in Canada making enquiry

We can't help you with your enquiry. We suggest you contact Ross & Co, our agents in Vancouver.

Message 2

From: Marketing manager
To: Large customer in a European country

We are moving to new offices on December 20th. The new office opens on December 27th. Our new address and telephone number is:

Message 3

From: Service Manager
To: Company in UK with large service contract

You will have read news reports of our merger with AVCO SA. Our service depts will operate independently for at least 12 months. Service calls should be made to AVCO, but our own engineers will continue to service your equipment.

Message 4

From: Mangani S.A.
To: Sales Dept, Rheingau Industrie A.G.
We have received your 198- catalogue and price list and are puzzled by the price changes to product Code No. F 55609. Can you explain why the price is ten times the previous year's price. Is this a printing error? Looking forward to hearing from

Message 5

From: Francis Martin, CIC, Paris
To: Mills and Green, Milton Keynes, UK
It doesn't look like we shall be able to sign that contract for the new order just yet. Our purchasing manager is uncertain whether our long-standing cooperation with Texmills can be jeopardized after so many years. It seems he wasn't aware of the dealing going on between the MD and Texmills at the time he was negotiating with Fred in Chicago.

Message 6

From: Personnel Manager
To: Fred Pannekoek, Head of Purchasing Department
It has come to my notice that the relationship between your personal assistant and yourself can be described as more than "friendly". Of course, I know you well enough to realize that you are fully aware that what you do in your private life is no-one's business but your own. However, given the nature of your work, and in view of the constant pressure on you at all times, I'm sure you appreciate my concern. In order to protect both your own name and that of your family, not to mention Ms Golightly's own reputation, I must ask you to terminate your relationship as soon as possible.

■ Whatever you're writing – a letter, telex, fax or memo – always try to think about your reader's reaction.

22

3 On the phone

Making different kinds of calls; taking messages.
Present tenses. Getting people to do things.

3.1 I'd like to speak to . . .

A 📼 Making a phone call isn't always easy – especially if you
don't know the person on the other end of the line very well . . .
You'll hear a caller trying to arrange an appointment with Dr
Henderson. Answer these questions about the calls:
  What went wrong?   How did each misunderstanding happen?
What *should* each speaker have done or said differently?

Here are some expressions you can use if you're on the phone:

> Hello, is that...?
> Can I speak to..., please.
> Hello, this is...calling from...in...
> Could you ask... to call me back, please?
> Thanks for calling back.
>
> Good morning, I'd like to speak to...
> Is... available, please? My name's...
> Could you give... a message, please?
> My number is...
> I'm so sorry, I've got the wrong number.

> Speaking.
> I'm afraid... is in a meeting/not in the office/still at lunch/on
>   holiday this week/away today/not available just now...
> I'll just find out if... is in the other office/available/back yet.
> What's your (extension) number?   I'll put you through to...
> Can I get... to call you back?   Hold on a moment, please.
>
> Oh hello,..., this is... speaking.

B 📼 Now imagine that *you're* trying to get in touch with Dr
Henderson, Head of Research at Felco Industries. Their number is
0044 234 32453. Listen to the recording and decide what *you* would
say in each situation. Dr Henderson is quite a hard man to find!

C Work in groups. Find out your partners' opinions:
  What is difficult about making a first-time call to a stranger?
  What can you do to make such calls easier?
  What can you do to establish a relationship more quickly?
  How can you make sure that the stranger knows who you are and
  what you want?

3.2 Getting people to do things

Listen to the recording and look at these examples.

REQUESTING In the first conversation the first speaker wants her colleague to do various things for her.

> I'd like you/him to..., please.
> Could you..., please?
> Do you think you could...?
> Would you mind -ing...?

> Sure.   Certainly.
> I'm sorry but...
> Unfortunately, ...
> I'm afraid I can't, because...

OFFERING TO HELP In the second conversation, the first speaker can see that his colleague needs assistance, and offers his help.

> Would you like/Can I give you... a hand/a lift?
> Would you like me to...
> Shall I...?
> Perhaps I can help? Can I help at all?
> If you need any help, just let me/us know.

> Thanks very much - if you're sure it's no trouble.
> That's very kind of you, yes. Could you...?
> No thanks, I can manage.
> That's very kind of you, but...
> No thank you, I'm just having a look/waiting for someone.

ASKING PERMISSION In the third conversation the first speaker is checking whether it is OK to do various things.

> May I...?
> Do you mind if I...?
> Can I...?
> Do you think I could...?
> Is it all right if I...?

> Yes, go ahead.   Sure.
> Certainly.
> No, I'm afraid not, because...
> No, I'm afraid you can't because...
> No, I'm afraid we aren't allowed to...

A Work in pairs. Imagine that you are temporarily sharing an office while your own separate offices are being redecorated. You don't know each other very well. One of you should look at File 5, the other at 11.

24

B  Work in pairs again. Half the pairs should look at File 20, the other half at 13. You will have to send some short *telex messages* to another pair and then *reply* to the ones you receive from them. Look at these examples first:

MESSAGE: *Please confirm receipt of samples, sent airmail on 6 February.*

```
GOOD MORNING. WOULD YOU PLEASE CONFIRM THAT YOU
HAVE RECEIVED OUR SAMPLES FOR THE PRINTING OF
PACKAGING AND LABELS, WHICH WE SENT BY AIRMAIL
ON FEBRUARY 6TH?
— BEST REGARDS —
```

REPLY: *Samples haven't arrived, please send further set by courier.*

```
UNFORTUNATELY YOUR SAMPLES HAVE NOT ARRIVED.
WOULD YOU MIND SENDING US A SECOND SET BY
COURIER, AS WE REQUIRE THEM URGENTLY?
— REGARDS —
```

C  Now find a partner who was a member of a *different* pair. Role-play four phone calls, each with the same purpose as the exchange of telex messages you have just dealt with.
To simulate the situation of a telephone conversation, the two people speaking must sit *back-to-back* like this:

— so that they can't see each other's faces.

3.3 Using the phone
Vocabulary

Work in pairs. Decide which of the verbs fit best in the following sentences. What other verbs could you use instead?

be over	call back/ring back	cut off	get through	give up
hang up	hold on	look up	pick up	put on	put through

1. The phone's ringing. Why don't you .... the receiver?
2. Mrs Scott isn't available at the moment. Can you .... later?
3. Can you .... Ms Dumas's number in the directory please?
4. I'm afraid she's with a client, shall I .... you .... to her secretary?

〉〉〉→

25

5. I'm sorry about that. I'm glad you're still there. We must have been .... for a moment.
6. Mr Green never seems to be in his office. I've been trying to .... to him all morning.
7. Could you .... for a moment, I'll just find out for you.
8. Is Graham there? If so, could you .... him .... please?
9. If the telephonist says 'Thank you so much for calling' and plays me that awful electronic music again, I'll ....
10. You'll never get New York at this time of day. If I were you, I'd ....
11. If an American telephonist asks 'Are you through?', she wants to know if your call ....

3.4 Can I take a message?

If you answer the phone and have to take a message, what information should you note down?

A [cassette] You'll hear three recorded phone calls. Listen to the calls and note down the message that is given.
The first is done for you as an example:

To: _Mr Février_   Date: _4 Sept_
MESSAGE:
    Mr Peter Schulz called from Vienna.
    Please call him today before 4 PM or any
    time tomorrow on 01 456 9924 re
    arrangements for congress in July
message taken by: _____J.B.K.____

Compare the way you have written down the messages with the way your partner has.

B Work in small groups. Imagine that you work for an international firm and that you need to appoint a new telephonist/receptionist as your present one is leaving soon.

What qualities are you looking for in such a person?
What skills should such a person possess?
What kind of training does such a person require?

C Draft a short advertisement for the position of telephonist/receptionist.

3.5 Present tenses

■ The PRESENT SIMPLE refers to 'permanent states or situations' and
to 'regular happenings or habits':
 We always *file* documents here and *send* copies to head office.
 He *lives* in London but *spends* every other week in New York.
 Does your company *deal* with the Far East?

These adverbs are typically used with the present simple:
always	generally	occasionally	frequently	sometimes	often
usually	normally	on a regular basis	regularly	twice a year	
once a week	every year	every two weeks	every other month		
once in a while	from time to time	never	rarely	hardly ever	
seldom					

■ The PRESENT PROGRESSIVE refers to 'temporary, developing or
changing situations':
 While *she's looking* for accommodation, *she's staying* with us.
 The market outlook for North America *is getting* better.
 Is anyone *taking* Mr Rossi's calls while *he's working* at home?

Some typical adverbs:
at the moment	now	just now	right now	this morning
today	presently (*US & Scots*)	at present	for the moment	

■ Some verbs (known as 'stative verbs') are NOT normally used with
the present progressive:
 I *realize* that their product *costs* less than ours, but . . .
 I *believe* he still *owes* us quite a lot of money.
 Do you remember how much each parcel *weighs*?
 Each package that we are sending *contains* 12 items.
 Our rate of discount *depends* on the quantity you order.

Typical verbs:
like	believe	belong	deserve	matter	own	prefer	fit
remember	realize	understand	owe	contain	measure		
weigh	cost	consist of	depend on	lack	appear	look like	

A Fill the gaps with a suitable verb from the list and (if possible) a
suitable adverb too. The first is done as an example.

analyze	*block*	*depend*	*look*	*pay*	*prefer*
require	*sound*	*speak*	*specialize*	*take*	*try*

 1. Her secretary .*generally takes*..... all her calls when she's out.
 2. We .... a 10% deposit for orders of this kind.
 3. He .... to be self-employed, rather than have a permanent job.
 4. The switchboard .... outside calls from this extension.

5. I .... the statistics so I can't give you a decision yet.
6. We .... to boost our sales in the Japanese market.
7. He .... rudely to me whenever I call him on the intercom.
8. He .... strange on the phone, but really he's very nice.
9. We .... our agents 12.5% commission on net sales figures.
10. Our firm .... in acquiring real estate in Southern California.
11. I know it .... like our original model, but we've updated it.
12. I can't give you a definite date: it .... on our own suppliers.

B Work in pairs. Write down *eight questions* that you can ask another student in the class, using present tenses. For example:

'Where do you live?'   'Where do you come from?'
'What book are you reading at the moment?'
'What do you think your husband/wife/friend is doing now?'

C Find another student and ask him or her your questions. If you get a very short answer (e.g. 'Italy'), ask more questions to get more details ('Where exactly . . . ?', 'What exactly . . . ?' etc)

3.6   Talking on the phone   *Discussion*

A When you're talking on the phone, remember that the person you're talking to may be having difficulties too.

■ Don't forget that the other person . . .
1. wants to understand you easily, so try to speak CLEARLY.
2. can't see your reactions, so always CONFIRM that you have (or have not) understood each point that's been made.
3. can't see you and doesn't know what a nice person you are, so make sure you sound POLITE and AGREEABLE.
4. hasn't got all day, so make sure your call is BRIEF.
5. is getting an impression of your firm while talking with you, so make sure that you sound EFFICIENT – your firm's image may be at stake, even if you're just taking a message.

Which of these five points do you and your partners feel *least* confident about if you have to make or receive a phone call in English? How can you increase your confidence, do you think?

B 🔲 We asked some business people this question: 'Do you make notes or a plan before an important phone call?' Listen to their comments. Which of their ideas do you agree with and why?

C If you agree that it is a good idea to plan ahead before making a phone call in English, look again at 2.8. Which of the ideas on planning a letter can be applied to phone calls?

3.7 Hello, my name's. . .

☎ Work in groups of three (or four). You will be taking it in turns to role play a phone call, while the third (and fourth) person listens in and comments on your performances. To simulate the situation of a phone call, the two people speaking must sit BACK-TO-BACK.

Student A should look at File 16, student B at 67, student C at 2 (and student D at 2):

■ IF YOU'RE 'ON THE PHONE', make notes before the call and during the call. Towards the end of the call, check with the other person that you have noted the important information accurately. In real life, you'd probably rewrite these notes immediately afterwards as a record of the call.

■ IF YOU'RE LISTENING to your partners 'on the phone', think about these questions while listening to the call:

- Does each speaker sound agreeable, polite and efficient?
- Do they sound natural and sincere?
- Does each speaker's tone create the right impression?
- Are they speaking clearly?
- Is the information they're giving correct?
- Is their grammar and pronunciation correct, as far as you can tell?
- Have they both covered all the essential points?
- **Is it the kind of call you would like to receive yourself?**

Comment on the call by giving 'feedback' to the two speakers.

(If you 'get lost' and don't know which File to look at next, ask your teacher.)

"You should use the phone more often, Mr Congreave.
It really makes you look like someone."

3.8 Give them a call! *Vocabulary*

A Fill the gaps with suitable words from the list.

area code (US)/dialling code (GB)   *bad line*   *busy (US)/engaged (GB)*
collect call (US)/transferred charge call (GB)   *dialling (GB)/dialing (US)*
enquiries   *extension*   *IDD/international direct dialling*
insert   *off the hook*   *out of order*   *outside line*
person-to-person call (US)/personal call (GB)   *phone book/directory*
receiver   *ringing*   *switchboard operator*   *unobtainable*
wrong number

1. Incoming calls to our firm are taken by the .... , who will put you through to the .... you require
2. 'I'm sorry to trouble you, I think I must have got the ....'
3. 'I'm sorry, I can't hear you very well, this is a ....'
4. 'I can't get through, their line always seems to be ....'
5. If you don't want to be interrupted by any phone calls, you can leave the phone ....
6. If you don't know someone's number you can use the .... or you can call directory .... (192 in the UK)
7. To make a call from a public telephone, lift the .... and .... a coin. Listen for the .... tone and dial the number. You will then hear a tone telling you that the number is .... If you've misdialled, you'll hear a tone telling you that the number is .... or that the line is ....
8. To make a call by .... from the UK: first dial the international code (010), then the country code, then the .... and finally the number you require.
9. 'Operator, I'd like to make a .... to New York, please. My name is Mrs Jane Wilson.'
10. 'I'd like to make a .... to Mr Bob Hill on this number: 456 8901.'
11. 'Hello, is that the switchboard? This is extension 67, can I have an .... please?'

B What would you tell a foreign visitor about how public phones in your country work?
What special facilities and numbers should they know about?

3.9 I've got some calls to make . . .

☎ Work in pairs. One of you should look at File 18, the other at 25. You'll be role-playing some more phone calls, so sit back-to-back again.

4 Reports and summaries

How to plan and write reports. Some advice on making notes. Practice in writing reports. Using the passive. Punctuation. How to summarize reports. Taking notes of conversations and discussions.

4.1 Writing v. telling

A Think about what you did yesterday or last Friday. If you work, describe what you did at work; if you're studying, describe what you did at college. Make notes about what you did. Now tell your partner and listen to what your partner tells you. Your teacher will now give you further instructions for a writing task.

B Work in pairs. Look at the map of a factory site where a robbery took place. Some of the buildings are marked, others are not. Try and guess the names of the unmarked buildings.

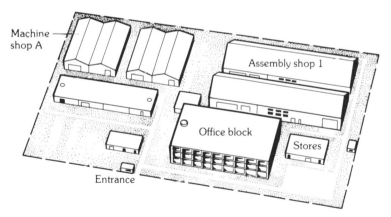

C ▭ You're going to hear reporters talking to three people who were on the factory site on the night of the robbery. Listen to the interviews and write in the names of the buildings on the map which are still unmarked. Mark in the place where the robbery took place and where the robber got into the factory. Mark on the map also where the people say they were. Compare your finished map with a partner. Listen to the interviews once more and make a note of what the various people were doing at the time. What did they do *after* the robbery?

D Prepare a report of what happened during the robbery, what the people were doing at the time and what they did after the robbery. In your report you should try and decide how the robbery took place and what made it possible.

E Work in pairs. What pieces of information have you both included in your reports and what pieces have you each left out?

F Work in pairs. What advantages do you see in writing? One of you should look at File 21, the other at 92. Later, discuss your findings in small groups.

4.2 Keeping it brief and to the point . . .

It is important in any writing – and especially in business – to be clear about the aims and purposes of your writing. In order that your reader can make sense of what you have written, follow these 'Golden Rules':

be *accurate*   be *brief*   be *clear*

They are easy to remember – as easy as A, B, C!

A Work in pairs. Read the following memo and imagine both of you are divisional personnel managers to whom the memo is addressed:
1. What do you think the managing director's aims were in writing the memo?
2. What – if anything – are you expected to do as a result of reading the memo?

MEMORANDUM

From: The Managing Director   *To:* Divisional Personnel Managers
Subject: Coffee-Making Facilities   *Date:* 27/4/—

There have been a number of comments about the amount of coffee consumed in our company. I do not want to sound as though I am against coffee-drinking; indeed our personnel consultants have emphasised how important coffee can be if you want an efficient and motivated office staff. But time-saving machines for making coffee do exist.
  We can expect a little opposition to the idea if we are not careful. You can never be sure how the office staff will react. They might well take it badly. In any case, we're thinking of putting in coffee machines. Please send me a report.

B   Look at the following report which was written after receiving the above memo from the MD. Do you think the report is what the MD asked for? How effective do you think the report is? Describe what you find good and what you find bad about it.

6/5/—

REPORT ON COFFEE-MAKING AND BREAKS

It is very interesting that the coffee-making habits of our employees have been noticed by other people in the company. It appears as if the time taken up by the making of coffee could be put to more productive use. We have also known for several years that there have been a number of problems connected with the motivation of our workforce, but the role played by coffee-drinking has so far not been clarified.

In one or two departments, staff seem to talk about nothing else but coffee breaks: how long is it till the break, whose turn is it to make it, etc. This unfortunate development has been discussed with the heads of department in my division on several occasions. They believe the subject of automated coffee machines, one for each department for example, is not very popular with a large number of staff. The staff think that the company would be trying to make money out of them. So I think that there is a grave danger that the actions of the management could be misunderstood.

Nonetheless, I feel that we should try and limit the coffee-breaks. We should try to prevent the staff from gathering round the coffee-making area and chatting for so long. I wonder if you have heard of the experience of our American sister company. They have a central coffee-making facility for all the divisional offices. This is then brought to the staff <u>at their desks.</u> In this way there is no need for a break. In theory this is surely one way of making working time more efficient.

C   Work in pairs. You probably agree that the managing director's intentions were unclear. What kind of report you write depends on how you interpret the memo.

1. Look at File 78 for a clearer specification of what the MD really wanted.
2. Draft a report with your partner.
3. Compare your report with the one above *and* with another pair's report.

4.3 First things first . . .

A Work in pairs. Consider some of the tasks involved in writing a report. Decide which could have helped to improve the MD's message in 4.2A. If you were writing a report which order would you do the things in? Ask your partner what he or she thinks should be done and in which order. Try to agree on a list. Number the items.

- Decide where you might need illustrations or diagrams.
- Check your grammar, spelling and punctuation and style.
- Write the body of the report.
- Summarize the report in a sentence.
- Decide what information is important and what is irrelevant.
- Write the introduction: state the subject, state the purpose, summarize findings.
- Consider the purpose of your report: who is it for, why does he or she want it, how will he or she use it?
- Check your illustrations.
- Arrange the points of information in a logical sequence and in order of importance. Make rough notes.
- Read the text aloud to yourself, or, better, to someone else.
- Ask someone else to look critically at your draft.
- Summarize the aim and emphasis of the report in one sentence.
- Write the conclusion (and recommendations).
- Collect all relevant material – notes, documents etc.
- Examine the draft. Does it do what the report is expected to do?
- Draft a working plan on a separate sheet of paper.

Has anything been left out which you think should have been included?

B Work in small groups. Discuss the order you decided on and the reasons why. How do your partners react to the ideas discussed?

"Damn it, Brookner, it seems to me your time could be better spent than by consolidating all your little notes to yourself into one big neat one."

4.4 A company report

Reading aloud

A 📼 Work in pairs. Look through the newspaper article and try
to decide what the missing words are. Listen to the recording and
complete the information missing from the article. Do you find the
report clear and informative?

GLAURI, the West German engineering and process plant group, is beginning to b.................... from its slimming down and c.................... saving measures, but is still cautious about future p.................... for orders.

Mr Erich Dietrich, chief executive, said that e.................... should recover slightly this f.................... year, despite the cost of the early r.................... scheme aimed at r.................... the workforce.

Glauri, a subsidiary of Metallco the metals, c.................... and trading concern, does not p.................... its exact earnings, but has said they d.................... last financial year as it went ahead with costly r.................... measures.

Glauri e.................... said that orders now were particularly difficult to p.................... because of the payments problems of developing countries, the uncertainty in the f.................... of the dollar and the drop in the oil price.

Mr Dietrich said that industrialised countries, including West Germany and the US were becoming more important sources of o.................... for Glauri.

D.................... orders accounted for 25 per cent of Glauri's t.................... orders in the last financial year and as much as 36 per cent so far this year.

There was a strong t.................... towards projects involving environmental protection, such as desulphurisation plants for power stations.

B Now one of you should look at File 41 and the other at 32, where
you will find a similar report to read aloud.

4.5 Using the passive

Grammar

A Work in pairs. Consider what is the difference in emphasis
between each of these pairs of sentences:

1. A room has been reserved for you at the Grand Hotel.
2. We have booked a room for you at the Grand Hotel.
3. The consignment was sent last week, so you should receive it soon.
4. We sent the consignment last week, so you should get it soon.
5. No capital is required if your company is well known.
6. You don't need any capital if your company is well known.

B Work in pairs. One of you should look at File 12, the other at 106. You will be using the passive to compare two price lists.

C Rewrite each sentence, starting with the words given, so that it means the same as the sentence on the left.

1. Six out of seven of the world's largest corporations use IBM computers.

   IBM computers...

2. We enclose payment together with our order.   Payment...

3. We will send the report as soon as it has been completed.   The report...

4. The customer should receive the delivery by Friday.   The delivery...

5. They may have notified him before the invoice arrived.   He...

6. The partners paid the staff every Friday evening.   The staff...

7. FCS marketed their new computer in Europe only.   FCS's new computer...

8. When he came back from lunch, the secretary had corrected and retyped the report.   The report...

9. They have enlarged the premises since my last visit.   The premises...

10. According to a recent report the group is making similar investments in other parts of the world.   Similar investments...

D Work in pairs. Look at the following sentences which might be found in a report. Why do you think the passive forms are used in these sentences? Would you like to receive letters or to read reports written like this?

1. It is suggested that the coffee machines should be installed so that the maximum time can be used for more productive work.
2. It is felt that Mr Brown is too old to continue in his present position.
3. It is regretted that the board of directors failed to inform the shareholders of the risks of investing in South Africa.

E Look at this text. Why do you think the passive is used here?

> First the wood is sawn into medium-sized pieces. Then it is transported to the machine shop where it is shaped and formed to make the characteristic table and chair legs. These are then smoothed and painted, before being packed into appropriate packages for onward shipment to the suppliers. The wood is often ⌐ ⌐ for this ⌐ ⌐

4.6 Punctuation

A What are the names of these punctuation marks in English?
Which name goes with which punctuation mark? The first one has
been done for you.

, ! " " / ( ) ? ' ' ; : . - —

1 comma ,	6 hyphen	10 colon
2 stroke/oblique/slash	7 dash	11 question mark
3 brackets/parentheses	8 exclamation mark	12 single quotes
4 semi-colon	9 full stop / period	13 apostrophe
5 double quotes / quotation marks / inverted commas		

B Complete these sentences by deciding which punctuation mark is
'explained' or 'illustrated'. For example, the words 'explained' and
'illustrated' in this sentence are between *single quotation marks* or
single quotes or *single inverted commas*.

1. The .... marks the end of the sentence.
2. If a .... is used, you know the sentence which you are reading hasn't
   finished yet.
3. Do people have as many problems with the .... , we wonder? What
   do you think?
4. A .... is used for word-division or word-joining.
5. And it should not be confused with another — longer — mark — the
   ....
6. Don't worry! The .... is no problem!
7. "..................... are used to show what someone actually said."
8. We have discussed several marks; we have given several examples; and we still
   have the .... to deal with.
9. Note: the .... can help to emphasize what is coming next:
   to list things: reports, letters, memos and so on.
10. If a person is not sure which word to use he/she can separate them by using the
    .... / .... / ....
11. And if they are using words (phrases or expressions) which are not of primary
    importance they can be placed between .... (.....................).
12. The ....'s use is rather limited, isn't it?

C Work in pairs. Look at the following text. Decide where to add
punctuation. You'll also need to add some Capital Letters.

memo from the md to all staff date 25th november 19— as a result
of the productivity survey carried out in the factory more rapid and
efficient ways of operating are now being applied in the factory
productivity has been increased by over 50 per cent the
management intends to apply these same methods to office staff in

order to reduce costs our company must adapt in a competitive world we aim to find ways of avoiding unnecessary actions by all staff we therefore propose to pay a months extra salary to any person who in the managements opinion has put forward the most practical suggestion to improve a particular office routine all suggestions should be sent to the mds office before the end of next month

---

4.7 Summaries and note-taking

A Work in pairs. You'll hear part of three conversations. Decide which of these notes goes with which conversation. Which of these methods of making notes do you prefer?

CONVERSATION NUMBER . . .

CONVERSATION NUMBER . . .

- suggest sending new invoice. . .   – deduct extra from total
- . . . wrongly billed. . .   – reason for 532 figure
- CK's last payment faulty. . .   – for two lots of TI40s instead of one

CONVERSATION NUMBER . . .

B You'll hear a man describing his job. Make notes, using one of the methods of writing personal notes shown above. Then draft a summary of what he says about his work.

4.8 Summarizing a conversation

It is important to take a note or make a record of all important conversations. The main points need to be clearly recorded so that another person can make sense of them (a record for the files).

A [cassette] Work in pairs. Look at these three extracts from summaries and listen to the recording. Which of the summaries do you prefer? Why?

1. **ROTAPLEX plc**   Fount Lane   Cowdray   Norfolk   CW3 7UJ
                        1 July 19—

    While on duty on the company stand a gentleman aged
    about 35 approached me and asked me how I was keeping.
    I replied that I was well and reciprocated the
    inquiry. He told me he was al~~ ~~pres~~ ~~ng ~~rn
    ~~ ~~t.

2. Notes on the Proprinta Exhibition
    To: TR Sales Manager (Tim Raven)
    From: BN (Bob Norman) Sales Representative

    Subject: Record of Consultation at PROPRINTA 30.6.—
    Firm: Happy Hidihis
    Person Met: Jim Brown. Procurement
    Nature of Inquiry: About R75

3. RECORD OF CONVERSATION AT PROPRINTA.
    Date 30.6.--
    1 Met Brown from Happy Hidihis
    2 He expressed interest in 10 R75s
    3 They want 15% discount on large order
    4. He says PRINTIX Inc will give him 15%.

B [cassette] Listen to the recording again. Draft a summary of the conversation in your own words, continuing one of the summaries above.

4.9 Summarizing a message orally

Giving the main points of a message or taking notes on what we are told or have heard is a very important skill when using English in business. Taking notes on what we've heard is more difficult than making notes on something we've read.

≫→

A Work in pairs. Which of this advice do you find useful?

1. Never write in complete sentences.
2. Don't use so many abbreviations that your notes are meaningless later!
3. Use key words like **because**, **therefore**, **but** or **and** to indicate the relations between ideas.
4. Use the dash – . It is the most useful punctuation mark in note-taking.
5. Use a lot of space – then you can expand your notes later. Put each idea on a new line.
6. Use the layout: paragraphs, headings and underlinings to help make the meaning clear.

B 🔲 Look at these messages. Listen to the recording and decide which message goes with which set of notes.

1

TELEPHONE NOTES

DATE .28/6/–– .... TIME .10.25 ....
MESSAGE FOR.... Peter Jones ....
....
FROM.. Station Hotel ....
MESSAGE receptionist..................
Single room with bath e w.c.....
confirmation of booking for....
29–30 June for Mr. Piccoli....
....
TAKEN BY .Christine Jackson ....

2

TELEPHONE NOTES

DATE 1.7/5/–– .... TIME 2.45pm ....
MESSAGE FOR. Ron Black ....
.Dispatch Department ....
FROM Mr. Akomba, Lagos ....
MESSAGE Components not on overnight...
flight from Stansted. Telex...
with longer instructions coming...
Please contact when...
.telex arrives ....
TAKEN BY .Pauline Frazer ....

3

TELEPHONE NOTES

DATE 3/2/–– .... TIME .11.10 ....
MESSAGE FOR. Donald Ashton, Finance ....
....
FROM.. Sally Courtney ....
MESSAGE Maria Doares' P.A. met at...
airport at Lisbon. Straight to......
industrias Conservas – quick tour....
of plant. Then talk with MD later...
Preliminary results first thing......
TAKEN BY .Pauline Frazer ....

4

TELEPHONE NOTES

DATE 24/4/–– .... TIME .9.30 ....
MESSAGE FOR. Michael Moore ....
.Purchasing Dept...................
FROM. Mr. Johannsen ....
MESSAGE Bicolor Uppsala calling........
tomorrow to see Research team. Can
he bring samples home interior paints
from Bicolor? Said you free about 11...
Must ring back and confirm ....
TAKEN BY .Christine Jackson ....

C Work in pairs. Take it in turns to tell each other what the telephone messages were about.

D 🔲 Listen to the second part of the recording. You'll hear some more phone calls – this time you'll have to make notes yourself.

40

4.10 Writing reports and summaries *Vocabulary*

Fill the gaps with words from the list.

circular   classify   clarify   cover   essentials   observe
recipient   submit   topic   transmit

1. The purpose of writing letters, memos and reports is usually to .... information from one person to another.
2. But before you can begin to write a report about anything at all, you need to .... the purpose for which you are writing it.
3. Before writing a report about a complicated process, you will find it helpful to .... it first for a period of time.
4. You will also need to .... all the data you have collected.
5. At the top of a memo or report don't forget to name the ....
6. You should start a new par. (paragraph) for each new ....
7. When you finally do write your report, the pieces of information you should never forget are the ....
8. The deadline is the latest time you can .... a report.
9. When you are writing a summary of what has happened, you should always try to .... the main points.
10. A letter that is sent to many different people in a company is called a .... (letter).

4.11 Communication in business *Discussion*

A Work in small groups. Arrange the following pieces of advice into those you think *helpful, unhelpful* or *untrue*, or just *OK*. Then, put them into the order you think most important for someone using English in business.
Add at least *three* more pieces of advice to the list.

1 Keeping written records is helpful for future reference.
2 If you make a mistake when you are writing a letter, you can correct it before sending it off.
3 Once you have said something, you cannot take it back.
4 If you speak to someone face to face, it is much easier to be honest.
5 Making a phone call is an easy way to solve a problem if you have no time to write a letter.
6 If you want to show the other person your feelings, then never write a letter.
7 If you are placing an order, then do it in writing.
8 If someone owes you money, it is no use phoning them up.

B Discuss which forms of communication you ought to / would like to be able to perform in English.

5 The place of work

Talking about where you work. Agreeing and disagreeing. Referring to the past. Describing a company's activities, organization and history.

5.1 Getting to know the place . . .

A Work in pairs. Look at this list and decide together which points are important when you're starting a new job:

- be punctual
- wear your smartest clothes (not trousers if you're a woman)
- go to the hairdresser's the day before
- smile at everybody you meet
- find out what the canteen food is like
- offer to pay for your own coffee
- make a note of everything anyone tells you
- ask if you can start work as soon as possible
- show your new colleagues pictures of your family
- if you're a smoker, don't smoke in an office you share with someone
- if you're a non-smoker, say you don't mind if the person you share the office with wants to smoke
- wait until you have been introduced before you speak to anyone else
- apply to go on a special training course
- ask where to get your luncheon vouchers
- inquire about the company pension scheme
- ask who is the trade union representative

B 🔲 You'll hear a new employee being told where the different offices are in the firm she has just joined.
1. Listen to the conversation and name the rooms shown with a ✱ on the plan on the next page.
2. Compare your answers with your partner's.
3. Discuss with your partner which of the things you talked about earlier would apply to Michelle.

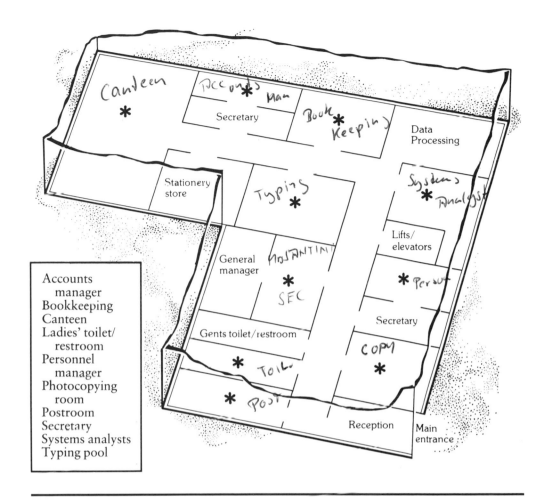

Accounts
  manager
Bookkeeping
Canteen
Ladies' toilet/
  restroom
Personnel
  manager
Photocopying
  room
Postroom
Secretary
Systems analysts
Typing pool

5.2 Agreeing and disagreeing
Functions

There are different ways of reacting to other people's opinions,
depending on how well you know the person and whether you agree
or disagree.

Look at these expressions for agreeing and disagreeing with
what someone has said.

If you want to agree with someone you can say:

> That's exactly what I think.
> That's just what I was
> thinking.

> In my opinion, office workers
> are not paid well enough.

> That's a good point.
> I agree entirely.

⫸→

If you want to disagree with someone:

Quite right, I couldn't agree more.
Yes, I'm all in favour of that.

I can see what you mean, but...
I don't think so, because...
I don't think it's a good idea...

Well, my opinion for what it's worth...

Maybe, but don't you think...?
That's true, but on the other hand...

A Work in pairs. Listen to the recordings and decide what the people in each conversation are talking about. Mark the expressions above that you hear the speakers using.

B Work in pairs. Look at these rather extreme opinions.

Smoking should be forbidden in offices.
All offices should have flowers in them.
All companies should offer their employees free lunches.
Overtime should be obligatory if the day's work is not done.

Make up a conversation about each topic using the expressions above. For example.
  'I think it would be a good idea if all firms had facilities for looking after pre-school children.'
  'I can see what you mean, but it would be a difficult thing to introduce.'
  or 'I agree entirely.'

C Work in groups of three or four. Ask your partners what they think of the following opinions of the actions of management and bosses. Decide which of the opinions you can agree on:

- people working in business should be told what to do and should do it without asking questions
- employees want to be recognized as people with their own (personal) needs
- employees have to be forced to work: otherwise they are just lazy
- managers need to closely control what employees do
- nobody wants responsibility at work
- if there are problems to be solved in a company, everybody should be asked their opinion before anything is done.

Then ask another group what they have agreed on and see if you agree. Can the two groups together agree on how management should act? Should it be authoritarian or co-operative?

5.3 Computers

Work in pairs. Complete each sentence with one of the words in the list.

disk   disk drive   display   hard disk   keyboard   menu
microprocessor   modem   monitor   mouse   operating system
printer   RAM (Random Access Memory)   ROM (Read Only Memory)
software

1. A *keyboard* is what you use to input information into the computer. It works like a normal typewriter.
2. The *disk drive* is where you place the disks to start the program.
3. The *monitor* shows what you type and the computer's calculations.
4. The *display* is what you can actually see.
5. The *menu* is a list of information that lets you choose what to do next.
6. The *printer* is used for making hard copies of what you can see.
7. Information is stored outside the computer on *disk*.
8. Many modern computers have a *mouse*, with which you can move an arrow to point at different parts of the screen.
9. The *microprocessor* is the heart of the computer and controls everything it does.
10. *Software* is another term for the programs you use on a computer.
11. A *modem* is a device which connects a computer to a telephone line.
12. As an alternative to putting information on a floppy disk you can use a *hard disk*
13. *ROM* are chips in the computer with permanent instructions and programs which you can't alter.
14. The *operating system* is a complex set of instructions which tells the computer how to carry out different tasks.
15. *RAM* is the facility the computer uses to store programming information temporarily. The bigger this is, the more complicated the tasks the computer can carry out.

"You know what I miss? Paper aeroplanes."

5.4 Explaining the company organization

A Look at the structure of the company in the diagram. Work in pairs. Guess what some of the missing job titles might be.

B [cassette icon] Listen to the recording and fill in the names and titles or job descriptions that are missing.

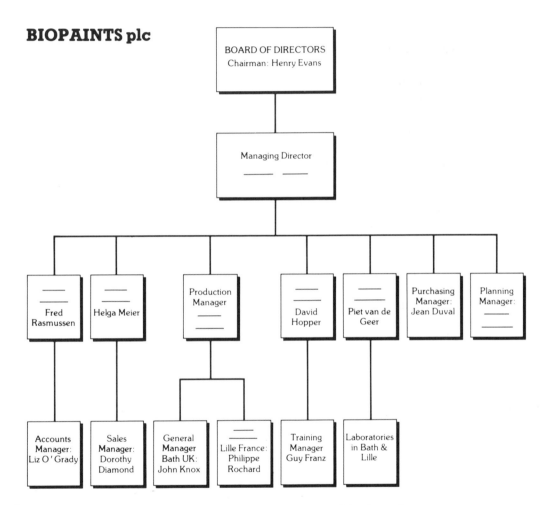

BIOPAINTS plc

BOARD OF DIRECTORS
Chairman: Henry Evans

Managing Director
——— ———

Fred Rasmussen

Helga Meier

Production Manager
———

David Hopper

Piet van de Geer

Purchasing Manager: Jean Duval

Planning Manager:
———

Accounts Manager: Liz O'Grady

Sales Manager: Dorothy Diamond

General Manager Bath UK: John Knox

Lille France: Philippe Rochard

Training Manager Guy Franz

Laboratories in Bath & Lille

C Which of the people mentioned are also members of the board? Discuss with your partner what other parts of the company have perhaps not been mentioned. For example, to whom would the following people report: The Public Relations Manager, the Works Manager, the Advertising Manager and the Accounts Manager. Say why you think so. What other kinds of company do you know?

D Work in pairs. One of you looks at File 19 and the other looks at 26.

5.5 What the company does . . .

A Work in pairs. Look at these symbols. Decide what areas of business you think they could stand for.
Which areas do some companies in your country belong to?
Discuss the kind of business or company *you* might find it interesting to work for.

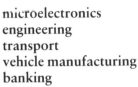

chemicals   microelectronics
retailing   engineering
shipping   transport
catering   vehicle manufacturing
insurance   banking
aerospace

B Now read the advertisement on the next page. It describes a company's development and its present operations. If you wanted to select a symbol for this company, which one would you choose?

C Work in pairs. Read the text once more and decide what information or events the following figures, numbers and years refer to in the text:

last five years
13 percent   13.8 percent   14.5 percent
30   50 percent
SF340
1890's   1930's   1985
47000
2.8 billions   4.4 billions   32 billions

D Work in pairs. Imagine that your company would like to know more about the Saab-Scania Group. As it suggests at the end of the ad, now draft a letter to the company asking the publicity officer / public relations department for further information.
When you have finished, compare your letter with another pair.

E Work in small groups. Discuss what advantages and disadvantages you can see in working for a company like the one described in the advertisement.

The Saab-Scania tradition points in one direction.

Commitment to the future.
We began manufacturing vehicles in the 1890's and aircraft in the 1930's. With the result that over a long period Saab-Scania has established a solid base of technical experience and engineering skill. In our areas of operation Saab-Scania has always been an innovative force.

This commitment to the future requires determined backing. For the last five years we have invested, on average, 13 percent of sales income in research and development, property and plant. Activities which have all been funded from within the Group.

In the field of specialized transport technology the symbol of Saab-Scania is the sign of tradition and financial strength.

The Saab-Scania Group manufactures automotive and aerospace products: passenger cars, trucks and buses, military aircraft, missiles, satellites and the Saab SF340 airliner. The Group also develops other advanced products in the fields of electronics, optics, sensors and image processing as well as in the area of energy technology.

We employ 47 000 people in locations in Sweden and 30 other countries.
In 1985 the Group sales were SEK 32 billions (GBP 2.9 billions) with profits of 2.8 billions (GBP 255.2 m.). Return on total assets was 14.5 percent, solvency (equity/asset ratio) was 50 percent and capital expenditure amounted to 4.4 billions (GBP 401.1 m.), equal to 13.8 percent of sales.

SAAB-SCANIA
Leaders in specialized transport technology.

For further information please write to Saab-Scania AB, Corporate Communications and Public Affairs, S-581 88 Linköping, Sweden.

48

5.6 Company news

Flaxco: last year's results

Extracts from the statement by
the Chairman, Paul Northfield:
'This year's re~~sult~~~ ~~the latest~~
~~·· ·· ·· ·~~

A Work in pairs. Write down some of the words and phrases you
think the chairman will use to describe his company's performance.
How do you think he will present them? Positively? Negatively?
What do the shareholders want to hear, do you think?

B 🔲 You'll hear the chairman of Flaxco Industries answering
questions put to him by journalists at a press conference. Does it turn
out the way you expected?

C Work in pairs. Which of these extracts from the company's
report are referred to in the press conference?

> . . . This year's results are the latest in an unbroken
> sequence of rapid growth over the last six years.
> . . . The successful penetration of major international
> markets has been the driving force behind the recent
> growth of the group.
> . . . The group has concentrated its resources and effort
> on medicines of the highest quality.
> . . . Our concentration on prescription medicines has
> enabled us to devote resources and management effort
> to the development of our main business. It has led to
> large increases in profits and earnings.
> . . . Our biggest research effort, by far, is in the UK . . .
> . . . but we are also expanding our basic research
> activity in Italy as well as in the USA.
> . . . Our group sells its products in one hundred and fifty
> countries through a network of seventy subsidiary and
> associate companies.

D Decide which of the points you heard discussed in the recording
are *not* mentioned in the report extracts.

5.7 Referring to the past *Grammar*

🔊 There are different ways of speaking about past events and actions in English. Study these examples:

1. Talking about something STARTING in the past but CONTINUING up to the present:

> How long have you been working for the company?

> I've been here since I left school.

> Have you finished that filing?

> Yes, I've just put the last letter away.

2. Writing or saying something has happened which is STILL RELEVANT for the present:
   We have received notification of your visit . . .
   We have booked a room at the Plaza Hotel for the 16th March 19—.

3. Referring to finished events that have a NEWS VALUE:
   We've signed the contract with OBM.
   Vandebrinck have at last patented their new automatic packing technique.
   I've invited Jacques Lacroix over for lunch to talk about the new site plans in Le Havre.

4. Referring to events which took place IN THE PAST:
   We despatched the shipment, as requested.
   They interviewed Roland Thoreau for the job, but he didn't get it.
   Because we did a lot of advertising, we sold a lot of products last year.

5. Sometimes the ways of referring to the past can be used together:
   – Have you been to the trade fair yet?
   – Yes, I have. I went yesterday.
   – And did you see anything worth buying?

6. The past and the present can be closely related:
   – Are you still working on that report?
   – Yes, I am. I've been drafting a new introduction.
   – Mr Casagrande has travelled all over the world, but now he's working for our office in Kuala Lumpur.

A Fill the gaps in these sentences with a suitable verb from the list, as in this example:

She's *been trying* to get through to head office all morning.

go   have   make   open   post   receive   search
send   start   stop   use   visit   work

1. Our company ....*has used*.... computers in its offices now for a long time.
2. We're very busy today. The phone ....*has*.... hardly ....*stopped*.... ringing since I arrived in the office this morning.
3. ....*Have*.... you ....*ever seen*.... Madrid before? Yes, I ....*was*.... there last year on business.
4. In 1986 our enterprise ....*opened*.... a factory in South America.
5. I ....*started*.... working here when I left school.
6. 'Is your secretary still looking for the file?' 'Yes, she *is searching*.... for it for the past twenty minutes.' *has been*
7. I'm sorry to keep you waiting. I *had to make* a phone call to Paris.
8. While you ....*were having*.... lunch, Mr Casagrande phoned.
9. We ....*sent*.... the letter to our parent company a week ago, but we *haven't received* a reply yet. *posted*
10. His firm ....*sent*.... him to their New York office and he ....*is working*.... there ever since.

B Work in groups of three or four. Find out about your partners' past: *place of birth, schools attended, where they lived, jobs* etc. What they did before starting their present job or starting college. What they have been doing until this moment in time.
MAKE NOTES ON WHAT YOU FIND OUT.

C Work in pairs with someone who was a member of a *different* group. Tell your new partner what you found out about the first group, referring to your notes to help you remember. Choose one of your partners' notes and try and find someone in the class who has a similar background to your partner.

5.8 A firm's history

A Work in pairs. Decide which are the largest and/or most important companies in your city or region. Make a list of ten you can agree on. (If you are in a multinational class what are the top ten firms in your country?) Make a list of the products they make or the services they supply, e.g. they manufacture cars, supply energy, finance etc.

⟫→

B Work in pairs. Look at the following two passages about two companies. Which of the headlines goes with which passage?

Planning and Building since 1849

Pioneering Tomorrow's Electronics

Philipp Holzmann AG has grown from a family firm to a highly reputable, major international concern.

In 1849 a company was established in Sprendlingen, near Frankfurt, by Johann Philipp Holzmann, primarily for railroad construction. Over the years, the company diversified its activities to all areas of building and civil engineering. As early as 1882, the company completed its first large foreign order – the main railway station in Amsterdam. This proved the starting-point for commissions from all over the world, including the construction of the Anatolian and Baghdad Railroads, and other major new rail links in East Africa. Subsidiaries set up by Holzmann in South America have built power stations, underground rail systems, municipal drainage schemes, bridges, and large buildings. These companies operated in Argentina, Brazil, Chile, Colombia, Peru and Uruguay. In 1917 Philipp Holzmann Aktiengesellschaft was founded, the same share-issuing corporation which exists today. During the Second World War, Holzmann lost a relatively large proportion of its business premises, operating facilities and construction machinery, as well as its foreign assets. Through great effort, foreign business was restarted by 1950. Since then some impressive construction projects have been carried out, particularly in the Middle East and Africa. These provide ample evidence of the company's capabilities in all areas of construction work. Through the J.A. Jones Construction Company of Charlotte, USA, and Lockwood Greene Engineers Inc. of Spartanburg, USA, Holzmann is once again well represented on the American continent.

Philipp Holzmann AG is today one of the largest German industrial concerns and one of the elite group of leading international construction companies.

Over the decades, the name of Siemens has become synonymous with progress. Since 1847, when Werner Siemens and Johann Georg Halske founded the Siemens & Halske Telegraph Construction Company in Berlin, the history of Siemens has been closely linked with the development of electrical engineering. While still a fledgling firm, Siemens & Halske spearheaded the evolution of telegraphy with the first pointer telegraph and the construction of an extensive telegraph network. In 1866 Werner Siemens invented the dynamo machine, laying the cornerstone of power engineering.

New ideas are an old tradition at Siemens. The company that grew out of the original Siemens & Halske is today a highly innovative leader in the world electrical and electronics market. Composed of Siemens AG and an array of domestic and foreign subsidiaries, the contemporary Siemens organization continues to set milestones on the road of progress.

Siemens maintains its own production facilities in 35 countries and operates a world-wide sales network. With more than 300,000 employees, it is one of the largest companies in the world electrical/electronics industry, having recorded annual sales of DM 54 billion in the 1986/87 fiscal year. Reliable and farsighted management is united with the youthful dynamism and zest for innovation that typify the company.

C Complete the information missing in this table.

Dates	What happened?	Who did what?
1847	*Siemens & Halske TCC*	*was founded by Werner S.)*
1849	*a company was establ.*	*by Joh. Phillip*
1866	invention of dynamo machine	*Werner Siem*
1882	first large foreign order completed	*comp. Holzm.*
1917	*Ph. Holzmann AG founded*	*Philip Holzm. comp: Holz.*
1955	foreign business restarted	*Siemens*
1984/85	recorded annual sales of *5.4.5 billion*	*Siemens*

Complete the following table:

Company	*Holzmann AG*	*Siemens AG*
Locations of company activities	*Sprendlingen near the*	*Berlin*
Activities of both companies up to 1940s	*railroad coads building underground*	*development of electrical engineer. points telegraph telegraph network*
Recent activities of the companies	*Construction comp. worldwide*	*electrical, electronics company worldwide*

D Work in pairs. One of you looks at File 23, the other looks at 40. You'll each have different information about another company.

5.9 Company world

Vocabulary

Fill in the gaps with words from the list.

administration   commerce   corporate   involve   launch
merge   phase   prosper   take over   white-collar

1. How many people are ...*involved*... in marketing the new product?
2. The latest model of our electric car will be ...*taken over*... on 1 January 19—.
3. When a firm begins to do badly on the stock market, plans are often made to change its .....*corporate*... structure.   ⟫⟫→

53

4. The management of contemporary corporations requires people who know how to ......*manage*...... .
5. Despite the problems in our sector our company expects to continue to ....*prosper*.... in the next twelve months.
6. Hong Kong has always been a centre of ...*administration*...
7. Giant companies which have been successful in the past have normally .... with their closest rivals.
8. In the course of the history of our company we have gone through several ....*phases*.... of development.
9. After a brief slump in annual growth they were ..*t*............... by a major competitor.
10. In order to deal with all the additional paper-work we need to expand the .... staff by several hundred.

5.10   The new office   *Discussion*

A   Imagine your office is about to be computerized.
Work in pairs and discuss your reactions. What advantages and disadvantages can you see in using electronic machines? Compare your experiences.

B   ⬜ You will hear some people talking about the effects that computers have had on their working lives. Match the summaries below to the speakers. How much have their lives changed?

4	6	1	3	7	2	5
Anita	*Peter*	*Roberta*	*Andrew*	*Edward*	*Monica*	*William*

   1. Without organizing jobs differently, introducing computers doesn't help.
   2. Computers create more work.
   3. Computers reduce everything to numbers.
   4. People begin to feel like machines.
   5. Future office work will be unrecognizable.
   6. Computer systems do not always function.
   7. The purpose of computers is not always clear.

C   Which of the points you discussed earlier were *not* mentioned in the recording?

D   Think of the offices you work in (or offices you have worked in at some time). Imagine that you have the authority and the budget to reorganize them – what changes will you make? What facilities will you introduce? What up-to-date equipment will you install? Draw a plan of your offices.

E   Design 'the perfect office'.

6 Import and export

Ordering and supplying goods or services.
Making enquiries. Answering enquiries and
making offers. Placing and acknowledging orders.
Getting and giving information. Talking about
the future.

6.1 Getting and giving information

A 🔲 In the recording a customer, Mr Rusconi, and a supplier,
Mr Garcia, are talking on the phone. You'll hear *two* versions of this
conversation. Which of these words describe the *impression* they each
give in the two versions?

friendly   informal   helpful   unhelpful   formal   cold
polite   rude

B Take a look at these useful expressions:

If you require some information you can say:

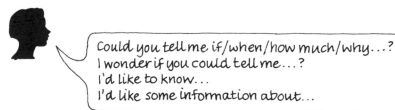

> Could you tell me if/when/how much/why...?
> I wonder if you could tell me...?
> I'd like to know...
> I'd like some information about...

Or you can write:

```
We require the following information...
Please let us know whether/when/how much...
```

When someone gives you some information, you can reply:

> Oh, I see.
> That's interesting.
> Really?
> Thanks for letting me know.

If someone asks you for information, you can reply:

> As far as I know, ...
> Well, in confidence, I can tell you that...
>
> I'm afraid I don't know.
> I've no idea, I'm afraid.
> I don't have that information available just now. Can I call you back?
> I'm not sure, I'll have to find out. Can I let you know tomorrow?
> I'm afraid I can't tell you that – it's confidential.

If you want to give someone some information you can say:

> I'd like you to know that...
> I think you should know that...
> Did you know that...?

Or you can write:

```
We should like to inform you that...
Here is the information you required...
```

If someone hasn't given you enough information you can say:

> Could you tell me some more about...?
> I'd like some more information about...
> I'd also like to know...
> When/How much/Why exactly...?
> There's something else I'd like to know: ...
> Can you give me some more details about...?

C Working alone, note down some information about:

- the companies *and* the people you have worked with
- your own home town *or* another town you know quite well
- your business career *or* your educational career
- your family and your personal relationships

Now join another student. Find out as much as you can about the information your partner has noted down.
Use the expressions above as you ask and answer the questions – and when avoiding answering.

D Work in pairs. One of you should look at File 17, the other at 42. You will each have some information to share with your partner about the products in a catalogue.

6.2 Making enquiries

ABOUT BROADWAY AUTOS

BROADWAY AUTOS is a subsidiary of BroadWay International Inc of Portland, Oregon. BROADWAY manufactures and markets two types of battery-driven electric vehicles: short-range delivery vehicles and one-person cars for disabled people. The vehicle bodies are manufactured in BROADWAY's own factory, but all other components including electric motors, batteries and wheels are bought to 2 month's stock and assembled in the factory. Over the years BROADWAY has built up a good relationship with its suppliers, most of whom have been working with them for many years.

YOUR ROLE:
You and your partner have just joined the Buying Department of BROADWAY AUTOS. Your boss is an American, Mr Fred North.

A 📼 You'll hear Mr North talking on the phone. What do you think he will ask you to do for him?

While Mr North is at lunch you notice this article in today's paper:

Arcolite to close Winterthur factory

ARCOLITE Electric AG have announced 200 redundancies at their long-established factory in Winterthur, Switzerland. Production will continue at their main plant in Lausanne, according to the announcement.

Arcolite's Director General, Mr Franz Anders, told our reporter: "This represents a rationalisation of our resources. We shall be creating 50 new jobs in our Lausanne plant. We have been wanting to expand on our Winterthur site for some time now, but this has finally proved to be uneconomic. I can assure our customers that there will be no interruption to supplies and we have sufficient stock to fill our current order book."

Arcolite shares fell from SF 3.220 to 2.975 on the Zurich Exchange after the announcement.

Decide together what you will say to Mr North when he gets back from lunch.

B To be on the safe side, Mr North wants *you* to find out about other suppliers. While he is away on a 10-day trip, you will be in charge. As no local firms can supply the product, you will have to contact possible suppliers abroad and ask for quotations.

Read the letter from Mr North to Jacques Roget, an old friend in the battery business, on the next page.

BROADWAY Autos

XXX Xxxxxxxx Xxxx, 62008 Xxxxxxxx, Xxxxxxx

TELEX 889765   TELEPHONE 0473 88999 (8 lines)

Jacques Roget
Rex et Cie
34 rue du Professeur Nicolas
35009 Clermont Ferrand
France   3 November 19—

Dear Jacques,

Lightweight Polymeric batteries

  I'm writing to you because we've been having a bit of trouble
with one of our suppliers who makes the lightweight batteries we
use to power our vehicles. I'm pretty sure you don't have a local
distributor of your products in this country, which is why I'm
writing to you direct to see if you can help us out. I did try to
call, but you weren't available.
  I'm sending some copies of our technical brochures so that you
can see what we need. Here's the specification:

Polymeric Batteries

Maximum Size: Height: 200mm   Depth: 200mm   Width: 300mm
Maximum Weight: 5 kg
Output: 1000 watts @ 12 volts
Rechargeable life at full power:8 hours
Labels: Each unit should bear a label giving:
    The output of the battery, its month and year of manufacture,
    your own company's name and country, a product code number and
    a unique unit number
Quantity: 4,800 units
Delivery: by 15 January 19—

  I'd appreciate it if you could quote us your best CIF price,
giving a full specification of your product and shipping date. Of
course our technical department would need to have some samples of
the batteries to test in our laboratories before we could place a
firm order.
  We usually deal with new suppliers on the basis of payment in
our currency by confirmed irrevocable Letter of Credit.
  Assuming the laboratory tests go well, and you can quote us a
competitive price, we'd certainly be able to place more
substantial orders on a regular basis.
  I'll be out of the office for a couple of weeks from tomorrow.
In the meantime, do get in touch with one of my assistants A—— or
B—— if you need any more information.
  Looking forward to hearing from you.
  Give my regards to Jeanne and the kids.

Best,

Fred A. North, Buying Manager

C Draft a short letter of enquiry explaining your needs, to be sent by airmail or fax to other battery companies.
Your letter will need to be written in a more formal, impersonal style than Mr North's. You should include this information:

- Introduce your firm and its products to the reader:

  We are...

- State the purpose of your letter, telex or phone call:

  We are seeking a supplier of...

- Give an exact description or specification of goods you require –
  size, weight, material, quantity, delivery, special features:

  This is the specification of the goods we require...

- Explain what you want the reader to do:

  Please quote us your best delivered/CIF price and shipping date.
  Before placing an order we would need to examine samples of the
  product.

- State the terms, methods of payment, discounts you expect:

  We usually pay by confirmed 60–day irrevocable letter of credit.

- End on an optimistic note and request an early reply:

  There is a good prospect of our placing regular orders.
  We hope to be able to place further orders with you.
  We look forward to receiving an early reply.

D When you have written your first draft, show it to another pair.
Look at their letter and consider these points:

Does it cover all the essential points?
Is the information correct?
Is it clear, concise and courteous?
Does it sound natural and sincere?
Will it create the right impression?

Is it the kind of letter you'd like to receive yourself?

When you have exchanged comments, write your final draft.

E Richard Duvall, the sales representative of one of your local suppliers, suggests you call his friend *Jim Dale*, the sales manager of Ramco Batteries in Manchester to ask for a quotation.

📞 Roleplay the phone call:
- Student A should look at File 96 for more information about the role of Mr Dale.
- Student B should make notes before making the call.

F In answer to one of your enquiries, you receive a letter from another firm, Artemis Batteries:

Artemis Batteries

33 Bbbbb Avenue, Cccccc
Telephone: 98 45 83   Telex 778303 TB   Fax 448908

Mr Fred North
Purchasing Manager
Broadway Autos
Xxxxxxxx Xxxxxx   9 November 19—

Dear Mr North,
   Thank you very much for your enquiry. We are of course very familiar with your range of vehicles and are pleased to inform you that we have a new line in batteries that fit your specifications exactly.
   The most suitable of our products for your requirements is the Artemis 66A Plus. This product combines economy, high power output and quick charging time and is available now from stock.
   I enclose a detailed quotation with prices, specifications and delivery terms. As you will see from this, our prices are very competitive. I have arranged for our agent Mr Martin of Fillmore S.A. to deliver five of these batteries to you next week, so that you can carry out the laboratory tests. Our own laboratory reports, enclosed with this letter, show that our new Artemis 66A Plus performs as well as any of our competitors' products and, in some respects, outperforms them.
   If you would like further information, please telephone or telex me: my extension number is 776. Or you may prefer to contact Mr John Martin of Fillmore S.A. in M——: his telephone number is 01 77 99 02.

   I look forward to hearing from you,
   Yours sincerely,

G Artemis can supply the product at 15% less than Arcolite's present price. Both Rex and Ramco are quoting 10% lower than Arcolite. Mr North wants to make Rex your *sole supplier*:

- Should you agree with him or should you argue the case for having more than one supplier?
- If Arcolite drop their price to the same level as Rex, should you then stick with Arcolite as sole supplier?

H Choosing a good supplier involves a lot more than just finding the lowest price:
   What does a buyer look for, besides a good price?

6.3 Sales and delivery

A Fill the gaps with suitable words from the list below.

backlog   bill of exchange   bill of lading   bulky   cash on delivery
cash with order   crates   deadline   grade   hold-up
inventory control (US) / stock control (GB)   margin   premium   retail
special delivery   surcharge   tender   triplicate
including value added tax   volume   wholesale

1. The profits made on a product vary according to the .... of sales and there is not normally a fixed profit .... on the unit price.
2. The .... price of this product (ie the price the consumer pays) is £13.99 incl. VAT (....................) – about 60% more than the .... price.
3. As we have been carrying out a(n) .... , there is a .... in processing orders. We apologize for any inconvenience caused by this ....
4. As part of the consignment is very urgent, we'll be making a .... of two of the twenty .... you have ordered.
5. We only supply .... one products of .... quality. Very .... consignments are shipped by sea. There is no .... for small orders.
6. They submitted a .... in .... , in accordance with our instructions, but it arrived after the ....
7. If you buy something by mail order it's normal to pay C.W.O. (........................), rather than C.O.D. (........................).
8. What's the difference between a B/L (........................) and a B/E (........................)?

B In foreign trade, prices are quoted using 'Incoterms'. Fill the gaps in these sentences. Use a dictionary if necessary.

1. **ex-works:** this price is the cost for the goods at the supplier's factory gate. The .... pays for freight carriage and insurance.
2. **ex-warehouse:** this price is the cost at the .... 's warehouse.
3. **FAS** Liverpool: this price includes all costs to a named port of shipment F........................ A........................ S........................ . The buyer pays for loading, onward shipment and insurance.
4. **FOB** Felixtowe: this price includes all costs of the goods F............ O............ B............ a ship (or aircraft) whose destination is stated in the contract.
5. **C & F** Kobe: this price covers Cost and F........................ , but not insurance, to a named port of destination in the buyer's country.
6. **CIF** Athens: this price covers C........................ , I........................ and F........................ to a named port of destination in the buyer's country.
7. **CIP:** this price is the cost of the goods, freight C................ , and I................ P................ by container to a named destination in the buyer's country.
8. **DCP:** this price is the cost of goods and transport, excluding insurance, D................ C................ P................ by container to a named destination.
9. **DDP** Zürich: this price is for all costs of the goods D................ D................ P................ all the way to the buyer's works or warehouse address.

6.4 Answering enquiries

Are you AFRAID... about security?

AntiSpy Products

**333 Rosedale Drive,
Bakersfield, CA 93002, USA
Telephone: 456/453 9000
Telex: 87869 Telefax: 9937**

AntiSpy Products have ALL the answers:

Afraid that someone has planted a bug somewhere?
The battery driven **AntiSpy**™ CJ4000P will detect any eavesdropping devices within 20 feet. Looks just like a Walkman and costs only $359.

Afraid that people may overhear your confidential phone calls?
The **AntiSpy**™ LR 44 "Octopus" portable telephone scrambler can be used anywhere in hotel rooms, phone booths etc. Disguised in an ordinary executive briefcase, it costs only $299.

Afraid that spies outside your building can "read" your computer screen? (Yes it can and does happen – we ourselves sell equipment that can do this!) Fit the **NEW AntiSpy**™ SP 700 computer screen protector to each PC or terminal and you can stop worrying. The SP 700 fixes to any computer screen and acts also as anti-reflection filter.

Special introductory price till May 1st while stocks last: $199 per unit or $499 for six. (Regular price $299)

All our prices are **carriage paid by air.**
Full no-argument money-back **guarantee** on all our products.
Send $50 for catalog. Refundable against purchase.
All major credit cards accepted.

A Work in pairs. Imagine that you both work in the export department of AntiSpy Products. It's your job to answer enquiries about your products. First, read the advertisement for your products above.

B Look at this OUTLINE. It gives some ideas for a 'typical' answer to an enquiry by letter, telex or phone – or even to a personal enquiry:

1. Thank the customer for their interest in your product(s) and confirm that you can (or can't) help
2. 'Sell' your product(s) and explain how it is suitable for your customer's needs
3. Say that you're sending a catalogue, price list, advertising literature etc

4. Explain how the customer can get 'hands-on' experience of the product(s):
   - offer to send samples or get rep to visit with samples/demo
   - state the location of distributor's showroom near enquirer's address
   - announce an exhibit at a forthcoming trade fair
5. QUOTE:
   - exactly what you are selling: confirm the specification of your product(s)
   - prices in buyer's or another hard currency, including terms of delivery (CIF, DDP, FOB etc) and validity:

   ```
   Total: 3450 US dollars CIF Incoterms
   The prices shown in this offer are valid for a period
   of 60 days from the date hereof
   ```

   - discounts: for cash/bulk etc
   - terms of payment: cwo / open account / letter of credit etc*

   ```
   Payment by irrevocable letter of credit in US dollars
   on a United States bank, allowing part-shipment,
   transhipment and house bills, and valid for 90 days
   from order date
   Payment with order by banker's draft or cheque on a US
   bank
   ```

   - shipping date

   ```
   The goods will be ready for shipment 3 to 4 weeks from
   receipt of your written order (and confirmation of
   your letter of credit)
   ```

6. End on an optimistic note and encourage the customer to phone or telex you *personally* for more information.

   - What would you *add* to the outline given above?
   - What would you prefer *not* to include?

C Look at File 115 to see a print-out of your current stock position and prices. You'll need to refer to this again during the activity. Using the information given in the advertisement and the printout, draft replies to enquiries #1 and #2 on the next page.

After you have written each draft, show it to another pair and get them to answer these questions:
   Does it cover all the essential points?　　Does it sound natural and sincere?
   Is the information correct?　　Will it create the right impression?
   Is it clear, concise and courteous?

   Is it the kind of letter/telex you would like to receive yourself?

* Terms of payment are covered in more detail in Unit 7

Enquiry #1 (extract from telex)

```
PLEASE SEND YOUR CATALOG AND CHARGE MY AMEX
#667589980 EXPIRY DATE AUGUST 15, 19--.
REGARDS HANSON, JOHNSON OIL, BRISBANE, AUSTRALIA
```

YOUR REPLY (by telex): Thank you for your enquiry. We're sending you our catalogue. We've debited your American Express card $50 US. The $50 will be discounted from your purchase. Please get in touch with me (name) if you have any queries.

Enquiry #2 (extract from telex)

```
DO YOU SUPPLY A PORTABLE LISTENING DEVICE
DETECTOR? IS THIS AVAILABLE FROM STOCK? PLEASE
QUOTE YOUR BEST DDP AIRFREIGHT PRICE FOR FIVE.
RGDS, PEREZ, ANDES MINING CO, BOGOTA, COLOMBIA
```

YOUR REPLY (by telex): Yes, from stock. Prices include shipping. Brief description of product. $50 secures our complete 120pp catalogue.

D 🔲 You'll hear a phone call: one of your colleagues is on the phone to Japan. Alter the stock position on your print-out in File 115 and then draft replies to Enquiries #3 and #4, this time as letters. Again, get another pair to evaluate each of your drafts.

Enquiry #3 (extract from letter)

```
I would like to know about the availability of a telephone
scrambler. If you have one, please let me know the price.
Is this product suitable for both tone dial and pulse
dial? Also is it suitable for different voltages?
```

YOUR REPLY: Yes. Quote prices. Available now / from Aug 15. Yes to both suitability queries. Catalogue $50.

Enquiry #4 (note from colleague)

A Mr. Ovambo from Lagos, Nigeria wants to know about the Screen Protector. He needs 10 for customers of his.

YOUR REPLY: Sorry we can't supply – import restrictions into Nigeria introduced in 1986. Our former distributors (Kano Security, Independence Square, Kano) may still have stocks.

64

E 🔊 You will hear one of your colleagues on the phone to Australia. Alter the stock position on the print-out and then reply to Enquiry #5.

Enquiry #5   (extract from letter)

```
Please quote your best DDP price and shipping date for 15
screen protectors, as advertised in High Life magazine. As
far as we know there are no restrictions on importing
these into Japan.
```

REPLY by letter or telex – you decide which.

F ☎ Now you will have to deal with Enquiries #6 and #7 on the telephone. One of you should look at File 59, the other at 105. Enquiry #6 concerns this telex:

```
WE REQUIRE URGENT INFORMATION ON BEHALF OF A
CUSTOMER ABOUT YOUR TELEPHONE SCRAMBLER. ARE THE
BATTERIES RECHARGEABLE ON 110 VOLT CURRENT? IS IT
TRUE THAT ITS OPERATION CAN INTERFERE WITH OTHER
PHONES IN THE SAME BUILDING? PLEASE PHONE US AFTER
12 NOON YOUR TIME.
REGARDS, AGENCIA LEON, MEXICO CITY
```

6.5 Importing and exporting   *Discussion*

A Work in groups. Find out about your partners' experiences of selling abroad by asking these questions:

- What proportion of your products are exported?
- Do you sell mostly in a small number of markets or are your sales scattered among many countries?
- Which overseas markets do you *actively* sell to?
- What proportions of your export business do you do directly with buyers and with agents or distributors?
- Is the documentation and shipping handled by a freight forwarder or by your own export department?
- What kinds of products sell well abroad?

B Now find out about their experiences of *buying* from abroad:

- What proportion of your materials or supplies do you import?
- What proportion do you import directly, or through agents or distributors?
- Do you often meet your suppliers from abroad, or do you deal 'at a distance' by phone, telex or letter?
- What materials or supplies do you buy from abroad, rather than from domestic sources?

■ If any of this information is a trade secret, you can avoid answering by using some of the techniques suggested in 6.1!

6.6 Looking into the future   *Grammar*

🔲 Different ways of talking or writing about future events in English have different meanings. Here are some examples:

PREDICTING future events:

> It will probably be difficult to get them to pay on time.
> Prices will/are going to go up if the exchange rate changes.
> By this time next year, our costs will have risen by 25%.
> If the exchange rates change, prices will/are sure to rise.
> We'll still be unloading the goods at 3 p.m.
> Please don't call after 12.30, Mr Carter will be having lunch then.

Describing a PLAN or ARRANGEMENT:

> I'm visiting/I'll be visiting Tokyo in November.
> She's arriving/She'll be arriving this evening.

Saying what you INTEND to do:

> I'm going to chase them up if they haven't delivered by Friday.
> I'm going to have lunch early today.

Making a PROMISE:

> I'll let you know next week.
> I'll make sure Mrs Hanson calls you back as soon as she's free.
> Mr Brown will pick you up at the airport.

Referring to FACTS (timetables or schedules):

> My plane for Buenos Aires leaves at 14.35
> When do you arrive in Mendoza?
> Next Friday is a public holiday in Argentina.

Talking about something that is going to happen VERY SOON:

> I'm just about to / just going to phone Sydney.
> They're just going to / just about to start the meeting.

■ It's sometimes more polite to use *will be doing*:

> When will you be calling Mr Lee in Singapore?
> Will you be seeing Mr Kwouk while you're in Hong Kong?

instead of: *When will you . . .?* or *Are you going to . . .?*

A   Fill the gaps in these sentences with suitable words.

1. We *shall be writing*............ .... to you to confirm this when we have checked our stock position.
2. What time .... train from Birmingham .... ?
3. Where .... Ms Carpenter before the conference?
4. .... a table for lunch? I think it would be wise to.
5. If I .... you before 5 pm, ... in your office?
6. .... me when the goods .... in your warehouse?
7. When .... typing the report? I need it as soon as possible.
8. What .... after the meeting this afternoon?
9. When .... to ACME Industries to confirm the order?

B   Work in groups of three or four. Find out about . . .
– your partners' plans or arrangements for tomorrow and the next few days.
– their ambitions: what they hope to achieve in their careers.
– what they think will happen in the world and in their country during the next few years.
Make notes on what you find out.

C   Work in pairs with someone from a *different* group. Tell your new partner what you found out in the first group.

6.7 Placing and filling orders

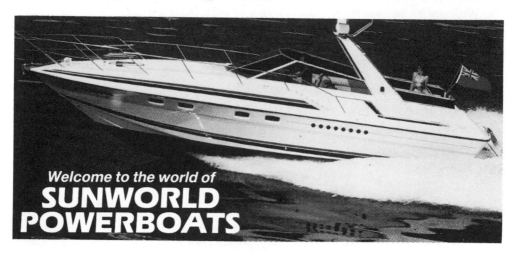

Welcome to the world of
SUNWORLD POWERBOATS

YOUR ROLE
You and your partner work in the export department of Sunworld
Powerboats. Mr Richardson, your boss, has found a promising new
customer in Central America. This customer doesn't speak English
well enough to deal on the phone in English, so you can only
communicate by telex or letter . . .

A   *Today is Friday, 12 July*
Look at this quotation, which you are about to telex to the customer.
Check it through to make sure there are no mistakes and make any
necessary alterations before transmission.

```
435677 NAVLI CR
789300 SUNWO T

OUR QUOTATION NO: 0067 12 JULY 19--    15:33
TO:  NAVES LIMON, PUERTO LIMON, COSTA RICA
FROM:   SUNWORLD POWERBOATS, T___

GOOD AFTERNOON. THANK YOU FOR YOUR ENQUIRY ABOUT OUR PB 5000
30-FOOT SUNVOYAGER. YOU ASKED US TO GIVE YOU OUR BEST CIF PRICE
FOR TWO OF THESE.
THE PRICE FOR TWO PB 5000 WITH SPECIFICATIONS AS IN OUR 19--
CATALOGUE PAGES 42-45 IS 179,800 (IN WORDS: ONE SEVEN EIGHT
THOUSAND NINE HUNDRED) UNITED STATES DOLLARS CIF PUERTO
LIMON.
IF YOU REQUIRE THE SPECIAL STAINLESS STEEL ANCHORS AND CHAINS
(OUR CATALOGUE NOS: 5567 AND 8876), THE TOTAL PRICE IS 187,850
U.S. DOLLARS.
THE GOODS WOULD BE READY FOR SHIPMENT 3 TO 4 WEEKS FROM THE
DATE OF YOUR WRITTEN ORDER. WE PACK EACH PB 5000 FOR EXPORT
IN A 40-FOOT OPEN TOP CONTAINER. WE UNDERSTAND FROM OUR
FREIGHT FORWARDERS THAT CARIBLINES HAVE A SCHEDULED SERVICE
TO PUERTO LIMON ONCE A MONTH.
WE WOULD APPRECIATE PAYMENT BY IRREVOCABLE LETTER OF CREDIT
```

```
CONFIRMED ON A T____ BANK AND VALID FOR 90 (NINE) DAYS FROM
THE DATE OF YOUR ORDER. THE PRICES GIVEN IN THIS OFFER ARE VALID
FOR A PERIOD OF THIRTY DAYS FROM THE DATE OF THIS TELEX.
WE LOOK FORWARD TO HEARING FROM YOU.
IF YOU REQUIRE FURTHER INFORMATION, PLEASE TELEX ME
PERSONALLY AND I SHALL BE PLEASED TO HELP YOU.
MR RICHARDS SENDS HIS BEST REGARDS.
BEST WISHES,


A____
SUNWORLD POWERBOATS
```

B *Today is Thursday, 18 July*

Look at File 86, where you will see the order from Costa Rica.
Check it against your quotation above.
Before you can give a firm shipping date, you will need to get a
delivery date from Alpha Marine, your supplier of anchors. Send
them a telex to order this item from their catalogue:

3456	**Anchor, stainless steel, 120kg**	DDP £135

C *Today is Friday, 19 July*

Your production manager promises both vessels packed for export in
containers on 22 August – if the special anchors are available. Look
at File 103 to see two telexes: one from Alpha Marine and the other
from your freight forwarders.
Send Naves Limon an acknowledgement of their order. Confirm the
terms of payment and delivery and quote a firm shipping date. Say
that you're sending a proforma invoice by airmail today.
Draft a short letter to accompany the proforma invoice.

D *Today is Friday, 13 September*

Two months have passed, you have shipped the goods and by now
they should have arrived. Unfortunately, there's a worrying headline
in today's paper:

Hurricane Suzy hits Caribbean

Look at File 55 to see a telex from Costa Rica. Reply to the telex and
take any other action you think necessary.

E *Today is Friday, 15 November*

Look at File 48 to see a memo from Mr Richardson and take
appropriate action.

F *Today is Friday, 20 December*

Send a Christmas message by telex to Naves Limon.

G *Today is Monday, 23 December*

Look at File 33 and take appropriate action.

7 Money matters

Reminding a customer of non-payment. Reported speech. Invoicing customers. Credit assessment. Payment by letter of credit. Dealing with cash-flow problems. Making international payments.

7.1 . . . what did he want to know?

Grammar

Look at the following examples of what you say when you report what someone has said.

- Notice the verbs that are used to introduce each report.
- The verb in the reported part is always in the past form, as are the time expressions.
- You normally report in the *third* person, unless you are talking about what you said yourself.

1 **In statements:**
   'I will not come to the meeting tomorrow.'→He said he would not come to the meeting the next day.
   'This is the first bad cheque we've had this month.'→He said that that was the first bad cheque they had had that month.

2 **In requests:**
   'Can we send you these invoices today?'→She asked whether she could send us those invoices the same day.
   'Will you audit the figures for this year please?'→They asked whether we would audit the figures for last year.

3 **In questions:**
   'When are you seeing my colleagues next week?'→He wanted to know which day they were seeing his colleagues the week after.
   'Which of these two statements of accounts is a true reflection of the firm's performance?'→They wanted to know which of those two statements of accounts was a true reflection of the firm's performance.

A Work in pairs. You have just received a telephone call from the credit controller in the Accounts Department of a supplier.
What did he want to know and tell you? Report the conversation to a colleague: the first two are done for you below.

1. Good morning! I'm sorry to ring you like this . . .

   He said he was sorry to ring but wanted to know...

70

2. But have you received our shipment of tyres?
   He asked whether we had received their shipment of tyres.
3. When did it arrive?
4. Are all the things you ordered included?
5. Did you get the invoice too?
6. Have you paid the invoice for the last shipment yet?
7. Because I haven't got a record of the payment.
8. Does the amount on the invoice correspond with what you ordered?
9. If it doesn't, we can give you a credit note to cover the difference.
10. Will you be paying the new invoice immediately?
11. Please try and send the cheque before the end of the month because our accounts department is considering changing the conditions of payment for future orders otherwise.
12. I hope we can continue working together.
13. And we hope to keep you as a regular customer despite any troubles you may be having.

This table summarizes some of the forms used in reported speech:

	Direct speech	Reported speech
VERBS	reports	reported
	is reporting	was reporting
	has reported	had reported
	shall (will) report	should (would) report
	may	might
	can	could
	must	had to
PRONOUNS	I	he, she
	we	they
	me	him, her
	mine	his, hers
	ours	theirs
	myself, ourselves	himself/herself, themselves
	this, these	that, those
ADVERBIAL EXPRESSIONS	now	then, at that time
	today	that day
	yesterday	the day before
	last week	the week before
	tomorrow	the next day
	next week	the following week, the week after
	here	there

B 🖭 You'll hear one side of a telephone conversation. Take notes and write down the report of the conversation you would give to your boss. ⟫→

71

Boss: What was that all about?
You: Well, I just rang Malaysian Fuels about their outstanding invoices.
Boss: What did they want us to do?
You: The credit controller . . .

C [image] One of you should look at File 38, the other at 57. You're going to be telling your partner about a conversation you had the other day.

7.2 Billing, invoicing

YOUR ROLE: You and your partner have been working in the Accounts Department of Universal Utensils for two weeks. Your boss Ms Keulemans has asked you to complete the bill for Vesta Vehicles. She has left you the following information.

A Complete the invoice after you have studied these documents:

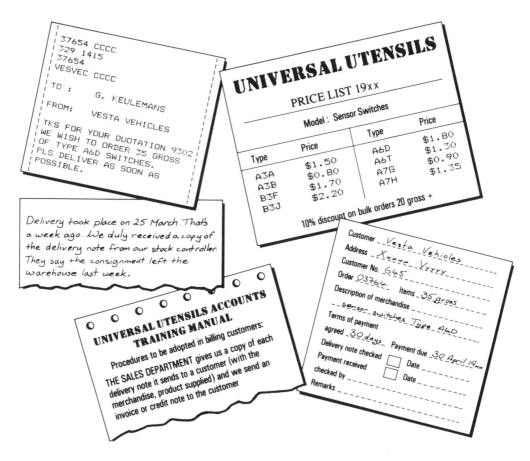

37654 CCCC
329 1415
37654
VESVEC CCCC

TO : G. KEULEMANS

FROM: VESTA VEHICLES

TKS FOR YOUR QUOTATION 9302
WE WISH TO ORDER 35 GROSS
OF TYPE A6D SWITCHES.
PLS DELIVER AS SOON AS
POSSIBLE.

UNIVERSAL UTENSILS
PRICE LIST 19xx

Model : Sensor Switches

Type	Price	Type	Price
A3A	$1.50	A6D	$1.80
A3B	$0.80	A6T	$1.30
B3F	$1.70	A7G	$0.90
B3J	$2.20	A7H	$1.35

10% discount on bulk orders 20 gross +

Delivery took place on 25 March. That's a week ago. We duly received a copy of the delivery note from our stock controller. They say the consignment left the warehouse last week.

UNIVERSAL UTENSILS ACCOUNTS TRAINING MANUAL
Procedures to be adopted in billing customers:
THE SALES DEPARTMENT gives us a copy of each delivery note it sends to a customer (with the merchandise, product supplied) and we send an invoice or credit note to the customer

Customer __Vesta_Vehicles__
Address _Xxxxx__Yyyyy__
Customer No. 645
Order 03764 Items 35 gross
Description of merchandise
__sensor_switches_Type_A6D__
Terms of payment
agreed _30 days_ Payment due _30 April 19xx_
Delivery note checked ☐ Date ____
Payment received
checked by ____ ☐ Date ____
Remarks ____

INVOICE FACTURE   RECHNUNG
          FACTURA   FACTUUR

Seller (Name, Address, VAT Reg. No.)		C.C.C.N No.
	Invoice No. and Date (Tax Point)	Seller's Reference
	Buyer's Reference	
Consignee	Buyer (if not Consignee)	
	Country of Origin of Goods	Country of Destination
	Terms of Delivery and Payment	

Vessel/Aircraft etc.	Port of Loading
Port of Discharge	

Marks and Numbers: Number and Kind of Packages: Description of Goods	Gross Weight (Kg)	Cube (M³)

Specification of Commodities	Quantity	•	Amount (State Currency)
		TOTAL	

	Name of Signatory
It is hereby certified that this invoice shows the actual price of the goods described, that no other invoice has been or will be issued, and that all particulars are true and correct.	Place and Date of Issue
	Signature

© SITPRO 1987 V5

B You've just found out that new prices have been in operation for two weeks. One of you looks at File 80 and calls up the customer; the other looks at File 74, for what John Granger says.

⟫→

73

C   Three days later you receive this letter from John Granger. Draft an answer to the letter.

Universal Utensils

Xxxxxxx   14 February 19—
Mmmmmmmmmm

Dear Sirs,

Account Nr. 645/Hrs/0098/Invoice No. 04276
_____

I regret to inform you that the above invoice contains a
mistake. It is almost certainly the case that the figure in
the invoice for the total has been multiplied by a
hundred. In view of our longstanding dealings with your
company, I am convinced that you do not expect me to pay
$98,000 for the last delivery of switches and electrical
components.

I would very much appreciate receiving a more reasonable
invoice.

Yours faithfully

John Granger
John Granger

Chief Clerk
Purchasing Dept.

D   A week later you receive a telex from John Granger (in File 56). Draft the acknowledgement which Mr Granger of Vesta Vehicles has requested: '_We thank you for your remittance of . . ._'

7.3   Payment by Documentary Letter of Credit

YOUR ROLE: Your boss, the accounts manager, has asked you to deal with the payment for a shipment of optical lenses from Greenberg Instruments, 2114   53rd Street, Hoboken, NJ, USA.

The method of payment agreed upon between the purchasing department and the supplier – Greenberg Instruments – is that of the Documentary Letter of Credit. This form of payment is not used very often in the accounts department, so to make sure you are following the correct procedure you look at this explanation in a bank's booklet on Documentary Letters of Credit.

A Look at the following document – a copy of a letter of credit.
Read the explanation of the various sections on the next page and
decide which explanation goes with which number.

BARCLAYS

Barclays Bank PLC
1 Union Court, London EC2P 2HP

date 20th July 19..

DOCUMENTARY CREDITS DEPARTMENT

SPECIMEN

(1)
IRREVOCABLE CREDIT No:- UTDC 65432
To be quoted on all drafts and correspondence.

Beneficiary(ies) (2)
Speirs and Wadley Ltd.
Adderley Road
Hackney, London E8 1XY

Advised through

Accreditor (3)
Woldal Ltd.
New Road
Kowloon, Hong Kong

To be completed only if applicable
Our cable of
Advised through   Refers

Dear Sir(s)
In accordance with instructions received from The Downtown Bank & Trust Co.
we hereby issue in your favour a Documentary Credit for £4108
(say) Four thousand, one hundred and eight pounds sterling (4)   available by your drafts
drawn on us (5)

at sight
for the 100% c.i.f. (6)   invoice value, accompanied by the following documents:-

1. Signed Invoice in triplicate.
(7) 2. Full set of clean Combined Transport Bills of Lading made out to
order and blank endorsed, marked 'Freight Paid' and 'Notify Woldal
Ltd., New Road, Kowloon Hong Kong'.
3. Insurance Policy or Certificate in duplicate, covering Marine and
War Risks up to buyer's warehouse, for invoice value of the goods
plus 10%.

Covering the following goods:-
(8)
400 Electric Power Drills

(9)   (6)
To be shipped from   London   to   Hong Kong c.i.f.

not later than (10)   10th August 19..

Partshipment not permitted   Transhipment permitted (11)

The credit is available for   presentation to us   until 31st August 19..

Documents to be presented within 21 days of shipment but within credit
validity.

Drafts drawn hereunder must be marked "Drawn under Barclays Bank PLC 1 Union Court,
London   branch, Credit number   UTDC 65432   "
We undertake that drafts and documents drawn under and in strict conformity with the terms of this credit will be
honoured upon presentation.

Yours faithfully,   R. E. Dancey

Co-signed (Signature No. 9847)   Signed (Signature No. 1024)

CRE 202 (replacing CRE 83, 606 series)   PLEASE SEE REVERSE

Subject to Uniform Customs and Practice for Documentary Credits Publication No. 400

Most Credits are fairly similar in appearance and contain the
following details:

☐ The terms of contract and shipment (i.e. whether 'ex-works',
'FOB', 'CIF', etc).
☐ The name and address of the importer (accreditor).

⟫→

75

- ☐ Whether the Credit is available for one or several shipments.
- ☐ The amount of the Credit in sterling or a foreign currency.
- ☐ The expiry date.
- ☐ A brief description of the goods covered by the Credit (too much detail should be avoided as it may give rise to errors which can cause delay).
- ☐ The name and address of the exporter (beneficiary).
- ☐ Precise instructions as to the documents against which payment is to be made.
- ☐ The type of Credit (Revocable or Irrevocable).
- ☐ Shipping details, including whether transhipments are allowed. Also recorded should be the latest date for shipment and the names of the ports of shipment and discharge. (It may be in the best interest of the exporter for shipment to be allowed 'from any UK port' so that he has a choice if, for example, some ports are affected by strikes. The same applies for the port of discharge.)
- ☐ The name of the party on whom the bills of exchange are to be drawn, and whether they are to be at sight or of a particular tenor.

The correct numbered order is given in File 98.

B 🔲 You'll hear a bank expert talking about some of the common mistakes that are made when people complete letters of credit. Fill in the items missing below:

Results of the survey:
Reasons for rejecting 25% of the documents:
- the letter of credit had ....
- the documents were presented .... the period stipulated in the letter of credit
- the shipment was ....

Documents were often inconsistent with one another in the following ways:
- the description (or ....) of goods on invoice(s) differed from that in the letter of credit
- the .... differed between export documents
- the .... shown on the invoice(s) and bill of exchange (draft) differed
- the .... differed between documents
- the drawing was .... than the letter of credit amount
- the letter of credit was .... the value of the order
- the .... was short
- there was an absence of .... , where required, on documents presented
- .... were used when not allowed

C Compare your answers. What are your own personal experiences with such discrepancies? What other problems like these have you had or seen? In what ways is what is described similar to or different from home trade or doing business with established and known customers?

7.4   Reminding a customer of an unpaid invoice

YOUR ROLE: You and your partner both work in the Accounts Department of Stateco.

A   *Today's date: Monday, 12 June*

1. 📼 You will hear a conversation between your head of department, Ms Benedetto, and the head clerk of Lateco, a customer who has not paid an outstanding bill. As you listen, make a note of some of the reasons given for the late payment.
2. Read this first reminder from Waitco to Stateco:

> 15 June 19—
>
> Dear Ms Benedetto,
>   According to our records payment of our invoice, no. 35823, sent to you last March, has not yet been made.
>   As specified on all our estimates and invoices our terms of business are 30 days net. Your invoice has now been outstanding for 90 days. In the case of unsettled debts of this duration it is our company policy to take legal action.
>   We would naturally prefer not to have to go so far. Would you please send us a cheque by return. In case you have lost or mislaid the original I am enclosing a copy of our invoice.
>   We look forward to receiving your payment by return.
>   Yours sincerely,
>
> *Pierre Lacoste*
>
> Pierre Lacoste
> (Credit Controller)

B   *Today's date: Tuesday, 20 June*

You still haven't received any payment on the invoice from Lateco. Write a first reminder to them. Decide which of the arguments in the letter above you can use in your own letter. You are not satisfied with what Lateco have said but you still want to give them a chance to pay up . . .

C   *Today's date: Thursday, 22 June*

Read this second reminder from Waitco to Stateco:

> 21 June 19—
>
> Dear Ms Benedetto,
>
> Account no. ST/PD 0053/Invoice no.35823
> _____
>
>   May we again remind you that this account is still overdue.
>   I would like to remind you also that our business terms are 30 days. We supply goods on the understanding of payment by the proper time.
>   May we ask you to settle your account by return.
>
> Yours sincerely
>
> *Pierre Lacoste*
>
> Pierre Lacoste
> (Credit Controller)

D *Today's date: Friday, 23 June*
You have still not received a cheque from Lateco for the overdue invoice. Draft a second reminder to them. Decide whether you can use similar arguments to those above.

E *Today's date: Monday, 3 July*
Read this letter from Lateco to Stateco:

28 June 19—

Dear Ms Benedetto,
    As you will remember from our telephone call, we have recently been experiencing a number of difficulties with several large customers. This has resulted in unfortunate delays in paying outstanding accounts.
    We are extremely sorry that your company has been affected by these developments.
    We are doing everything possible to rectify the situation. Indeed we hope to be able to settle our debts within the very near future.
    I would very much appreciate it if you could bear with us patiently, as I am sure that liquidation on our part would not be in your interest either.
    I shall inform you of further developments before the end of the month.

Yours sincerely

John Brown

John Brown
(Chief clerk, Accounts)

F *Today's date: Tuesday, 4 July*
Draft a request for deferred payment to Waitco, explaining the cash flow problem caused by Lateco ('a major customer of ours').

G *Today's date: Monday, 10 July*
Read this letter from Waitco to Stateco:

7 July 19—

Dear Ms Benedetto,

Account no. ST/PD 0053/Invoice no.35823

    We refer to your request to postpone the payment of our account.
    In view of the long period of trading we have enjoyed with your company we are prepared to allow you a further 30 days. We must however insist that the account is paid within seven days following 10 August.

Yours sincerely

Pierre Lacoste

Pierre Lacoste
(Credit Controller)

Draft a reply to Lateco's letter of 28 June above.

17 July 19—

Dear Ms Benedetto
    Please find enclosed the outstanding cheque for...
    We would like to thank you for your sympathetic and
understanding actions. We shall do everything in our power
to settle our accounts as promptly as possible.

    Yours sincerely

    John Brown

    John Brown
    (Chief clerk, Accounts)

H   *Today's date: 19 July*
A cheque arrives with the letter from Lateco and now you can . . .
send a cheque with a letter to Waitco.

"And now, with a lighthearted look at the year's trading figures . . ."

7.5 Dealing with cashflow problems

A Look at these customer order records of the firm Intertex.
What have they ordered before?
Have they paid regularly in the past?

ORDERS	Customer: INTERTEX		No: 0339
Date	Order	Invoice	Date pd
5/11/XX	100 bales cotton	MS/56/0321	15.1.XX
9/12/XX	2000 mtrs fabric	MI/67/521	17.2.XX
20/1/XX	1600 mtrs fabric	MC/01/465	19.3.XX
28/2/XX	98 bales cotton	PL/43/284	

Work in groups of *three* pairs.

B ▶️ You and your partner are credit controllers of a company involved in international trade.
Pair A should look at File 113, pair B at 15 and pair C at 52.
You'll find information about the company you work for and the record of orders from a customer. Answer these questions:
  What have they ordered from you in the past?
  Have they paid regularly in the past?
Discuss with your partner what to do about the outstanding payment.

C ☎ Each member of the pair will play a different role:

One of you plays the role of credit controller of your firm. You phone up the buyers' head clerk or accounts manager:
- Ask about the non-payment of the invoice – it is now 30 days overdue.
- Ask how long the delay will last and what they intend to do about it.
- Ask them to confirm in writing that they're unable to pay yet, but that they're willing to do so when circumstances permit.

The other member of the pair plays the role of accounts manager of your firm. You'll receive a phone call from the credit controller of your supplier, asking about an outstanding invoice.
- Explain why you haven't yet been able to pay the bill.
- Or explain that you've sent a cheque or some other form of payment and it must have got lost in the post.
- Or explain that your firm has cash flow problems which make it impossible to pay at the moment.
- Ask for a postponement of the payment deadline.

D Draft the letter or telex together explaining why you need more time to pay the outstanding bill. Send the letter to your supplier.

E Read the letter you get from your buyer. Is it the kind of letter you'd like to receive yourself? Decide what action to take.

7.6 How much did you say that was? *Reading aloud*

A Work in pairs. Dealing with money and payments usually
involves numbers and figures; here are some expressions using
numbers. Decide which of the expressions in words below go with
which figures. Which items are left over? Write out the numbers for
these.

1. Invoice No. 508/19G
2. a gross profit of 14.5%
3. 31 August 1993
4. the list price is £41,337
5. profit before interest and tax of £1,457,000
6. an annual rate of interest of 26.8%
7. a handling charge of 1½%
8. total interest charges of £3.66
9. $673m operating profits

a) three pounds sixty-six
b) fourteen point five per cent
c) twenty-six point eight per cent
d) forty-one thousand three hundred and thirty-seven
e) one million four hundred and fifty-seven thousand
f) seventeen hundred and ninety-five
g) six hundred and seventy-three million
h) the thirty-first of August nineteen ninety-three
i) three point six six
j) one and a half per cent
k) five o eight stroke nineteen G (five zero eight oblique nineteen G)
l) one and a quarter per cent

B Listen to the recording and complete the information
missing from the report below. Compare your answers. Decide with
your partner how you would write the numbers in words.

Volvo earnings rise by .... in ....quarter

Volvo, the Swedish automotive, energy and food group, increased its profits by .... in the first quarter of .... despite a fall of 5 per cent in group turnover.

Profits after financial items rose to .... ($345m) compared with SKr 2.21bn in the first quarter of last year.

The group was helped by a .... foreign-exchange gain on loans – compared with a gain of SKr 30m a year earlier – as well as by interest earnings of SKr 109m – compared with .... in the first quarter of last year.

Operating profits were virtually unchanged at .... compared with SKr 2.1bn in the first quarter of .... Volvo expects to make a productivity gain this year of at least 5 per cent.

The group's liquid funds, inflated by the record profits of the past two years, climbed to .... by the end of the first quarter from SKr 14.4bn a year earlier.

Volvo profits, at least in the short term, have been hedged against the impact of the falling dollar, but the lower dollar exchange rate shows clearly in the group's sales figures. Volvo turnover fell 5 per cent to SKr 20.66bn from SKr 21.8bn in the first three months of last year despite a substantial rise in the volume of car sales...

⟫⟫→

C Use the information you now have to work out the following amounts:
1. the difference in profits between this year and last year
2. the increase in the foreign-exchange gain on loans
3. the change in operating profits
4. the rise in liquid funds
5. the amount which the company's turnover fell by

D 🎭 One of you looks at File 104, the other at 79.
Dictate the details of the invoice/air waybill to your partner. Your copy is unclearly photocopied. Find out what the missing details are from your partner.

7.7 The results were good . . . *Read and discuss*

Work in pairs. Look at the extracts from the Managing Director's report and the charts and notes about GKN.
Find the answers to these questions:

1. What does the sum of £68 million refer to?
2. How high were GKN's profits?
3. Where in the world was the firm's trading surplus greatest?
4. How did the total group sales compare with the previous year?
5. What was the reason for the difference?
6. How large is the amount of total dividends for the year?
7. How much depreciation was deducted from Group Sales?
8. What was the second largest deduction from Group Sales for?
9. What percentage of group sales were achieved outside the UK?
10. How much interest did the group have to pay? Why?
11. What does the sum of £68 million refer to in the calculation of the company's trading surplus?
12. How large is the capital expenditure programme referred to?

The results for 1986 overall were good. While total group sales and trading surplus were lower than the previous year, this was largely because of the transfer of our special steels and forgings operations to be part of United Engineering Steels, the company jointly owned by the BSC and ourselves. The pre-tax profits at £132 million matched those of the previous year which were themselves a record.

In the business sectors, however, the trading results were mixed.

The automotive sector was not uniformly bleak, however, and passenger car sales were buoyant generally. Our factories producing car components had a good year, particularly our transmission companies on the continent. There, the trading surplus rose by £21 million to a total of £77 million. Similarly in the UK our transmissions company, Hardy Spicer, performed well. It is being helped by a large capital expenditure programme to install flexible automated production lines. The £9 million first phase has been completed, and the second stage costing £13 million is being implemented. The result is that Hardy Spicer can compete with Japanese landed prices which should help secure future business.

GROUP SALES £2059m

UNITED KINGDOM £814m 40%

CONTINENTAL EUROPE £721m 35%

REST OF WORLD £73m 3%

AMERICA £451m 22%

TRADING SURPLUS £146m

UNITED KINGDOM £34m 23%

CONTINENTAL EUROPE £77m 53%

REST OF THE WORLD £7m 5%

AMERICA £28m 19%

Group Sales for 1986 amounted to £2059 million pounds.
From this figure the costs of running the business had to be deducted:

£599 million for wages, salaries and related costs;

£1246 million for materials and services;

£68 million for depreciation of plant, buildings and equipment;

That left a trading surplus of £146 million.

From the **trading surplus of £146 million**:

Interest on bank borrowings and other loans to finance the business amounting to £43 million had to be deducted;
£29 million pounds were added back from investments and GKN's share of profits in related companies.

That produced a **profit before tax of £132 million**.

GKN then had to pay taxes amounting to £51 million and £13 million pounds to minority shareholders.

This resulted in **earnings of the year of £68 million**.

GKN paid its shareholders a dividend on their investment which amounted to £31 million, and extraordinary items amounted to £36 million mostly arising from the sale of Steelstock and restructuring of the French autoparts distribution division.

This left **£1 million which were transferred to reserves** for putting back into the business.

Which company in your own country could you compare with GKN?
In what ways were/are its performance similar/different?

7.8 **Where the money is . . .**   *Discussion*

A   Work in pairs. Answer the following questions. What is publicly owned and privately owned in your country – in the UK – in the USA? Consider services and manufacturing. Make a list of:

POST / TELEPHONES / AIRLINE / RAILWAY SYSTEM / BUS TRANSPORT / MOTORWAYS / GAS / WATER / ELECTRICITY / STEEL PRODUCTION / COAL / TV / RADIO . . .

Shareholders as a percentage of total population

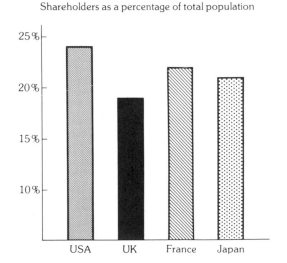

B Look at the chart and find out what your partner's reactions are
to these questions. Then compare your answers with the rest of the
class.

1. How does the percentage of shareholders in your own country compare to the figures in the chart?
2. Who does industry belong to in your country?
3. Who are the shareholders?
4. How does the government in your country treat state enterprises.
5. What are the advantages of having privately owned companies?
6. What are the advantages of having nationalized industries?
7. Which individual industries and services do you think should or should not be nationalized or privatized?
8. What is the most important objective of a company – making profit, providing a service, or something else?
9. What do you think of companies which give their employees a share of the profits or shares?
10. Where would you invest your money, if you were rich enough?

7.9   Financial terms   *Vocabulary*

Fill in the gaps with words from the list.

endorse   funds   incur   lack   overheads   proceeds   royalties
standing order   subsidies   write off

1. Many companies receive .... and other revenues from their numerous inventions used by other firms.
2. The family purchased the site with the .... from their sale of securities and other assets.
3. But they .... large tax debts when the head of the family died.
4. Some developing countries are fortunate if the banks .... their long outstanding debts.
5. When demand for their goods falls, it is difficult for small companies to reduce expenditure on .... such as rent and energy costs.
6. In the last fiscal year many American companies suffered from a .... of cash and had to borrow heavily.
7. Many became insolvent because they didn't have sufficient liquid .... to pay back the loans they had taken up.
8. Payment is authorized only on presentation of a cheque .... on the back by the payee.
9. Customers with regular bills of fixed amounts may pay by ....
10. Many governments are offering companies favourable .... to open factories in underdeveloped regions.

84

7.10   Dealing with foreign currency and money abroad

A   Work in pairs. Read the article below which advises British
people on what sort of money to take with them when travelling
abroad. Answer these questions:

1. How many different methods are mentioned? Which?
2. Which method is recommended most highly?

On the money-go-round

MONEY – usually the lack of it – is a universal problem for travellers. Whatever the amount they take there is a variety of ways to carry it. Since each has both advantages and disadvantages, a combination of two or three is advisable, the mixture depending on financial circumstances as well as destination.

Traveller's cheques: will be replaced if lost or stolen, theoretically within 24 hours. You pay 1 to 1.5 per cent of the value of the cheques (and maybe a fixed handling fee if you are buying in any of the 20 plus foreign currencies) but usually get a better rate when cashing them. In any of the Americas be sure to carry dollar cheques.

Foreign currency: carry a small amount (for taxis, porters, telephone calls, snacks) until you can get to a bank. Most UK banks need advance notice of your requirements, otherwise change sterling at the airport or port (though exchange rates are less favourable).

The commission and rate of exchange do vary but shopping around is rather impractical. Some countries (in particular Greece) restrict the amount of their currency that you can import. You should also carry some sterling for necessary expenses when you return.

Postcheques: Each cheque, when accompanied by a Postcheque Card (included free with your first order of cheques) can now be used to draw up to £100 in local currency from 90,000 post offices in most of Europe and around the Mediterranean as well as Hong Kong, the Bahamas and Japan.

Credit cards: Access (linked to Mastercard in the US and Eurocard in Europe) and Barclaycard (linked to Visa) are accepted in nearly 5 million outlets each though they vary in their acceptability – Barclaycard, for example, is stronger in France, Spain and Italy, whereas Access is most useful in Germany and the US. Their acceptance in Continental petrol stations, too, is not always certain.

They may also be used for cash advances and instead of a deposit on car hire.

Charge cards: American Express and Diners Club are less widely accepted than credit cards and the interest-free settlement period is shorter but there is no pre-set spending limit. In addition to the initial starting and annual fee for the cards, both charge a one per cent processing charge for bills converted back into sterling.

Eurocheques: can be used to withdraw local currency as well as pay for hotels, restaurants, garages and other services in nearly five million, mostly European, outlets. The cheques, made out to the exact amount you require, are then debited to your account in the same way as a domestic cheque.

Individual cheques can be cashed for up to a maximum of £100 or the equivalent in local currency.

There is no limit to the number of cheques you can use to make a purchase. You pay around £3.50 for the card and there is also a commission of 1.25 per cent on the value of the transaction, plus roughly a 30 pence handling fee per cheque.

David Wickers

B   Now read the article once more and answer the following more
detailed questions:

3. What happens if you lose your travellers cheques?
4. Where should the British traveller exchange sterling into foreign currency?
5. Why is the British traveller advised to carry sterling?
6. Where can you use Postcheques?

⋙→

7. What are the advantages of credit cards?
8. What disadvantages do charge cards have?
9. How do you pay for Eurocheques?
10. What is the limit of a Eurocheque?

C Compare the information in the article with your list of advantages and disadvantages. What differences are there?

TOURIST RATES

£1 buys

Australian dollars	2.18
Austrian schillings	21.65
Belgian francs	64.80
Canadian dollars	2.13
Danish kroner	11.79
French francs	10.40
German marks	3.08
Greek drachmas	243.00
Holland guilders	3.47
Irish punts	1.15
Italian lire	2290.00
Maltese pounds	0.57
New Zealand dollars	2.51
Norwegian kroner	11.22
Portuguese escudos	248.50
Spanish pesetas	202.50
Swedish kroner	10.74
Swiss francs	2.56
US dollars	1.78
Yugoslav dinars	3350.00
Yen	227.00

D Look at the exchange rates and convert these sums into sterling and then into US dollars:

10 New Zealand dollars
900 Danish kroner
340 Swiss francs
620 Portuguese escudos
75 Holland guilders
490 Canadian dollars
85 Maltese pounds
73 Australian dollars

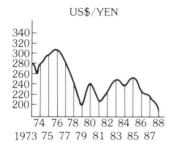

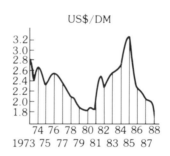

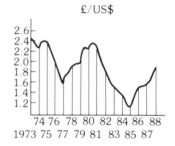

E Look at the fluctuations of the currencies above.
1. Between 1973 and 1980 how big/small has the drop/rise in the exchange rate of the DM, the Yen and the £ been?
2. And between 1981 and 1984?
3. When was the greatest drop of the £? Of the DM? Of the Yen?
4. Compare the situation with today. How much has the $ been devalued or re-valued against the Yen in the past year / 6 months?
5. How much has your own currency fluctuated against the currencies mentioned above.
6. Why do exchange rates change?

Exchange rate fluctuations are a problem for buyers abroad and also for sellers abroad. They are also a problem for travellers abroad. What problems have you had / do you know of in connection with movement in exchange rates? What consequences can they have? For companies, countries, industries, individuals, etc?

8 Delivery and after-sales

Dealing with problems.
Conditional sentences.
Coping with complaints and errors.

8.1 We all make mistakes – sometimes!

Work in pairs or small groups. You and your partner(s) work in the
buying department at Zenith International. You have just got back
from holiday. While you were away Max, the 19-year-old son of your
director, was in charge of your office.

1. Read this note you left for Max before you went away:

    ```
    Max, please place order for 45 x 100 metre reels
    of 40mm MCL88 cable from UNIFLEX SpA in La
    Spezia, Italy. All details in files. This is a
    repeat order - just copy the previous one and
    change the dates.
    ```

    and this note that Max has left for you:

    MCL88 cable ordered as you instructed. Price seems to have gone
    up since last order – I assume this is OK. Uniplex seem to have
    moved from La Spezia to Pisa. Their new address is:
      Uniplex srl., Viale Dell'Industria 131, 56100 Pisa
    Best wishes
      Max
    P.S. Hope you had a good holiday!

    What do you think may have happened? What should you do?

2. Listen to a telephone message that was recorded on the
    answering machine yesterday.

3. Look at File 99 to see two more documents, including a telex that
    has just arrived.

4. Uniplex's price is $7\frac{1}{2}\%$ higher than UNIFLEX's. What are you
    going to do? Will you stick by Max's order, which will upset
    UNIFLEX SpA?
    Will you try to negotiate a lower price from Uniplex? Or is it
    better to explain to Uniplex what has happened, apologize and
    cancel the order?

⟫→

5. 📞 or 👤 When you've made your decision, role play the two phone calls or visits: one to Piero Conti at Uniplex srl and the other to Lucia Donato at UNIFLEX SpA.
   Plan each call or visit, by making notes before you begin.

6. Draft a telex or fax to Uniplex and another to UNIFLEX, which you could have sent *instead of* phoning or visiting them.

7. Send your telexes or faxes to another group and ask for their reactions and comments.

8. Explain to the rest of the class (or another group) how you dealt with the problems.

9. Draft a short report on how you dealt with the problems for the attention of your boss – who is Max's father!

8.2 Complaints and apologies   *Functions*

If you want to make a complaint to a person you don't know well, be careful! A direct complaint or criticism in English can sound rude or aggressive to an English-speaker.

It may be best to mention the problem more indirectly by saying:

> I'm sorry to have to say this but...
> I'm sorry to bother you but...
> I think you may have forgotten...
> It may have slipped your mind, but...
> There may have been a misunderstanding about...

In some situations, but only if you're talking to someone you know really well, it may be necessary to say, more directly:

> What are you going to do about...?
> I'm not at all satisfied with...

And in extreme cases, if you've already tried more polite methods, you may even have to threaten someone like this:

> Look, if you don't send your engineer to repair the machine we will be forced/obliged to cancel our next order.

> Unless you pay the account within seven days, we will place the matter in the hands of our solicitors/attorneys ...

88

📼 You'll hear four phone calls or conversations. Note down what the *PROBLEM* is in each case and what *ACTION* is to be taken. Then compare your notes with a partner.

If someone complains to you, or if you think they're likely to complain, it may be wise to apologize (even if it wasn't really your fault) and then promise to put things right by saying:

> Sorry, my fault.
> I'm very sorry. I didn't realize.
> There has been a slip-up/problem in our —— department.

```
We are very sorry about the delay/mistake ...
We wish to apologize for ...
Please accept our apologies for...
```

And you can accept someone's apology by saying:

> That's all right!
> It's perfectly all right.
> It really doesn't matter.

If things have gone wrong, the person you're talking to will want to know the *reasons*. He or she may assume someone in your firm is to blame and that they have been:

lazy, inefficient, incompetent, slow, careless, impolite, forgetful *or* unhelpful

If you don't want to accept responsibility or blame someone else, you could explain that the problem is due to:

a clerical error, a computer error, a typing error, a keyboard error, a misunderstanding, a bad telephone line, pressure of work, temporary staff *or* a shortage of staff

What other *excuses* can you and others in the class think of?

A Work in pairs. Look at these extracts from four letters. Complete each sentence and decide what you would say in your reply to each letter if it was *your fault* in each case.

```
... we are concerned that the order we placed by letter on 8
June may have got lost in the post. Could you please ...

... the order has not yet arrived at our warehouse, even though we
received advice of shipping from you ten days ago. Would you ...

... according to your scale of charges the price of a double
room with bath is $55 including tax. However, on checking my
account later I discover that I was charged $69.50 per
night. Will you please ...
```

⟫→

```
.... our order was for 80 boxes containing 144 items each. Each box
we have opened so far contains only 100 items. Will you please ...
```

B 🎭 Now imagine that the same four problems are being
discussed on the phone. Role-play each conversation with your
partner. Take it in turns to be the client or the customer.

C 🎭 One of you should look at File 24, the other at 61. This
time you will be dealing with some problems that might arise
when working with an English-speaking colleague. Here are some
useful expressions you can use:

I'm sorry to mention this, but . . .
I'm not quite sure how to put this, but . . .
There's something I've been meaning to tell you: . . .

8.3   Friday afternoon: delivery problems

Work in pairs or in small groups to discuss what action you would
take in these situations.
In each case, imagine that it's Friday afternoon . . .

1st problem

You are a manufacturer. Last month you placed an order for some
special alloy components for your manufacturing process with Ocean
View Components Inc. of New York. The goods were delivered on
Monday. Now it's Friday, 3pm.

📼 Your production manager, Mr Robinson, has left a message for
you on the telephone answering machine. Make notes as you listen to
the recording.

On a previous occasion, in connection with a different order, you sent
Ocean View this telex:

```
RE: OUR ORDER TR 678

LAST MONTH WE ORDERED FROM YOU 120 BOXES OF YOUR
ARTICLE NO. 231. YOU PROMISED DELIVERY ON 30 MAY
19__. SO FAR WE HAVE NOT RECEIVED THIS SHIPMENT
AND HAVE NOT HEARD FROM YOU.
PLEASE ARRANGE FOR IMMEDIATE SHIPMENT AND INFORM
US WHEN THE SHIPMENT WILL ARRIVE HERE.

REGARDS,
PAT BROWN, PACIFIC INTERNATIONAL
```

And you received this answer from Ocean View:

```
RE: YOUR TELEX NO 0097 DATE 05/06/__

WE ARE VERY SORRY FOR THE DELAY. THIS IS BECAUSE
OUR SUPPLIERS SHIPPED TO US LATE. THEIR SHIPMENT
ARRIVED LAST WEDNESDAY AND YOUR ORDER IS BEING
PACKED FOR EXPORT NOW.
WE WILL SHIP GOODS JUNE 9 EX NEWARK TO ROTTERDAM.
GOODS WILL ARRIVE LONDON JUNE 17.
AGAIN, WE ARE VERY SORRY, BUT IT WAS BEYOND OUR
CONTROL.
BEST, FRED DUVALL, OCEAN VIEW SUPPLIERS.
```

1. Decide together what you are going to do. How will you solve the problem Mr Robinson told you about? What will you tell him? Will you telephone Ocean View, telex them or send them a letter? What will you say or write?
2. Draft a letter or telex – or write notes for a phone call.
3. Compare your solutions and drafts with another pair or group.

2nd problem

You are a distributing wholesaler. You have been waiting for an order to arrive and you receive this letter about it:

```
                                        Your order ref 57/BEH

Dear Ms S_____

I am writing to apologise for the late delivery of this order.

We normally pride ourselves on keeping to our delivery dates, but
in this case the order was more complex and time-consuming than
we had anticipated.

Our revised delivery date is now Friday, November 22. Our truck
will arrive at your warehouse after lunch and unloading will take
approximately 1 hour.

We hope that this revised date and time is suitable and we
greatly regret any inconvenience that may have been caused.

Yours sincerely,

J. Lorenzini
Export Sales Director, Medco Industries
```

The problem is that Friday afternoon is a *very* busy time in the warehouse. However, the sooner you get the goods from Medco, the sooner you can supply your own customers.

1. Decide together what are you going to do this time. How will you solve this problem? What will you say or write to Medco?
2. Draft a letter, fax or telex to Medco – or write notes for the phone call you will make.
3. Compare your solutions and drafts with another pair or group.

3rd problem

You are responsible for Export Customer Service. Look at these
documents: A is a memo from Mr Frost, your delivery manager,
B is part of a fax from your customers, Arctic Refrigeration.

A We have just had Arctic Refrigeration on the phone about the order we sent out last week. They say that the goods were damaged when they inspected them, but they didn't notice this till two days after delivery. My driver got their signature to confirm that the shipment was in good condition on delivery. My guess is that Arctic's people caused the damage and they are trying to blame us. They are claiming credit of $255 on their next order. Please sort this one out before the end of today, Friday.

B Your delivery manager was most unhelpful on the
telephone. He implied that <u>we</u> are responsible for
the damage caused by your driver! My warehouse
manager informs me that this man unloaded the
shipment without sufficient care for the fragile
nature of the contents of the cartons.
   We expect to receive $285 credit on our next
order. A detailed list of the damage is on page
2 of this fax.
   Please reply to this fax by return.

1. Decide together what you are going to do. How will you solve this
   problem? What will you tell Mr Frost? What will you say or write
   to Arctic Refrigeration?
2. Draft a letter, fax or telex to Arctic Refrigeration – or write notes
   for the phone call you will make.
3. Compare your solutions and drafts with another pair or group.

Class discussion

What other problems might
occur with deliveries? Does
anyone have any horror stories
of cases of bad delivery
problems? Tell the class how
the situation was dealt with.

*"Someone has
complained about our
product, you don't
happen to know what
we make, do you, Miss
Hopkiss?"*

8.4 What if . . . ? *Grammar*

🔲 *If* sentences are used to describe or imagine the consequences of events. There are three types of conditionals:

TYPE 1 [*If* + present, followed by *will*] is used to imagine the consequences of events that are likely to happen or to describe the consequences of events that always happen:

If our flight isn't delayed, we'll have lunch before the meeting.
If you press the red button, the machine will stop.

TYPE 2 [*If* + past, followed by *would*] is used to imagine the consequences of events that are very unlikely to happen or events that cannot possibly happen:

What would you do if you won a lot of money in a lottery?
If I was (*or* were) in charge, I would give myself a rise.
If you placed your hand in there, the machine would stop automatically.

In some situations, either Type 2 or Type 1 may be used:

I would go to the USA next summer if I could afford to. (. . . but I won't be able to save up enough money)
I'll go to the USA if I manage to save up enough money. (*more optimistic*)

TYPE 3 [*If* + past perfect, followed by *would have*] is used to speculate about the consequences of events that happened or began to happen in the past:

If I had known this work was going to take so long, I wouldn't have started it before the weekend.
If there hadn't been a spelling mistake in the letter of credit, the order would have arrived on time.

A Work in pairs. Fill the gaps using the verbs below:

accept	arise	become	break down	call	carry out
check	contact	decline	do	flourish	foresee	have
inform	make	realize	remain	see	send	understand

1. If I ....*have*........ enough time, I ...*'ll finish*..... the report tonight.
2. If the machine ...., we .... your service engineer at once.
3. If your guarantee still .... valid, any repairs .... free of charge.
4. If they .... a lower bid last month, we .... it rapidly.
5. If you .... how angry my boss gets, you .... how I feel.
6. What .... you .... if you .... a colleague stealing substantial quantities of stationery from your office?
7. If they .... to pay up, we .... them a threatening letter.
8. If I .... extent of the damage, I .... all our insurance policies.
9. If any crucial problems .... at the docks, please .... me personally.
10. If the nation's economy .... next year, the trade gap .... narrower.

Notice the difference in meaning between *if* and the conjunctions underlined in these examples:

> I'll be there to meet him <u>when</u> his plane arrives.
> (*But notice we'd say:* . . . <u>if</u> his plane arrives before midnight.)
> You can assume I'll be arriving on Thursday, <u>unless</u> you hear from me to the contrary. (= if you don't hear from me)
> I'll wait here at the airport <u>until</u> she arrives.
> I'll take an overnight bag <u>in case</u> I have to stay the night.

B Complete these sentences, using your own ideas:

1. Please don't turn off the machine till *it has finished its cycle.*
2. The machine will operate 24 hours a day unless....................
3. Installation must be carried out by a qualified person in case....................
4. I'll call you from the airport when....................
5. We will replace any faulty parts free of charge if....................
6. Our engineer can make any minor adjustments to the machine when....................
7. I'll take an overcoat with me on my trip in case....................
8. She's in a meeting. Please don't interrupt her unless....................

C What are the underlined contractions in these sentences short for? Rewrite each sentence using the full forms that you'd use [→ you would use] in a formal letter:

1. I <u>won't</u> keep you long if <u>you're</u> very busy.
2. <u>I'll</u> help you collate the files if you <u>haven't</u> got enough time.
3. <u>What'll</u> you do if you <u>aren't</u> feeling very well tomorrow?
4. <u>What'd</u> you do if you <u>couldn't</u> get in touch with the engineer?
5. <u>I'd</u> feel pretty angry if <u>he'd</u> spoken to me like that.
6. <u>I'd</u> have (<u>I'd've</u>) finished yesterday afternoon if <u>I'd</u> had enough time.
7. I <u>wouldn't</u> have spoken so sharply if <u>I'd</u> known that <u>it'd</u> upset him so much.
8. If <u>I'd</u> forgotten to send the order <u>I'd</u> be feeling rather stupid.

■ Although you will need to understand other people using contractions like 'I'd've done it', you may prefer to use the full forms in your own speech if you find them easier.

D Look at the headlines from newspapers of the future on the next page.

1. Discuss which events are *possible* and which are *very unlikely.*
2. Speculate what the consequences of each event might be.
3. Think of several consequences of each event. For example, if you think the first is highly unlikely, you might say:

> 'If there was (*or* were) ever a single world currency, there would be no more problems with exchange rates.'

4. Report your most interesting ideas to the rest of the class.

UNO agrees on single worldwide currency

Office cleaning by robots

Banking services to become a state monopoly

World customs duties and tariffs abolished

Substantial shortage of applicants for office jobs

Income tax rises to 50%

New type of nuclear power stations completely safe

A computer on every school pupil's desk

Unemployment rises to 50%

Number of retired people exceeds working population

Voice-operated word-processor: no need for a keyboard

8.5 Delays, faults and problems   *Vocabulary*

Fill the gaps in these sentences with suitable words from the list.

attorneys (US)/solicitors (GB)   boycotts   cash against documents
Chamber of Commerce   circumstances   claim   compensate
documents against payment   expired   lawsuit   load   major   merchandise
minor   modification   negligence   overseas   quotas   rebate   refund
regulations   reject   storage   sue   take legal action   truck   void

1. If any *merchandise* is faulty the buyer can .... it and demand a ....
2. If the goods are damaged in transit, the suppliers may have to .... the clients. If so, they can make an insurance .... to recover this cost.
3. As it is their liability and the damage was due to the .... of their packers, we can .... against them, but a .... will be very expensive.
4. If they don't replace the goods that have defects, we'll place the matter in the hands of our .... and .... them.
5. The consignment will be sent by .... on a RoRo ferry. If there is any damage to the ...., we will offer you a .... on your next order.
6. Our own technician can carry out .... adjustments. But call the suppliers' service engineer if a .... repair or .... is required.
7. The guarantee .... last year and, unfortunately, our service contract was not renewed and is now ....
8. Due to unforeseen ...., we couldn't clear the goods through customs, so we paid a .... charge while they were held in a bonded warehouse.
9. Exporters have to know about any trade restrictions involved in......................... trade, such as federal or governmental .... and .... or ....
10. They also have to know the meaning of terms like C.A.D. (........................) and d/p (....................). The local .... can provide useful advice to exporters.

95

8.6 After-sales problems

Discuss each of these problems in pairs or in small groups. Imagine that you work in the Buying Department.

1st problem

The machine shop supervisor has left this message on your desk:

> The HD 440 tooling and cutting machine that we bought from Fox Industries Inc. last year has been causing a lot of trouble. We had a service visit last month and before that it was working fine. Now it's making a lot of noise, there's a lot of vibration, it's going slower and worst of all the accuracy is no longer satisfactory. Please contact Fox and get their man to call a.s.a.p.*

(* short for: as soon as possible)

You have recently complained to Fox Industries about their service on another machine. Here is the letter you sent their Export Sales Manager a few days ago:

May 20, 19—

Dear Mr Reynard,

As you know, we have bought several machines from your company and have been quite satisfied with their performance. We have even recommended Fox machines to other companies. Recently, however, the standard of your after-sales service has got much worse.

Our two HD 55Cs were installed in 1984 and your regular twice-yearly service together with our own maintenance programme has kept them in perfect working order. When there was a breakdown, your service agents used to send an engineer at 48 hours notice. Now the situation has changed and the engineer promises to come in 'about 10 days' and is unable to tell us exactly when he will be arriving. Last week he arrived at 4 p.m. on Friday afternoon and our own maintenance engineer was unable to leave work until your man had finished.

Let me say that we are not satisfied with this state of affairs. We have already spoken to your service agents about this, but there has been no change so far.

We look forward to hearing from you and hope that you can promise an immediate improvement in your after-sales service.

Yours sincerely,

1. Decide what action you should take in this situation.
2. Draft a suitable letter or telex – or notes for a phone call.
3. Compare your draft or notes with another pair or group.
4. When you have done this, look at File 116.

2nd problem

You recently bought some cheap electrical components from Coyote
Enterprises. The quality seemed to be up to standard . . .

1. 📼 Your boss is talking to your Sales Manager on the phone.
   Listen to the call and make notes.
2. Decide what action you should take in this situation.
3. Draft a suitable letter or telex – or notes for a phone call.
4. Compare your draft or notes with another pair or group.
5. 📼 Listen to the conversation and make notes.
6. Decide what further questions you would ask Mr Wiley.

3rd problem

This time, imagine that you are the *supplier* of the goods. Read this
telex from one of your customers:

```
YOU ASSURED US THAT THE EQUIPMENT WOULD BE
MODIFIED FOR CONDITIONS IN THIS COUNTRY. WE HAVE
FOUND THAT THE HARDWARE DOESN'T WORK ON OUR
VOLTAGE, WHICH IS 110 VOLTS, 60 CYCLES. PLEASE
SUPPLY US WITH SUITABLE TRANSFORMERS BY
AIRFREIGHT OR REPLACE THE EQUIPMENT WITH A
MODIFIED VERSION. ALTERNATIVELY, WE CAN OBTAIN
TRANSFORMERS LOCALLY AT YOUR EXPENSE.
PLEASE REPLY IMMEDIATELY WITH YOUR DECISION.
```

1. What action are you going to take?
2. Draft a suitable letter or telex – or notes for a phone call.

4th problem

Imagine that you are the *supplier* of the goods. Read this letter from
one of your customers:

```
The equipment seems to be working smoothly after
the installation problems. Unfortunately, my
works manager informs me that the handbook sent
with the machine has got wrongly bound.
Apparently, pages 25-50 are missing and 1-24
are included twice!
    Please send us a replacement at once by
airmail or courier.
```

1. What action are you going to take?
2. Draft a suitable letter or telex – or notes for a phone call.

8.7 Satisfaction and loyalty?

A Work in groups. Find out your partners' answers to these questions:

- How do you, as a customer, deal with bad after-sales service?
- Suppose someone complained about *your* after-sales service: how would you deal with this?
- Does anyone in the group have any 'horror stories' of cases of particularly bad after-sales service?

B Look at this card, which was enclosed with a computer product. Find out your partners' answers to the questions below:

THANK YOU!

We value you as a customer and want to thank you for your business. We hope you will be pleased with your purchase and would like your feedback. Please don't hesitate to call or write us.

Please remember to fill out your warranty card and return it promptly to DOVE Computer. The card is used to register your name in our automatic update service.

Thanks again from the
Employees at DOVE Computer

- Why was this card used, do you think?
- How would you have reacted to receiving it?
- What goods or services could such a card be used with?
- Would customers in your country like to receive a card like this?
- What are the advantages of ensuring customer satisfaction and encouraging customer loyalty? (A loyal customer is someone who buys regularly and supports your firm and its products.)
- What other methods can be used to maintain your customers' goodwill and promote your firm's good reputation?

C Design a similar Thank You card to be packed with your own firm's product (or with another product you're familiar with). You may prefer to draft an extra paragraph that can be added to your guarantee card instead.

9 Visits and travel

Travelling on business and looking after foreign visitors: making travel and accommodation arrangements, having a meal. Organizing a conference. Narrating. Using to___ and -ing forms.

9.1 'A trip to the States . . .' *Listening*

You'll hear some recordings of a number of typical situations in which business travellers find themselves during a trip abroad. Listen carefully and answer the questions. After each part you'll be able to role-play a similar situation.
[These recordings were all made on location in the USA.]

1 Going by Air

📼 You'll hear the traveller enquiring about flights and then checking in for his flight.
Listen to the conversations and fill the gaps in the summaries:

The traveller is at a travel agent. He wants to fly from San Francisco to .... on September .... The best rate the travel agent can offer is a .... -day advance purchase at $ .... one-way or $ .... round trip. The traveller wants to return on .... He must pay for the tickets by September .... but decides to pay for them ....

The traveller is checking in at Pittsburgh Airport for a flight to .... The clerk tells him that his flight number is .... and he has seat number .... , next to the .... His flight boards from Gate number .... , at .... and the flight leaves at ....

👥 Work in groups of four or five. Two of you should look at File 39, the others at 60. Imagine that you are passengers and staff at an airport information counter.
In the first half the time's 07.30, in the second half it's 10.00.

2 Accommodation

📼 You'll hear the traveller in two situations: first at an out-of-town motel and then at a hotel in New York City.

⟫→

Listen to the conversations and fill the gaps in the summaries:

AT THE MOTEL The motel room costs $........................ including tax. The room has a TV, a .... bed and a phone with d........................ d........................ To use the phone the traveller has to pay a .... of $........................ He has to fill out the register with his name, address and the .... number of his .... Breakfast, consisting of c........................ and d........................ , is served from .... to .... His room number is .... The traveller pays $........................ in ....

AT THE ROYALTON HOTEL Rooms at the hotel cost from $........................ to $........................ , not including .... The traveller asks for a .... room. The hotel clerk suggests a room in the .... of the hotel at $........................ . This room has bath and shower. The traveller wants to stay for .... nights. His room number is .... The traveller pays $........................ by ....

Work in two large groups. Half of you should look at File 58, the others at 44. You will be playing the roles of guests and reception staff at the Hotel Miramar. Change roles halfway.

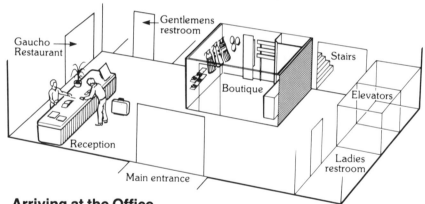

3 Arriving at the Office

You'll hear the traveller being received by Jim Randall, his host in Chicago.
This time you must imagine that *you* are the traveller and reply to Mr Randall's questions.
Your teacher will pause the tape after each question for you and the other members of the class to suggest suitable replies. Then you'll be able to hear the traveller's actual replies.

Work in pairs. Role-play the same situation as the one you heard in the recording. One of you should play the role of visitor and the other the role of host or hostess. Imagine that the visitor has flown in from another continent to visit *your* city.

100

9.2 International travel

You may depend on a travel agent or your firm's travel department to
make your travel arrangements, but there may still be times when you
want to change an itinerary for a visitor or yourself – or when things
don't quite go according to plan.

 Here are some phrases you might need to use:

> I want to fly to Miami on the 10th of next month, returning on
> the 20th.
> I'd like to reserve a seat on Flight number GJ 414 to Milan.
> I'd like to change/reconfirm my reservation on Flight number
> AR 770 on the 16th of this month.
> I need to get to the airport/railway station/railroad station
> as quickly as possible.
> One coach class/round trip/one-way to Houston, please.
> One first class/club class/tourist class return/single to
> Glasgow, please.
> Can I reserve a rented car / a hotel room at the other end?
> Is it too late/early to check in for Flight number IE 009?
> Which platform/track/gate does the 13.40 to London leave
> from?
> Can you tell me what time Flight number SQ 60 is due to
> arrive/depart?
> Can you tell me why there's a delay on Flight number SZ 111/the
> flight to Osaka/the 17.35 train for/from Birmingham?

A Work in pairs. Look at these situations.
Who would you speak to in each case to get the information you
require?

What exactly would you say in each situation?

- You've heard that flight BZ 431 is delayed.
- You want a rail ticket to Manchester.
- You want to reconfirm your seat on flight TR 998.
- You want a plane ticket to Berlin.
- You're in a hurry to get to Manchester Airport from the
  convention centre.
- You've arrived at the airport three hours before your flight.
- You have three minutes before your train leaves.
- You've heard that the 17.55 train has been cancelled.
- You want to make sure of a hotel room in Madrid before your
  flight departs.

⟫→

B Work in groups. Discuss these problems with your partners:

What action would you take in each situation?
Who would you speak to?
What would you say to that person?

1. You arrive in good time at the airport but discover that you have lost your ticket. The ticket clerk says your name is not on the computer.
2. You find that your travel agent has entered the wrong check-in time on your itinerary and you have missed your flight. Your host is meeting you at the airport but by now he will have left home for the airport.
3. You are a non-smoker but the only seat available on the plane is in the smoking section. After take-off you find that your neighbour is a chain smoker and he doesn't speak English.
4. You are on a business trip to India. You have a meeting tomorrow morning in another city. Will you take the overnight express or the plane at 6 am? They both arrive at 8 am.
5. You arrive at Melbourne Airport, Australia, for a one-week visit. The immigration officer tells you that you may not enter the country because your vaccination certificate is not valid.
6. You are departing from an airport abroad. You are stopped by a security guard, who clearly thinks you look very suspicious.
    She asks you these questions:
    'What has been the purpose of your visit?'
    'Where have you been staying?'
    'Who have you been in contact with?'
    'Who packed your case?'
    'Before you open the case, please tell me exactly what it contains.'
7. You want to get home before the weekend. The only flight tonight is on an airline with a bad reputation. Your favourite airline has no flight until tomorrow.
8. Your train has missed the connection and now you're going to be an hour late for your appointment. You do have time to make one quick phone call.
9. You are driving a rented car down a country road in an English-speaking country. You hear a bang and stop at once to find that you have a flat tyre. You open the boot but there is no spare. In the distance, you can see a car approaching . . .
10. You are on your way by car to give a presentation to which people from ten different firms have been invited. 50 km from your destination you stop to fill up with petrol. You pay and drive off, but 200 metres down the road the car stops and you realize that you have filled up with diesel fuel.

In some cases you may think 'It all depends . . .' – but what exactly does it depend *on*?

9.3 Narrating

If you're with a guest or your host, having a meal or a drink or travelling together, you can't spend all your time 'talking shop' (talking about business). Much of the time you'll be chatting or socializing. An important part of socializing is telling people about things that have happened to you – unusual, amusing or interesting experiences you've had.
In this section you'll be able to practise and improve your story-telling skills in English.

A 🔲 You'll hear some stories about travel. Decide whether the statements below are **true** or **false**, according to the stories – you'll probably need to hear the recording twice.

New York
1. The first story is about Mr and Mrs Perry's troubles in New York.
2. The couple intended to spend the weekend together.
3. They didn't find each other until the Sunday afternoon.
4. The misunderstanding was due to the reception clerk's carelessness.

Scandinavia
5. The leaflet about hotels in Oslo was very useful and informative.
6. The colleague's suitcase was taken from Stockholm to London.
7. The suitcase did not contain anything valuable.

Asia
8. At first the passengers were not angry about having to wait.
9. Once they got on the plane the passengers stopped feeling worried.
10. By the time they were near their destination, they felt calm again.
11. The plane was unable to land because the landing gear was faulty.
12. In the end the plane landed safely and no one was hurt.

Here are some expressions you can use when exchanging stories:

I'll never forget the day...
Did I ever tell you about...
The worst journey I ever made was...
I had a surprise / I had a fright the other day when...

That's interesting!   That's amazing!
Really!   How awful!
How embarrassing!   How terrifying!

What happened then?   Why did you do that?
What did you do then?   What did you say then?
How did you feel then?

⟫→

B Now it's your turn to tell some stories. When you're telling a story, it may be a good idea to exaggerate a bit and invent details to make the story more exciting or interesting!

1. Work alone. **If possible, do this preparation at home *before* the lesson.** Try to remember two stories you can tell about each of these subjects. Make notes.

   Think of an amusing, frightening, surprising or embarrassing experience you have had . . .
   . . . on a journey by car, plane, train or bus.
   . . . in a hotel.
   . . . while having a meal.
   . . . while meeting or looking after a visitor.
   . . . at work.

2. Work in groups. You will probably find, once you get started, that your partners' stories will remind you of other experiences you have had. If so, tell these stories too.

3. Work in pairs. Look at the pictures below: they can be interpreted in many different ways. Imagine that it is the story of a day that *you* spent travelling – can you work out what happened? Use your imagination to add plenty of details (about the meals and the people you met, for example).

4. When you're ready, join another pair and tell them your version of the story. You could perhaps begin like this:
   'The car was in the garage for repair on the day I had to travel to . . .'
   and maybe you could finish like this:
   '. . . and when I got back to my room I wrote some letters and went to sleep.'

9.4 Looking after a visitor

A Even if you don't travel on business yourself, it's quite likely you may have to greet, meet or eat with visitors from abroad. Here are some things you might have to do when looking after an English-speaking visitor. Which of these activities have you done or might you have to do one day? Put a √ beside the things you might have to do.

- Picking a visitor up at the airport or station
- Accompanying the visitor to his or her hotel
- Helping to fill in forms in your language
- Translating or interpreting for a visitor
- Explaining to a visitor how to get somewhere
- Accompanying a visitor on part of his or her journey
- Showing a visitor round your office or factory
- Introducing a visitor to your colleagues and superiors
- Eating and drinking with a visitor
- Explaining how to use the public transport system
- Explaining local customs and habits
- Helping a visitor with problems
- Showing a visitor the sights and tourist attractions
- Explaining the economy and industry of your area
- Helping a visitor with shopping
- Seeing a visitor off at the airport

Join a group and tell your partners about your experiences.

B MEETING A VISITOR

 These phrases can be used when meeting or being met:

> Hello are you Mr/Mrs ___? I'm ___.
> Welcome to ___.
> It's a great pleasure to meet you.
> I've been looking forward to meeting you.
> How was your journey/flight?
> I think we'll go to your hotel / our office first ...
> ... my car's outside / we'll take a taxi / we'll take the airport bus.
> Can I take (one of) your bags? Can I help you with your luggage?
>   I'll just find a trolley / a porter for your bags.
> Is there anything you'd like to do before we...?
> Would you like a drink or something to eat before we...?

> Sorry I'm so late – there was fog at Schiphol / an engine failure
>   outside Cologne / a traffic jam north of Florence.
> I hope you haven't been waiting too long.
> Before we set off, I'd like to have a coffee/beer/sandwich.
> I'd just like to make a quick phone call, if that's all right.
> Very smooth. / Not too bad. / Pretty tiring. / Absolutely exhausting!

 Work in pairs. Imagine that one of you is arriving and the other waiting at the airport.

1. Before you start, decide together who you are: your names and jobs, where you are and the reasons for the visit.
2. Role-play the whole scene, right up to leaving the airport.
3. Change partners and role-play the scene again.

C GIVING DIRECTIONS

Here are some phrases you can use when giving directions:

> It's a bit complicated, I'd better show you on the map.
> It'll take about 20 minutes on foot.
> Go to the right as you leave this building and turn left when you get to the
>   town hall.
> Keep straight on and go across the river. You'll see the railway station
>   on your right / on the right.
> Continue along that road for three blocks till you come to a church.
> Opposite the church there's a big square. The restaurant is down a
>   little back street on the other side of the square.
>
> You can take the tram — it's the number 89 which says 'ZOO' on the
>   front. You'll need to get a ticket from the machine before you get
>   on. At the fifth stop you get off and cross the road and walk on for
>   about 100 metres. The restaurant is on the left, you can't miss it.
>
> Drive straight on until you see the blue signs that say 'CITY.' Follow
>   these signs as far as the lake and then turn right and drive along
>   the lake for about 5 km. The restaurant is on the right just after the
>   first village, you can't miss it.

Work in pairs. Play the roles of host and visitor.
The visitor needs to know how to get to all the important parts of
your town or city. Draw a rough street plan before you start – or
draw the map for the 'visitor' as you explain how to get to each place.
Change roles so that you each have a turn as host.

D LOCAL KNOWLEDGE
It's a good idea to get to know your own city or town from a visitor's
point of view – this may be quite different from your view as a resident.

What do you know about your own city? Do you know . . .
>   where a visitor could go on a free day, or at the weekend?
>   when the museums and art galleries are open?
>   how a visitor can get tickets for a concert or show?
>   where a visitor can rent a car?
>   which restaurants serve typical local dishes?
>   where a visitor can buy local specialities to take home?
>   when the bus to the airport leaves and how long it takes?

Work in pairs. Imagine you'll soon be welcoming two people from
the other side of the world, who haven't left their own country before.
They're coming to work with you for a few months.

1. Make a list of customs and habits that will seem strange and which will be
    different from their country. What will you explain to them about . . .
    *   eating (popular dishes, meal times, etc)
    *   public transport (how do you get tickets, for example?)
    *   shopping (where to buy groceries and clothes cheaply)
    *   work (clothes to wear, office hours etc)
    *   entertainments (where can you go dancing, for example?)
    *   sports (where can you play tennis, work out or swim, etc?)

2. 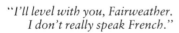 Now form a group of four with another pair. Imagine that the others are
    newly-arrived foreigners, who need to be briefed on habits and customs in your
    country.

3. Half-way through, your teacher will tell you to change roles.

4. Make a list of fifteen famous local names: ones that are well-known in your
    country but less well-known abroad.
    2 national politicians   2 local politicians   2 historical figures
    2 TV personalities   2 movie stars   2 entertainers or artists
    2 big names in local industry or commerce

5. Join one or two other pairs. Explain to the members of the group why the
    people who are on your list but not on theirs are well-known – imagine they are
    foreigners who are unfamiliar with your country.

*"I'll level with you, Fairweather.
I don't really speak French."*

9.5 To be or not to be . . . or be-ing?? *Grammar*

Most learners of English have difficulty with the -ing form ('the gerund') and to__ ('to + infinitive').
Study these examples and fill the gaps in the sentences below.

-ing AS THE SUBJECT OF A SENTENCE:
  Travelling abroad can be exhausting. Meeting people can be tiring.
  .... a new city can be exciting.
  .... in hotels can be lonely.
  .... from the airport to the city is easy.

-ing AFTER PREPOSITIONS:
  Is anyone interested in playing tennis this evening?
  I can't get used to* living in a different time zone. (*to is a preposition here)
  I'm looking forward to* .... the USA next summer.
  It's unwise to travel by air without .... a reservation
  You can find out if flights are delayed by .... the airport.

VERBS + **-ing**:
  enjoy   finish   dislike   avoid   give up   don't mind
  practise   delay
  I've finished reading that report. I'm trying to give up smoking.
  I avoid .... by car on business.
  I dislike .... in airport lounges.
  I always enjoy .... unusual foreign food.

VERBS + **to__**:
  learn   manage   mean   choose   forget   can't afford   help
  pretend   need   didn't mean   expect   hope   offer   refuse
  want   agree   promise   I'd like   recommend   encourage
  train   teach   allow
  I'd like you to give me a hand with these files.
  They promised to phone me back. He didn't mean to be rude to you.
  I can't afford .... at the Ritz.
  We decided .... the weekend at the seaside.
  We managed .... two seats on tomorrow's flight.

VERBS + **-ing** *or* + **to__** WITH NO DIFFERENCE IN MEANING:
  begin   start   continue   intend   hate   like   love
  prefer   propose
  She began to make/making enquiries. I love to eat/eating Chinese food.
  She hates .... alone in restaurants.
  Which plane do you propose .... ?
  After the meal we continued ....

VERBS + **-ing** *or* + **to** WITH A DIFFERENCE IN MEANING:

stop to ↔ **stop -ing**
Please stop making that noise, it's driving me mad! (= don't continue . . .)
We stopped to get some petrol and have some lunch. (= stop in order to . . .)
Their boss told them to stop .... personal calls on the office phone.
I was half-way through the report but I had to stop .... the phone.

remember to ↔ **remember -ing**
'Did you remember to call our agents in Rio yesterday?' (= not forget . . .)
'I don't remember you asking me to, Bob.' (= have a clear memory of . . .)
Please remember .... us a telex to confirm the details.
I remember .... her last year at the sales conference.

try to ↔ **try -ing**
'I'm trying to open this box, but I'm just not strong enough.' (= try with difficulty or without success)
'Try hitting it with a hammer, that might work.' (= try this method . . .)
We tried .... you on the phone but you weren't available.
Why didn't you try .... me at home? You've got my number.

to AFTER ADJECTIVES:

pleased   glad   surprised   disappointed   relieved to . . .
I was pleased to receive your invitation.
They were relieved to hear the plane had landed safely.
I was glad .... my old colleague at the conference.
We were surprised .... that the fare was over $500.

interesting   kind   hard   essential   difficult   easy to . . .
It was interesting to see the factory. It's hard to get a visa for Burma.
It's easy .... from the airport to the city by public transport.
It was very kind of you .... me at the station.

too . . . to *and* **. . . enough to**
She was clever enough to guess the answer. My coffee is too hot to drink.
The parcel was too .... to be sent by post.
I want to be early enough .... a good seat on the train.

A   Work in pairs. Underline the correct alternatives in these
sentences. The first is done for you as an example.

1. Eat/**Eating**/To eat ... the local food and ... drink/drinking/to drink ...
   the local wine made me feel ill the next morning.
2. We were very annoyed ... find out / finding out / to find out ...that customs
   formalities took so long.
3. I'm afraid I didn't remember ... post/posting/to post ...the letter.
4. I try ... avoid/avoiding/to avoid ... go/going / to go ... abroad during the
   summer.
5. On the way to my host's house I stopped ... buy/buying / to buy some
   flowers.

≫→

6. After a long day, I was looking forward to ... have/having ... a drink, a shower and a rest.
7. If you go to live in another country it can take a long time ... get/ getting / to get ... used to ... adapt/adapting ... to the way of life.
8. Have you managed ... get/getting / to get ... me a seat on tomorrow's flight?

B Fill these gaps with suitable words, using **-ing** or **to __**:

1. We'll delay .*leaving*......... until we hear the weather forecast.
2. Which hotel would you recommend me .... ?
3. It's essential .... a visa if you intend .... the USA.
4. Would you like .... the evening with me and my family?
5. It wasn't easy .... an interpreter who spoke both Chinese and Japanese.
6. He was talking to me about .... Japan next spring.
7. .... is not allowed in public buildings in this country.
8. There's a disco in the hotel. The music started .... at 11 pm and it stopped me .... till 3 am.
9. I tried .... have a shower, but there was no hot water.
10. We agreed .... in the hotel lobby at 8 o'clock.
11. The 07.15 plane is too early for me ....
12. It's been a lovely evening! Will you allow me .... the wine?
13. Thank you very much. It was very kind of you .... me.
14. Would you like me .... a lift to the airport in my car?
15. I don't mind .... when I'm abroad.
16. I usually enjoy .... when I'm away from home.

9.6 Accommodation

If you know a hotel and you've stayed there before, you probably just send them a telex like this to book a room:

```
TO:  HOTEL CONCORDE, TOULOUSE

PLEASE BOOK THREE ROOMS WITH BATHS FOR THE NIGHT
OF MONDAY 1 APRIL. ARRIVING 20.00 HOURS.

HARRY MEIER
ACME INTERNATIONAL
GENEVA, SWITZERLAND
```

But if you're visiting an unfamiliar city, and if you require more information about the hotel, you may need to telephone them.

110

A 📼 You will hear Mr Meier's secretary phoning the Hotel Concorde. Answer these questions about the call and make notes:
   Why did the secretary phone instead of sending a telex?
   What information did she get from the hotel?

B Work in pairs.

1. ☎ One of you should look at File 76 the other at 68. You'll be calling a hotel to book a room.
2. Do the roleplay again, with reversed roles.
3. Draft a letter or telex to the Stafford or the Ritz confirming the reservation you made on the phone.

A quiet haven in a corner of St. James's

The Stafford

In a quiet corner of St. James's is a small hotel which up to now has been known only to a select clientele. Its exquisite furnishings and decor retain all the charm and elegance of an Edwardian town house. Every bedroom is furnished and decorated in a different style and many guests ask for "their own room" each time they stay with us.

For business The Stafford is a perfect venue. The American Bar is an ideal place to meet for a quiet drink and the Restaurant is unsurpassed for business entertaining. More formal or confidential meetings can be held in one of our Private Salons which can accommodate up to 30 people.

For further information, please write or telephone Clive Bullock. The Stafford, St. James's Place, London SW1A 1NJ. 01-493 0111. Telex: 28602.
The Stafford Hotel. Discover it for yourself.

Gentlemen, may we recommend a small hotel overlooking Green Park

Ever since César Ritz built his famous hotel in Piccadilly to create "the most fashionable hotel in the most fashionable city in the world", it has been a firm favourite with business travellers coming to London. Many regard it as the finest business address in London. With only 128 rooms, The Ritz offers a friendly, personal service which is second to none.

The famous Ritz Restaurant, described as "the most beautiful dining room in London" is perfect for business entertaining be it breakfast, lunch or dinner. For private meetings or business functions there are luxurious suites available.

Telephone Carol Thomas on 01-493 8181 or write to The Ritz, Piccadilly, London W1 for further details.

**The Ritz.
Where it's a
pleasure to
do business.**

THE RITZ
PICCADILLY · LONDON

111

C Work in groups. What kind of hotel do you (or would you) prefer to stay in on a business trip? How is it different from a holiday hotel?

Imagine that you are designing a new business hotel: the first of a new chain, catering for *mid-budget* business travellers.

1. Decide on the basic concept of your 'product':
   Atmosphere: 'modern' or 'traditional' or 'intimate' – or a new concept . . .?
   Location: city centre, out of town or in a quiet back street?
   What kinds of people do you want to come to your hotel?
   The staff: will there be a high ratio of staff to guests or will there be an emphasis on self-service?

2. What facilities will you offer? Make a list. Here are some ideas to start you off:

buffet-style breakfast	cocktail lounge	24-hour coffee shop
fitness centre / gym	free car parking	good towels
jacuzzi & sauna	photocopying	room service 24 hours
secretarial service	self-service cafeteria	swimming pool
video movies	fresh fruit and flowers in bedrooms	

   restaurant serving local specialities   + *your own ideas* ....

3. Arrange the facilities you have listed *in order of importance*.
   Then decide which you will offer – offering them all would price your product out of the mid-budget market!

4. When your group has designed 'the perfect business hotel', describe your product to another group or to the whole class.

9.7 At a restaurant

A   Imagine that you're at a restaurant with a foreign visitor who can't understand some of the items on the menu.
Work in pairs and play the roles of visitor and host or hostess.
If possible, get a menu from a local restaurant – or start by composing a menu of your own national dishes.

Here are some useful expressions:

> Can you tell me what . . . . . . is?

> These are starters, these are main courses, and these are desserts.
> Yes, it's a speciality of this region. It's a sort of . . .
> Yes, that's something rather special. It's a kind of . . .
> Well, that's difficult to explain. It's a bit like . . .
> I'm afraid I don't know what that is. I'll ask the waiter/waitress.

> That sounds very nice. I'll have that, please.
> I don't really like the sound of that.
> I'd like to have . . . . . . to start with, followed by . . . . . .

Christmas Fayre Menu

FRESH MELON AND ORANGE COCKTAIL
POTTED SHRIMP SALAD
served with Garlic Butter
HOME MADE TOMATO SOUP
finished with Cream

★

BLACKCURRANT WATER ICE

★

GRILLED HALIBUT STEAK
topped with Anchovy Butter
ROAST ENGLISH TURKEY
with Chestnut Stuffing, Chipolata, Bacon Roll and Cranberry Sauce
BREAST OF CHICKEN WIMBORNE
in a pepper and mushroom sauce
GRILLED RUMP STEAK
with mushrooms and tomato
(at £1.00 extra)
Market Day Vegetables with a potato dish is served with all main course dishes

★

CHRISTMAS PUDDING WITH BRANDY SAUCE
FRESH FRUIT SALAD
SHERRY TRIFLE

★

COFFEE WITH MINCE PIES

★

PRICE £9.95 PER PERSON to include NOVELTY CRACKERS

B Work in groups. Imagine you're having a meal at a restaurant in an English-speaking country. Look at the menu above. Decide what you're going to have and then call someone to take your order. While you're waiting, keep talking to each other, as if you're really having lunch or dinner together.

9.8 Organizing a conference

Work in groups. Imagine that you're organizing a weekend conference for about 50 delegates, from the evening of Friday 22 May to lunchtime on Monday 25 May. Four foreign speakers have been invited and you'll need to write to them in English.

1. Discuss what arrangements you'll have to make for the conference. Make a list of the things you will have to do.
2. Work through the activity, following the instructions below.

⟫→

March 16

What's happened so far . . .

You have provisionally booked 30 double and 10 single rooms at the three-star Hôtel du Lac. This hotel has a hall for up to 75 people and three seminar rooms that hold 30 people each. The conference will consist of lectures (in English) in the hall and simultaneous seminars for smaller groups in the other rooms. Four foreign guest speakers have provisionally agreed to take part: their lectures will be on the Saturday in the main hall. So far, 10 weeks before the conference, you have 23 firm bookings from delegates and 14 provisional ones.

1. Draft a letter to the foreign speakers, giving this information:
    - Confirm dates and venue of the conference.
    - Ask for title and 100-word summary of their talk.
    - Explain the accommodation arrangements – 'You will have sole occupancy of a double room with a view of the lake. Your accommodation and full board will be paid for by us.'
    - Explain about expenses: 'we will refund your expenses by cheque in our currency or by T/T to your own bank'.
    - Ask them to book APEX tickets, not standard fare.
    - Make the hotel and the conference sound attractive.
2. Show your draft letter to another group and make any amendments you think are necessary.
3. Write a final draft of the letter.

March 30

1. Now, two weeks later, the four speakers have been in touch with you. They each have special requests:

Mr Santini phoned to say that he had understood he was getting a fee for the talk and not just expenses. I said you'd phone him or send a telex today.

```
FOR THE LECTURE I WILL NEED AN OVERHEAD PROJECTOR.
WILL THERE BE PHOTOCOPYING FACILITIES ON SITE?
I AM NOT VERY HAPPY ABOUT THE HOTEL ARRANGEMENTS. I WOULD PREFER
MORE LUXURIOUS ACCOMMODATION THAN THE CONFERENCE HOTEL. COULD
YOU BOOK ME INTO A FIVE-STAR HOTEL INSTEAD, PLEASE?
REGARDS, THOMAS BRINKMANN.
```

```
     I've decided to bring my family over for a week.
During the conference I'll stay in the hotel but my
family will need accommodation for the weekend and
then for the four of us for the week after the
conference (till May 30). Can you find us a 3-
bedroom self-catering apartment near the lake?
     Thanks for your help.
    Looking forward to seeing you in May.
```

Janet Hennessy

And you will hear a recorded message from the fourth speaker, left on the answerphone early this morning.

2. Discuss with your partners how you will deal with each request, bearing in mind these points:
   - You haven't budgeted for any speaker getting a fee.
   - There is a four-star hotel, the Bellevue, about 1km from the conference hotel but each speaker is getting a very nice double room with view of the lake at the conference hotel.
   - Holiday apartments in the village cost £100–150 per week.
   - You can only pay expenses in cash if you know exactly how much in advance. (He should phone or telex when he knows how much the tickets will cost.)

3. Draft a letter or telex to each speaker.

April 13

1. Now it's time to send out the programme of the conference.
   Decide when each of the speakers will be lecturing on Saturday May 23:

9.00–10.30	11.00–12.30	14.00–15.30	16.00–17.30

2. Draft a letter to the four speakers, giving this information:
   - Tell each speaker when they will be speaking
   - Give details of their accommodation:

We've booked you a nice room with a balcony overlooking the
lake. There's a marvellous view of the mountains when the
weather is clear.

   - Give instructions on how to get to the hotel from the airport or
     station:

When you arrive at the Airport get a rail ticket to A___ and
take the train that goes to the Main Station. Change there
to a local train going to D___ (platform 14 every half
hour). A___ is the 7th stop. The Hotel du Lac is right
opposite the station. Allow one hour for the journey.

   - Say that you're looking forward to meeting them and that there
     will now be about 70 delegates.

3. Join another group and discuss what you did in this activity.

9.9 Flying down to Rio

Work in groups. Use the information below to arrange a business trip
for a traveller in South America. You'll need to decide on the
itinerary, taking in all the cities shown. The trip should be as short as
possible, and there should be a meeting or a flight every day. Your
flight arrives in Rio on Thursday 16 August at 05.00 and it's best not
to arrange a meeting for that day. Imagine that *you* are the traveller.

You have already booked a stand at the trade exhibition in
Florianópolis: this starts in the afternoon on August 24 and ends on
August 27. The rest of the time you will be based in Rio and will need
to make day trips to other cities within Brazil. Trips outside Brazil
will require at least one overnight stay. Flights back home are at
22.30 on Tuesdays and Saturdays.

August						
Su	Mo	Tu	We	Th	Fr	Sa
			1	2	3	4
5	6	7	8	9	10	11
12	13	14	15	16	17	18
19	20	21	22	23	24	25
26	27	28	29	30	31	

September						
Su	Mo	Tu	We	Th	Fr	Sa
						1
2	3	4	5	6	7	8
9	10	11	12	13	14	15
16	17	18	19	20	21	22
23	24	25	26	27	28	29
30						

Public Holidays

Argentina: Aug 17
Brazil: Sept 7
Chile: Sept 18-19
Peru: Aug 30
Uruguay: Aug 25
Venezuela: Aug 15

You have to meet the following people, and you will need the best part of a day with each one of them:

CITY	NAME	AVAILABILITY
Belo Horizonte	João Jardim	Tuesdays only
Blumenau	Flora Fischer	August only
Brasilia	Ivan Itaparica	Sept 3 onwards
Rio de Janeiro	Anna Almeida	Thursdays or Fridays only
	Berta Baena	Saturdays only
	Edisón Echevarria	any day
	Nelsón Neves	second week of September
São Paulo	Doris Dias	August only
	Maria Martin	any day
Bogotá, Colombia	Klaus König	Sept only
Buenos Aires, Argentina	Hectór Hudson	end of August
Lima, Peru	Carla Castro	August only
Montevidéo, Uruguay	Gregorio García	any time
Santiago de Chile	Lucia Lluch	Sept only

(You'd also like to fit in a weekend break at the Iguassu Falls, if possible.)

Look at the map and airline timetable on the next page.

Flights to and from RIO DE JANEIRO, Galeão Airport
(except flights to/from São Paulo)

Rio to/from SÃO PAULO	Every 30 mins to/from Santos Dumont Airport	(first flight 06.30, last flight 22.30, duration 1 hour)

Rio to/from BRASILIA	Every 90 mins (first flight 06.00, last flight 22.00, duration 1 hour)

Rio to BELO HORIZONTE	06.00	08.00	10.30	18.00	14.30	17.15	(duration 1 hour)
Belo Horizonte to Rio	07.00	09.00	13.15	14.30	18.00	20.30	(duration 1 hour)

Rio to FLORIANÓPOLIS	07.00–09.50	14.00–18.00
Florianópolis to Rio	08.40–12.15	20.30–23.15
Florianópolis to Montevidéo	10.15–14.00 (Wed only)	

Rio to IGUASSU FALLS	09.15–12.30	11.00–14.15	16.00–21.25
Iguassu Falls to Rio	15.30–18.45	17.30–20.45	20.30–23.30
Buenos Aires to Iguassu Falls	18.00–19.45		

Rio to BLUMENAU	12.00–15.50
Blumenau to Rio	08.55–12.55

◇ NOTE: Blumenau is about 2 hours by taxi from Florianópolis

Rio to BUENOS AIRES	08.45–11.55	16.15–20.45	
Buenos Aires to Rio	08.30–13.00	16.00–21.15	18.00–20.50

Rio to MONTEVIDÉO	08.45–13.50
Montevidéo to Rio	16.20–20.50
Montevidéo to Buenos Aires	16.20–17.10

Rio to SANTIAGO DE CHILE	08.00–12.50
Santiago to Rio	14.15–20.30

Rio to LIMA	11.00–14.15 (Sun)	22.00–01.00 (Wed)	17.30–22.00 (Sat)
Lima to Rio	12.50–20.15 (Mon)	11.50–17.25 (Wed, Fri)	14.40–20.15 (Sat)

Rio to BOGOTÁ	12.00–16.05 (Sun)	12.00–17.35 (Wed)
Bogotá to Rio	21.40–05.40 (Mon)	21.40–07.05 (Thu) [both connect with 08.00 to Santiago]

1. Draft a letter or telex to one of the people arranging a meeting on the day you've decided.
2. And, if you have been unable to fit anyone in to the itinerary, write to them explaining why they have been left out.
3. Draft a telex to the Hotel Cambridge in Santiago, booking a room for one or two nights.
4. Tell another group about the itinerary you have worked out and explain why you've made the decisions you've made.

A 🔲 We asked some experienced business travellers for advice.
Listen and make notes.
- Which of the advice do you agree with or disagree with?
- Add some more pieces of advice you'd give to a first-time traveller.

B Work in groups. Find out about your partners' experiences and
feelings about these aspects of travelling abroad:

Staying in a hotel	Living out of a suitcase
Driving a car abroad	Eating in restaurants abroad
Travelling by train	Long-haul and short-haul flights
Visiting new places	Weekends away from home
Jet lag	Waiting for a delayed flight

Which are enjoyable, or exciting?
Which are stressful, annoying or depressing?
What difference does it make if you're on holiday (travelling for
pleasure) and not travelling on business?

C Supposing you had to travel across the Atlantic or Pacific at your
firm's expense, how would you choose to go: on an ocean liner,
supersonic by Concorde – or first class with your own national
airline?

👥 How would you justify this to your finance director?
What would he say to persuade you to fly Economy Class?
Role-play the conversation between the two of you.

10 Marketing and sales

Marketing a product: market research and promotion. Selling a product: sales talk, meetings and demonstrations. Comparing and contrasting. Possibility and probability.

10.1 Local products

Discussion

Work in groups. Think of eight products (goods and services) that are produced or provided in your city or region and answer the questions below:

1. a brand of beer or a soft drink
2. a grocery product (breakfast cereal, health food, etc)
3. an industrial product (machines, consumer goods, vehicles, etc)
4. a service (cleaning, temporary employment bureaus, etc)
5. a place of entertainment (theatre, cinema, etc)
6. a public service (telephones, mail, transport, etc)
7. an educational service (maybe the course you're doing now?)
8. a financial service (bank, insurance company, etc)
9. another well-known local product: ....

– What competition does each product face? (This may not be another brand, but another type of product: people may prefer to buy clothes instead of going to the cinema, for example.)
– What is the image of each product?
– What is the image of the company that produces it?
– How strongly or weakly is each of the products marketed?
– Where is each product advertised?

10.2 What is marketing?

A Fill the gaps in these sentences, using the words from the list.

creative process   design   distribution   end-users   first
hire purchase   image   labels   mail order   need   opportunities
outlets   patterns   place   posters   price   product
production-orientated   profitably   promotion   range   rival
satisfy   strengths   threats   weaknesses

1. What is marketing? Marketing is the .... of satisfying customer needs ....
2. What is 'the marketing mix'? It consists of 'the four P's': providing the customer with the right P............ at the right P............ , presented in the most attractive way (P............) and available in the easiest way (P............).
3. What is 'a product'? A product is not just an assembled set of components: it is something customers buy to .... a .... they feel they have. The .... and the .... of the product are as important as its specification.
4. What is 'price'? The product must be priced so that it competes effectively with .... products in the same market.
5. What is 'promotion'? The product is presented to customers through advertising (TV commercials, ... , etc), packaging (design, ... , etc), publicity, P.R. and personal selling. See 10.8 for more on this topic.
6. What is 'place'? Your product must be available to customers through the most cost-effective channels of .... A consumer product must be offered to .... in suitable retail .... , or available on .... or by ....
7. What is meant by 'S.W.O.T.'? A firm should be aware of its S............ and W............ and the O............ and T............ it faces in the market place.
8. Why are firms becoming more customer-orientated and less .... ? Because new products must be created to meet the changing .... of customers' needs – a firm can't rely on the success of its existing .... of products. The customer and his or her needs must come ....!

B Work in pairs. What opportunities and threats does your firm face in the next 2–3 years?

"Well, gentlemen, we've got a stunning new logo and a marvellous publicity campaign ready. We just need to come up with a product."

121

10.3 Comparing and contrasting *Grammar*

First, look at these rules:

ONE SYLLABLE   Adjectives with one syllable form their comparatives and superlatives like this:

    cheap → cheaper → the cheapest
    large → larger → the largest
    plain → plainer→ the plainest
    bright → brighter → the brightest
    [Exceptions: good → better → the best   and   bad → worse → the worst]

TWO SYLLABLES   Some adjectives with two syllables form their comparatives and superlatives like this:

    pretty → prettier → the prettiest
    happy → happier → the happiest
But many form their comparatives and superlatives like this:
    costly → more costly → the most costly
    striking → more striking → the most striking
    useful → more useful → the most useful
But some can form their comparatives and superlatives like this:
    common → more common/commoner → the most common/commonest
    clever → more clever/cleverer → the most clever/cleverest

THREE SYLLABLES   All adjectives with three or more syllables form their comparatives and superlatives like this:

    attractive → more attractive → the most attractive
    profitable → more profitable → the most profitable
    expensive → more expensive → the most expensive

A   What are the comparative and superlative forms of these adjectives?

correct, accurate, precise, reliable   new, modern, up-to-date
convenient, economical, flexible   warm, friendly, kind
optimistic, happy, cheerful   pessimistic, unhappy, gloomy
funny, amusing, lively, witty   possible, likely, probable, certain

B   Look at these sentences and the pie chart on the next page:

- White is **the most** popular colour for cars in Britain.
- Red is **the second most** popular colour for cars in Britain.
- White is a (**much/far**) **more** popular colour **than** blue.
  or Blue is a (**much/far**) **less** popular colour **than** white.
  or Blue **isn't as** popular a colour **as** white.
- Gold cars are **not** (**quite**) **as** popular **as** yellow ones.
  or Yellow cars are **a bit/little more** popular **than** gold ones.
- Yellow cars are (**just**) **as** popular **as** brown ones.
- Green seems to be **the least** popular colour for cars in Britain.
  or Green is **the most** unpopular colour for cars in Britain.

122

- About **twice as many** brown cars are sold **as** black cars in Britain.
  or **Half as many** black cars are sold **as** brown cars.
- **More/far more** red cars are sold **than** green cars.
  or **Fewer/far fewer** green cars are sold **than** red ones.
  or **Not as many** green cars are sold **as** red ones.
- **Most** British people would never dream of buying a green car.

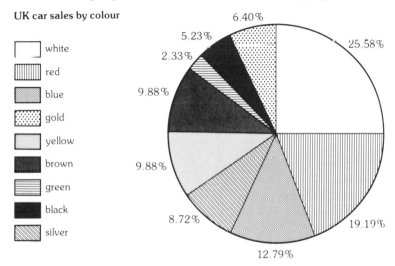

UK car sales by colour

- white
- red
- blue
- gold
- yellow
- brown
- green
- black
- silver

6.40%
5.23%
2.33%
9.88%
9.88%
8.72%
12.79%
19.19%
25.58%

C Write some more, similar sentences about the information given in the pie charts below and on the next page.

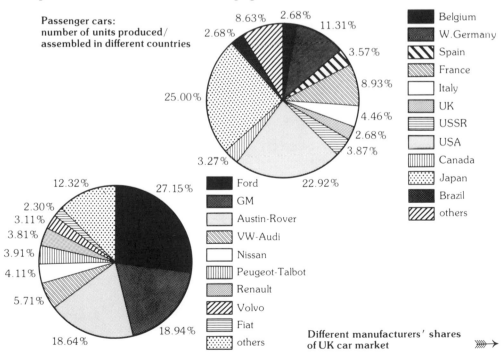

Passenger cars: number of units produced/ assembled in different countries

8.63%   2.68%   11.31%
2.68%   3.57%
25.00%   8.93%
4.46%
2.68%
3.27%   3.87%
22.92%

- Belgium
- W.Germany
- Spain
- France
- Italy
- UK
- USSR
- USA
- Canada
- Japan
- Brazil
- others

12.32%   27.15%
2.30%
3.11%
3.81%
3.91%
4.11%
5.71%
18.64%   18.94%

- Ford
- GM
- Austin-Rover
- VW-Audi
- Nissan
- Peugeot-Talbot
- Renault
- Volvo
- Fiat
- others

Different manufacturers' shares of UK car market ⟫→

123

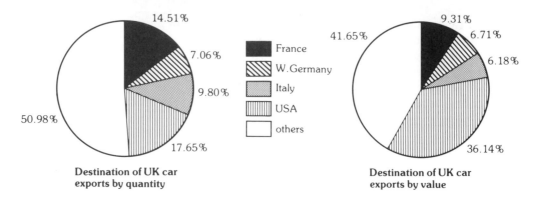

14.51%
7.06%
9.80%
17.65%
50.98%

France
W.Germany
Italy
USA
others

Destination of UK car exports by quantity

9.31%
6.71%
6.18%
36.14%
41.65%

Destination of UK car exports by value

D Any product gives various 'benefits' to the customer: these may be functional or practical (speed, power, efficiency etc) or psychological (attractive appearance, making the customer feel happy or proud, etc):

Feature ———▶ Benefit
A is more .... than B, which means that .... *Positive benefits*
B isn't as .... as A, which means that .... *Negative benefits*

Look at the three products compared here. Discuss the 'features and benefits' of each product, like this:
The Acme 77B is available in bright colours,
    which means that it will be an attractive feature of your room.
The Acme 77B isn't as powerful as the other fans,
    which means that it won't keep you so cool.

	Rolac 241	Samco Airblast	Acme 77B
fan diameter	24 cm	17.5 cm	35 cm
power consumption	20 watt	30 watt	75 watt
mosquito/fly killing	yes	yes	no
settings	3	2	4
speeds (r.p.m.)	600/1000	1000/1500	200/750
air output (m³/minute)	45	25	40
colours available	beige only	white or black	5 bright colours
country of manufacture	Italy	France	Taiwan
retail price	£17.99	£24.50	£14.99
wholesale price per 100	£104.55	£152.00	£85.00

E Work in groups. Ask your partners these questions:
What benefits does *your* firm's product give?
What will it do for the customer?
How is it different to or better than the competition?

10.4 Arranging a sales meeting

Work in pairs. Mr Müller, your boss or colleague, has asked you to
do some things for him while he is away. This is one of them:

Please write to Gafco in Brussels, arrange meeting on 24 May. Preferably late morning. Offer lunch date if René Van Hoorn is available.

A Read this information on the customer record card:

COMPANY	Gafco. S. A.
ADDRESS	153 avenue Louise, 10078 Brussels, Belgium
TELEPHONE	010 32 2 75 75 75
HOW TO GET THERE	15 mins by taxi from Central Station or tram 34 stops opposite
CONTACT	Purchasing Director René van Hoorn
ASSISTANT	Assistant to Purchasing Director Jean Meyer
LAST CALL	December 12, 19--
SALES LAST YEAR	Jan-Mar $57,876 Apr-Jun $46,982 Jul-Sept $65,893 Oct-Dec $32,456
SALES THIS YEAR	Jan-Mar $44,986
SPECIAL COMMENTS	René speaks French, Flemish & German but prefers to do business in English. Don't talk about his family. Jean authorised to confirm, not originate orders.

B Draft a letter to the customer. Here are some phrases you can use:

```
Mr Müller has asked me to write to you on his behalf.
He would prefer a late morning appointment if that is
    convenient to you.
Would you be free to meet him and to have lunch on...?
Please confirm that the date and time I have suggested are
    suitable.
```

C Read another pair's letter and reply to it by telex in the role of
Jean Meyer. Here are some phrases you can use:

delighted to join you for lunch   looking forward to seeing you
be expecting you here at 11.30   discuss changes to your specifications

D 📞 Read the other pair's telex. Then one of you should look at
File 114, the other at 70.

10.5 Sales talk

A 🔲 Work in pairs. You will hear part of an interview between
a sales engineer and her client, then answer these questions:

- How do you think the deal for 404X's or 404PS's was closed?
- Do you think both people were satisfied with the meeting so far?

⟫→

- How are the clients *you* know more difficult to deal with than Mr Ray?
- What would you have done differently if you'd been (a) the sales engineer and (b) the client?

B Which of the points in this text do you agree or disagree with?

Anyone who has contact with customers is a sales person – that includes the telephonist who answers the phone and the service engineer who calls to repair a machine. So that probably includes you!

The relationship between a sales person and a client is important: both parties want to feel satisfied with their deal and neither wants to feel cheated. A friendly, respectful relationship is more effective than an aggressive, competitive one.

A sales person should believe that his product has certain advantages over the competition. A customer wants to be sure that he is buying a product that is good value and of high quality. No one in business is going to spend his company's money on something they don't really need (unlike consumers, who can sometimes be persuaded to buy 'useless' products like fur coats and solid gold watches!).

Some sales people prefer a direct 'hard sell' approach, while others prefer a more indirect 'soft sell' approach. Whichever approach is used, a good sales person is someone who knows how to deal with different kinds of people and who can point out how his product will benefit each individual customer in special ways. A successful sales meeting depends on both the sales person and the customer asking each other the right sort of questions.

C What sort of questions are most useful in a sales meeting?
- What *answer* is each of these questions likely to provide?
- Which of the questions are likely to give more useful information?

'Do you think the product is too expensive?'
   'What are your reactions to the prices I've quoted you?'
'Is the machine designed to operate 24 hours a day?'
   'Tell me about the operation of the machine.'
'Are you worried about the question of reliability?'
   'Are there any particular points you're worried about?'

D 🔲 Work in pairs.

1. Student A should look at File 22, and student B at 8. You'll be taking part in a meeting between a sales person and a customer.
2. When you have finished the meeting, find someone from another pair who has been playing the same role as you.
   Imagine this person is a *colleague* and report to them on the meeting you've just had. Then rejoin your original partner.
3. Now student A should look at File 8, and student B at 30.
4. After the second meeting, report to a 'colleague' from another pair who has been playing the same role as you.
5. Draft a short report on one of the meetings you had, describing what happened and the outcome. Imagine that this report will be read by your superior, who is away this week.

10.6 Marketing your own region

In this activity you will be deciding how to market a product you're very familiar with – your own region. Look at these ads:

A Work in pairs. Look at the statistics below. How much of this information is relevant to marketing your own region? Your customers may be British people *or* people who would otherwise go to the UK. Compare your ideas with the rest of the class.

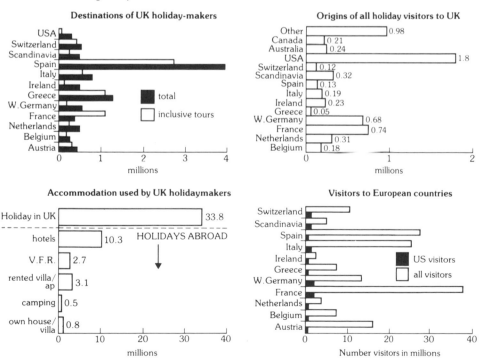

B   The class is divided into three groups. Group A should look at
File 62, Group B at 28 and Group C at 46.

1. Each group will have to design a questionnaire about the region and its
    competitors and then conduct interviews with consumers (i.e. potential
    visitors).

2. When your group has designed its questionnaire, each member of the group
    should stand up and go round the class finding 'members of the public' (from
    other groups) to interview. Ask each of them the questions in your
    questionnaire.
    [If possible, this should be continued out of class, with the questions translated
    into your own language if necessary.]

3. Report back to your group. Make a simple table using the information you have
    collected.

4. Each group reports its results to the whole class.
    Make notes on the important points made by the other groups.
    Ask questions on any points they haven't made clear.
    or
    Form new groups of three or four, consisting of one member from each of the
    original groups. Find out what each of the groups discovered.

5. Draft a report summarizing your group's findings, including a table or chart.
    Show this to a member of another group and ask for comments.

6. Work in groups, consisting of one member of each of the original groups.
    Decide together:

    *   Who are your (potential) customers?
    *   What are the main attractions of your product?
    *   What are the main attractions of the competition?
    *   What is the 'unique selling proposition' that makes your product special?
    *   How can you inform customers about your product?
    *   What positive points about your region should you stress?
    *   What misconceptions about your product should you try to correct?
        For example, if people think your region is 'flat and boring' or 'hot and
        dusty', how can you persuade them they're wrong?

7. Work as a whole class or in two large groups. Devise a marketing strategy for
    your product. How can you improve your product's image and promote it to
    the customers?

8. Think of a good slogan for your product. Draft a short text for an
    advertisement in a British newspaper or magazine.

10.7 Promoting a Total Product

The promotion of a product involves considering it as a 'Total Product': its brand name, presentation, labelling, packaging, instructions, reliability and after-sales service are all part of the total product; a product which is a service must be clearly 'visible' to the customer.

A 📼 You'll hear part of a lecture. The lecturer is talking about brand names that sound strange or ridiculous to British ears or which were changed for the British market. Mark the brand names below with a √ if they are on sale in the UK, or with a × if they are not on sale in the UK under that name.

Soft Drinks: Pocari Sweat   Calpis   Psschitt   Sic
Food: Bum potato crisps   Mother biscuits
Portable radios: Party Boy   Yacht Boy   Tiny 320   Weekend 360
Cars: Cedric   Gloria   Rabbit   Ritmo   Strada
       Kadett   Astra   Nova   Corsa   Golf
       Camry   Cherry   Bluebird   Starion   Sunny
Vacuum cleaners: Vampire   Compact Electronic
Computers: Einstein   Dragon   Compaq   Macintosh
           Apple   Banana   Lemon   Apricot   Golden Delicious

Can you think of examples of foreign brand names that are unsuitable in *your* country?

B Work in pairs. As Marketing Manager for Pyramid GmbH, you commissioned a French translation of the instructions for a new product. Without consulting you, your assistant had 20,000 copies printed. Read this fax from your distributors in France:

```
Dear Herr Gebhardt,

     Today we had another ten minutes filled with laughter,
thanks to your samples of instructions in French that we
received today. They are full of linguistic errors which
would make the product unsellable on the French market.
     This is not the first time that we have drawn your
attention to this. We refer you to our memo "Notes on
Instructions in French" dated July 3, 19--. We are relying
on you to use your influence to prevent this happening
again.
     We certainly hope that you have not yet had these
leaflets printed because such literature will put us on a
level with importers of low-quality products from overseas
- and our customers will not be amused.
     Sincerely yours,
     Jeanne Devalier
P.S. I tried to phone you about this but you were not in
the office.
```

⋙→

1. ☎ Role-play the telephone conversation between Herr Gebhardt and Mme Duvalier that would have taken place if Gebhardt had been in the office.
2. Draft a letter or telex from Pyramid GmbH to Amneris S.A., apologizing and explaining what action you're taking.
3. Draft a memo to all members of staff at Pyramid GmbH reminding them that all translations of instructions must be submitted to you so that they can be checked by the distributors in the relevant countries before printing. This also applies to *any* literature that is enclosed with the product.

C Here are five genuine extracts from instructions in English. Find the errors and then correct them.

1. **If the iron is standing on it's heel, pull the tank away from the iron**

2. Position stabilisation shelf on pins an tighten keyways
   Prevent snapping out bey screwing locking bolt

3. Even if the oven is provided with self-aeration, it is necessary that the furniture disposes of a chimney for the natural ventilation so as to exhaust the heat passing throught the oven thermal insulation.

4. So, no readjusted is usually required if you use the unit in the country where you brought it.

5. Finally lets summarize certain advices for a goog and safe procedure:
   – Clen away any grease or piant which covers the part
   – Never lay the vaiorus cables on parts which has just been welded

■ Promoting a product involves developing a '*Unique Selling Proposition*' ('USP'): the features and benefits which make it unlike any of the competing products.
There are four stages in promoting a product ('AIDA'):

1. attract the *Attention* of potential customers
2. arouse *Interest* in the product
3. create a *Desire* for its benefits
4. encourage customers to take prompt *Action*.

D Study the ads on the next page and answer these questions:

- What kinds of customers is the advertisement directed at?
- What exactly is the product being 'sold'?
- What is the 'Unique Selling Proposition' of each product?
- How well does each ad succeed in the four steps of 'AIDA'?
- What changes would have to be made to the style or tone of the ads to make them suitable for your country?

E 📼 You'll hear some radio commercials. Answer the same five questions about them.

YOU ARE WHAT YOU DRINK.

SPA

L'EAU PARFAITE

Now he saved so much with his Young Persons Railcard, he could afford to see her every weekend.

...a Young Persons Railcard for £15 and get a third off rail fares for a whole year. See the leaflet for full details.

Young Persons Railcard.

Young Persons Railcard 1987 press advertisement

Made in Hong Kong.

You can't put anything past this fellow. He's one of the hundreds of thousands of bright, energetic, and striving children who will provide the next generation of leadership for one of the world's economic miracles. The financial capital of Southeast Asia, conduit to China, a thriving business centre that provides goods, services, and ingenuity to a waiting world.

No other company in Hong Kong is as directly involved in every facet of life, and business, as Hutchison Whampoa.

For more information on the strength, and depth, of our local and international capabilities, please contact us directly.

Hutchison Whampoa. Part of today's world.

Hutchison Whampoa Limited

UK The Lord Derwent I. V. O., 9 Queen Street, London, W1X 7PH HK Mr. A.t. van der Linden, Hutchison House, 22/F, Hong Kong.

131

10.8 Promotion

A There are many ways of attracting customers to your product and of keeping your name in the public eye.
Fill the gaps with suitable words from the list.

brochures   catalogues   contribute   direct mail   display   effective
extent   hands-on   image   impact   key accounts   leaflets
packaging   point of sale   press conference   press releases
public relations   publicity   recommend   representatives   reputation
showrooms   specific   stand   toll-free   trade fairs and exhibitions
trademark   word of mouth

1. Sales literature – .... , ... and .... can describe
    your product in more detail and give more information than an advertisement.
    Potential customers can be sent .... literature by post.
2. .... advertising – displays in retail outlets (supermarkets, chain
    stores, etc) can attract the attention of potential customers.
3. .... – labels and presentation increase the .... of your product.
4. Sponsorship – you can .... to the cost of a sporting or artistic event, where
    the brand name or .... of your product is displayed prominently.
5. .... – potential customers can come to your premises and see a .... or a
    demonstration of your products and get .... experience.
6. .... – your company takes a .... or mounts an exhibit to enable
    customers in the same trade to see your products and talk to your ....
7. .... – the public are informed of a new development through
    newspaper articles. You can inform the press by issuing .... or by
    holding a .... , so that reporters can question your spokesperson.
8. .... – PR can ensure that your firm keeps a high profile, and that
    people are aware of your good .... and attractive ....
9. .... – existing customers tell their friends or colleagues about your
    product and hopefully .... it to them, so that they want to buy it.
10. Telephone selling – your staff can call customers, or customers can call a ....
    number to request sales literature or ask for .... information.
11. Personal selling – your rep can visit customers: this is the most .... method
    of promotion, but also the most expensive. Travelling to meet a prospect may
    not always pay off. Your .... would be visited frequently.
12. If you are marketing a service it must be 'visible' – your prospective customers
    must be fully aware of the .... of your service and its benefits.

B Work in pairs. Consider these products. Which methods are used
to promote them? Which methods would probably *not* be suitable?

new houses	a family hotel	a conference centre	cheese
an airline	a magazine	computers	bicycles
an exhibition	cigarettes	rail travel	medicines
coal	petrol	a circus	a zoo

10.9 A sales demonstration

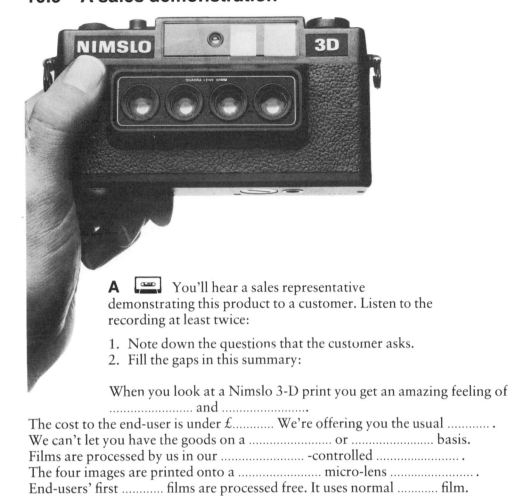

A 📼 You'll hear a sales representative demonstrating this product to a customer. Listen to the recording at least twice:

1. Note down the questions that the customer asks.
2. Fill the gaps in this summary:

When you look at a Nimslo 3-D print you get an amazing feeling of
.... and ....
The cost to the end-user is under £............ We're offering you the usual ....
We can't let you have the goods on a .... or .... basis.
Films are processed by us in our .... -controlled ....
The four images are printed onto a .... micro-lens ....
End-users' first .... films are processed free. It uses normal .... film.
You look through the viewfinder, press the .... and the ....
exposure and focussing .... takes care of the rest.
We're running a national .... , so end-users will be fully
aware of the product and keen to ....

Here are some expressions you can use during a sales demonstration:

> I'll just show you...
> You'll see that...
> Take a look and you'll notice that...
>
> If I could just show you...
> You'll notice that...
> If you just come a little closer...

> Could you tell me/us...   I'd like to know...
> What sort of delivery time / discount are you offering?

》》》→

B   Think of a new product you've recently bought – preferably something that's not too large to take to class with you.
1. List the features and benefits of the product.
2. Make notes on how it works.
3. Take your product to class and demonstrate it to your group.

10.10   Possibility, probability and certainty   *Functions*

If you are certain about something you can simply say:
    It will happen or *It won't happen*   *It happened* or *It didn't happen*
    It's true or *It isn't true*
If you are not certain you can simply say:
    It may happen or *It might happen* or *It could happen*
    It may be true or *It might be true* or *It could be true*
    It may have happened or *It might have happened* or *It could have happened*

But in many situations you'll probably want to express your meaning more exactly or emphatically. You may want to show the DEGREE OF PROBABILITY:

100% probability: **Certain**	75% probability: **Likely**	50% probability: **Possible**	25% probability: **Unlikely**	0% probability: **Impossible**

I'm sure that these sales figures are accurate. **100%**
The figures must be accurate.
There's no doubt that the figures were carefully checked.
The figures must have been thoroughly checked, so I'm absolutely sure/certain that they're accurate.

Our sales in the USA are likely to go up next year. **75%**
I expect that our sales in Canada will go down.
I wouldn't be surprised if our sales in Mexico went up.
It's quite possible that our sales in Peru will go up.
Our sales in Argentina may well remain static.

There's a chance that we'll manage to break into the UK market.
It's (just) possible that your forecast is over-optimistic.
I'm not sure if the figures that I've noted down are accurate.
There may have been some kind of mistake. **50%**

Singapore probably isn't a very profitable market for us.
I don't think that we'll be able to sell in Japan.
Thailand is unlikely to be a good market for our product.
I doubt if we'll be able to make any sales in Korea. **25%**

I'm (quite) sure that it isn't worth appointing an agent in Zambia. Sales in Tanzania can't have been worse than they are now. Uganda definitely isn't a good market for our product. These figures couldn't possibly be accurate! 0%

A 🔲 We asked a number of people to predict events they thought might happen in the next twenty years or so.
1. Listen to what they said and make notes.
2. Discuss each prediction with your partner. Use the expressions in the examples above to say how likely you think each event is to happen.
3. Write one sentence to give *your* view on each prediction.

B Work in small groups. Sales and marketing often involves spotting *TRENDS* and deciding what may happen next in the market place. Imagine that you are marketing the products shown below, what trends do you and your partners foresee in the next few years?

ships	printing	publishing	holidays	air travel
fruit	typewriters	health foods	cigarettes	banking
fast cars	small cars	office clothes for men and women		

C Work in small groups. Some of the information given here is true and some is untrue. Use the expressions above to say how probable *you* think it is that each statement is true.

1. The world's largest advertising agency is Japanese.
2. The world's greatest consumers of coffee are the Swedes.
3. The world's largest employer is a French company.
4. 99% of all businesses in Japan and Switzerland employ an average of 15 people.
5. The world's biggest manufacturer of motor vehicles is the USA.
6. Over $1 billion a year is spent on advertising in the USA.
7. The world's largest airport is Dallas – Fort Worth, Texas.
8. Most Japanese companies pay professional trouble-makers not to cause trouble at their shareholders' meetings.
9. The airport that handles the second largest number of international passengers in the world is JFK, New York.
10. The average person over 15 smokes 1,750 cigarettes annually.
11. The world's no 1 exporting country is Japan.
12. It cost Esso $200 million to change its name to Exxon in 1972.
13. The world's biggest restaurant chain, McDonald's, serves about 1.5 million hamburgers a day at its 9,000 restaurants.
14. The world's largest food company is Swiss.
15. The world's busiest port is New York.
16. The world's greatest beer drinkers are the West Germans.

10.11 What would *you* do?

Work in groups. How would you deal with these customers:

• **Mr A** always keeps you waiting 20 minutes when you've made an appointment to see him. He never looks at the literature you leave with him but seems equally unfamiliar with your competitors' products. He seems very cautious and says he has to consult his colleagues before making a firm decision, but regardless of this, when you make your next visit he always says he hasn't had time to do so.

• **Mrs B** regularly places small orders with you, but could order substantially more. Instead, she orders from your main competitor. She seems to enjoy telling you that your products are too up-market for her customers. Your product range is very competitive, and anyway you do have a more down-market range that you know she knows about. She always says she's in a hurry, but can still find the time to criticize your company.

• **Mr C** keeps raising objections to your products: he says they are too expensive, that he's worried about your after-sales service, that your new technology may not be reliable, that your design may not appeal to his customers. Just when you think it's time to close the deal, he raises yet another random objection and declines to place an order.

What would you do if you worked in marketing for these firms:

• **Dentallo** is a medium-size firm making toothpaste and toothbrushes. Your Dazzle toothpaste and Protect toothbrushes are market leaders in the domestic market, but due to heavy competition from multi-national companies with big advertising budgets you are no longer able to reach your export sales targets. Market research shows that a large proportion of consumers abroad find your product image is old-fashioned and dull, though your prices are lower than the competition.

• **Elysium Sport** is a company that produces clothing for cycling clubs, athletics and football clubs. In the home market, you have so far managed to hold your own against cheaper competition from South-East Asia, because your customers appreciate the quality of your products and because you can produce short runs of customized garments (using a patented printing process) with their logo or badge. At present, you only export a small amount, but you would like to find a gap in the overseas market where your kind of product would sell well.

11 Meetings

Taking part in group meetings, informal one-to-one meetings, and more formal committee meetings. Discussion techniques. Prepositions of place and direction.

11.1 Discussion techniques

In a meeting, you may want to find out what the other members of the group think. You can ask them for their views by saying:

> What are your views on this, John?   Do you agree, Mary?
> Mr Brown, what do you think about this?   Ms Smith, what's your opinion?

If you want to interrupt someone and put forward your own opinion you can say:

> If I could just make a point here...   Could I make a suggestion?
> Sorry to interrupt, but I'd just like   It seems to me that...
> to say that...

If you want to make sure the others in the group have understood or find out if they agree with you, you can say:

> Do you see what I mean?   Are you with me?
> Don't you agree, James?   Are we unanimous?
> Don't you think so, Mrs Robinson?   Does anyone object?

If you don't understand what someone has said, you can say:

> Sorry, could you say that again,   Sorry, I didn't quite understand.
> please?   Sorry, I'm not quite with you.
> I'm sorry, I didn't catch what you
> said.

A   You'll hear a recording of a staff meeting about introducing flexible working hours. Listen to the recording twice:

1. Notice how the expressions are used in the meeting.
2. Tell your partner which of the opinions you agree with.   ⟫→

B Here are twelve opinions about meeting: put a tick
(√) beside the ones you agree with and a cross (×) beside the ones you
disagree with. Then find out what your partners think about each of them.
Try to use the expressions above in your discussion.

DO YOU AGREE?

1. More time is wasted at meetings than in any other business activity. ☑
2. The purpose of meetings is to decide when the next one will take place. ☒
3. A meeting is a group of people who can decide nothing alone and who
   decide together that nothing can be done. ☒
4. It's better to send everyone a memo about a new procedure than to have
   a meeting about it. ×
5. Meetings help everyone to feel personally involved in decision-making. ☑
6. It's better for the boss to make a decision than to have a meeting. ☑
7. The most important person at a meeting is the chairman. ☑
8. The most important piece of paper at a meeting is the agenda. ☒
9. Most meetings are unnecessary, they're just a way of making people
   think they're important. ☒
10. It's better to talk to each person individually than to have a meeting. ☒
11. A meeting may be the only chance the members of a group actually have to
    see each other face to face. ☑
12. Meetings lead to better decisions, because of the exchange of ideas. ☑

11.2   Planning a meeting

YOUR ROLE   You work in the Inter-Company Marketing Division
of Archimedes Inc, based in Paris. The quarterly meeting of your 15
marketing managers in Europe is always held in Paris. The next
meeting will take place on the last Friday of next month.

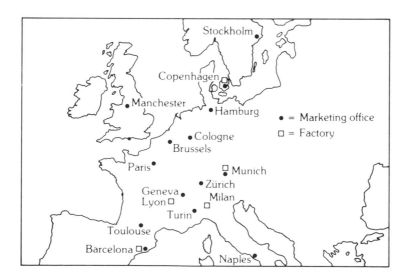

1. Work in pairs. Read these fax messages from your home office in Chicago and from two of your branches in Europe:

From Claire Brewster, Archimedes Inc, Chicago

The next meeting of European marketing managers should be either in Turin, Italy, or Munich, West Germany. We all need a change from Paris and must prevent our European operations becoming too centralized. Both these cities are closer to more of our other European branches and they are much less costly in terms of accommodation.
Please get in touch with your managers and find out which of these two venues they prefer, then let me know.

From Andy Denman, Archimedes Ltd, Manchester

I hear from you that our next meeting is not to be Paris, but in Turin or Munich. I am very much against this change of venue as there are no convenient direct flights from here to either city. This change would add two days to my busy schedule.

from Isabelle Sellier, Archimedes SA, Geneva

You say that our next meeting is to be in Turin or Munich, instead of Paris. As far as I'm concerned, Turin is preferable because we are having a meeting with our Italian colleagues in Milan on the last Wednesday of next month.

2. 🔲 Listen to the recorded messages from Zurich, Barcelona and from your assistant, Michele Lombardini. Make notes.

3. Decide with your partner where next month's meeting is to take place.

4. 🔲 Listen to a recorded phone message from Chicago.

5. Draft *three* memos announcing the date and place of meeting: to be sent to those who voted for Turin, Munich and Paris, respectively.

6. ☎ Change partners with another pair. Role-play a phone call to Isabelle Sellier in Geneva or Hans-Ruedi Frommer in Zurich, explaining the reasons for your decision. Make notes *before* you make the call.

7. Go back to your original partner and report what happened during the call.

8. Draft an agenda for this quarter's meeting, putting these items in logical order:

Any other business	Ideas for new products
Lunch	Matters arising
Minutes of last meeting	Report from Claire Brewster (USA)
Reports from each member	Welcome by host manager
Relaunch of Archimedes SA44	Streamlining inter-office procedures

9. Work in groups. Compare your agenda with another pair. Do you have the items in the same order? How important is the arrangement of items on an agenda? Does every meeting need an agenda?

11.3 Speaking at meetings

Here are some expressions that are used in a committee meeting.
The more formal expressions are marked with an asterisk (*):

What does everyone think about this?
Let's put this to the vote.*

I suggest that...
I propose that...
I move that...*

I agree with that suggestion because...
I'm for the motion because...*

I don't quite agree with that point because...
I'm against the motion because...*

I think it's time to adjourn the meeting.*
I think we're running out of time.

Is there anything else we should discuss?
Is there any other business?*

A Work in groups. You are members of a staff committee
investigating ways of improving working conditions in your offices.
After the meeting your proposals will be submitted to a management
committee.
1. Decide who will be 'in the chair' and who will take the minutes.
   Before the meeting starts, the chairperson should look at File 47,
   the others at File 14, 65 or 100.
2. Hold the meeting.
3. Write a short report of your meeting, giving your proposals to the
   management committee.

B Now imagine that you are members of the management
committee who have been sent the report (written by one of the *other*
groups, not your own).

1. Study the report and discuss the proposals it contains. Decide who
   is to chair your meeting and who will take the minutes. Before the
   meeting starts, the chairperson should look at File 47, the others at
   File 88, 9 or 37.
2. Hold the meeting.
3. Draft a memo to all members of staff, explaining what action you
   intend to take on their proposals. Send this memo to the group
   you received it from.

C Work in pairs. Role play a one-to-one meeting between a
manager and a staff representative to discuss the management
committee's memo.

11.4 Do we really need a meeting? *Discussion*

A Think of the meetings you have attended recently:
- How would you have structured them differently?
- Were they a waste of time?
- What would happen if people didn't hold meetings?

B Work in small groups. Look at these problems and decide the best way of dealing with each problem. Which would be best?

- a one-to-one meeting of two of the people involved,
- a meeting of four or five of the people involved,
- a meeting of about ten of the people involved,
- a meeting of *everyone* involved,
- or should just *one* person decide what to do and then inform everyone by phoning or sending a memo?

1. A large, influential customer continually pays late. Your sales manager and credit controller have politely and repeatedly complained but this hasn't made any difference. The time has come to decide what to do about this.
2. In a small factory the older workers are ignoring safety rules and encouraging the younger ones to do the same. Some of these rules may be excessively cautious and the older workers' production rates are very good.
3. In a medium-size factory, groups of workers operate as teams. One group has been getting poorer results than the other teams and verbal warnings have had no effect.
4. The firm is having a bad year and it will probably be necessary to make five members of the office staff redundant. The normal policy is 'last in – first out'.
5. Someone has been leaking information about your firm's products to your competitor. It may be a member of your staff or one of your preferred suppliers.
6. The board requires a report on your department's long-term plans over the next ten years.
7. The territories covered by your sales force have been unchanged for ten years. A revision of the boundaries might make the team more efficient.
8. There is to be a company picnic next month and everything has to be planned and organized.

Discuss the alternatives like this:
'If you had a meeting of four people, the others might feel that . . .'
'If the manager sent everyone a letter, everyone might . . .'

C What do you enjoy and dislike about meetings?
How do you feel about speaking at a small meeting – and at a larger one?

11.5 Place and direction
Grammar

Look at this plan of the offices of PrepCo International:

POSITION
at the back of
at the bottom of
at the top of
behind
between
in the corner of
in the middle of
next to
on the edge of
on the left of
on the other side of
on the side of
on top of
opposite

DIRECTION

across	past
away from	round
between	through
into	towards
out of	

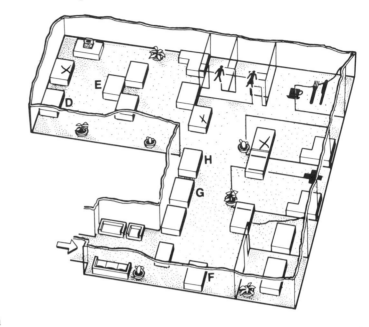

Maria Braun's desk is near the canteen, just opposite the toilets.
If you go towards the toilets, you'll see her desk on the right —
there's a cactus plant just in front of it.
Bill Allan's desk is at the far end of the building. Turn left at
Maria Braun's desk and then go past a cactus and another
plant. His desk is next to the computer.
Bob Carter's desk is opposite Maria Braun's, just outside the
toilets.

Imagine that you are in the reception area of PrepCo International. A
visitor from another branch wants to know where various people
work . . .

A Look at the examples in the speech balloon above. Put a name tag
on the desks of Bill Allan (A), Maria Braun (B) and Bob Carter (C), to
show where they sit.

142

Here's a list of all the people who work in PrepCo's offices:

<u>PrepCo International</u> MEMBERS OF STAFF

```
Mr Bill Allan   Miss Maria Braun   Dr Bob Carter   Mr Jimmy Dante
Dr Kevin East   Mr John Forster   Mr Ted Greenwood   Mr Erik Hansen
     Mrs Jane Isaacs   Ms Lotte Jørgensen   Miss Diane King
     Ms Pat Lawrence   Miss Collette Mercier   Mr Alex North
     Mrs Paloma Orlando   Ms Anna Prince   Mr Charles Queen
     Mr Diego Romero   Dr Emilia South   Miss Valerie Taylor
```

B Write down what you'd say to the visitor to help him or her to find these people: Mr Dante, Dr East, Mr Forster, Mr Greenwood and Mr Hansen (Letters D to H on the plan).

C Work in pairs. One of you should look at File 90, the other at 101. You will be finding out from each other where everyone else at PrepCo works.

D Work in pairs. Explain to your partner how to lay out a letter in the style used in *your* firm.
How is this different from the style used in Britain or the USA?
Where *exactly* do you put the date, address, signature etc?
How are envelopes laid out differently?

E Work in groups. Imagine that you're going to hold a committee meeting (or a board meeting) in your classroom.
Decide:
- how you will rearrange the furniture
- what extra furniture you'll require
- what other equipment and stationery you'll require

Make notes and/or a plan of the room.
Describe *exactly* where you'll put everything you need for the meeting.

11.6 One-to-one meetings

A 📼 You'll hear part of a one-to-one meeting.
What do you think happened at the end of the meeting?
How was it different from a social meeting between friends?

B Work in groups of four. Each group should consist of **two pairs.**
You'll be role-playing a meeting between a client and salesperson
discussing the idea of using your school or institute as a venue for a
seminar or conference.

1. Throw a coin to decide which pair will play the role of salespersons (PAIR A,
   representing the school or institute) or clients (PAIR B, representing the
   conference organizers).
2. PAIR A: Draft a letter or telex to the clients to suggest a meeting.
   PAIR B: Make a list of the requirements you have for your seminar/conference.
   What facilities will you require?
3. PAIR A: Decide how well your school or institute can cater for a seminar or
   conference. How many participants can be comfortably accommodated in the
   premises? What facilities can you offer? How will you deal with
   accommodation for the delegates?
   PAIR B: Read the letter or telex you receive and reply to it, agreeing to a meeting.
   Send the reply to the other pair.
4. ☎ Phone the other pair to confirm or discuss the arrangements for the
   meeting.
5. PAIR A: Draft an agenda for the meeting.
   PAIR B: Draft a list of questions you will ask the salespeople.
6. 🎭 Each member of PAIR A goes to meet a member of PAIR B to have private
   one-to-one meetings.
   Imagine that the client and salesperson already know each other, but you
   haven't met for quite a while:

> Hello, thanks for agreeing to see me.
> Hello, it's good of you to come and see me.
> It's good to see you again.
> Shall we get down to business?
> There are a few questions I'd
>   like to ask: ...

> Well, I think that covers everything.
> I think that's about all for the
>   time being.
> So do we agree that..., then?
> I'll put these proposals down in
>   writing and send them to you.

7. Make notes on your discussion and the decisions you reached.
8. After the meetings, report back to your partner.
   How did you get on? What was the outcome of your meeting?

11.7 Let's have a meeting!

A 📼 You'll hear some people talking about things that happen at meetings. Make notes. Decide with your partners which are the worst things – and which don't really matter.

B You will be holding a meeting to organize . . .

A SOCIAL EVENT FOR YOUR CLASS:
a class picnic, a party, a social evening or an excursion.

1. First of all, draft an agenda. The meeting should cover the date and duration of the event, what form it should take, who will be invited, transport, catering, who will be responsible for organizing it, how the work of preparation will be shared, etc. Each proposal should be a separate item on the agenda.
2. Form two large groups. First, group A will hold a meeting while the members of group B take notes. Later, group B will hold the meeting, while members of group A take notes.
3. Decide who will chair the first session. Set a time limit. If time runs out before the meeting has reached its conclusions, the meeting should be adjourned (to be continued after class).
4. Before the second session, each member of group B should show (and explain) their notes to a member of group A.
5. Decide who will chair the second session. Set a time limit. If time runs out before the meeting has reached its conclusions, the meeting should be adjourned (to be continued after class).
6. Each member of group A should show (and explain) their notes to a member of group B.
7. Discuss what you might do differently (and better!) if you could hold your meetings again. What did you find difficult to do in the meeting?
8. Compare your notes with another member of your own group to make sure that you noted all the important points.
Draft a report of the meeting. Summarize the discussion and show the decisions that were reached. Include details of the time, date and duration of the meeting, and the people who were present.

12 Operations and processes

Describing simple and everyday operations.
Describing work and business operations.
Giving instructions. Explaining. Using Modal verbs.
Dealing with production problems. Talking about
automation and robots.

12.1 Explaining a process. How do you . . . ?

A Work in pairs. Look at the diagram of the wooden garden table.
Decide how you think the components of the table fit together.
Which parts is the table made up of? How many parts are there?
How do the components combine to form the parts of the table?
Use *all* the components shown.

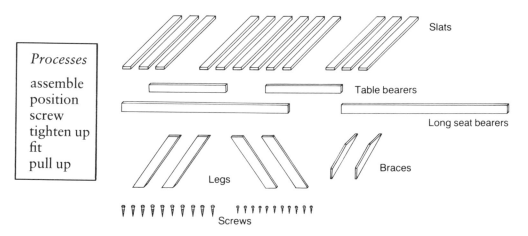

Processes

assemble
position
screw
tighten up
fit
pull up

Slats

Table bearers

Long seat bearers

Braces

Legs

Screws

B Work in groups. Compare your ideas with another pair. Then look
at File 112, which contains a photograph and diagram of the table.

C 🔲 You will hear a salesperson explaining how easy it is to
assemble the table. Make notes on the steps involved.

D Work in pairs. Explain to your partner how a machine which you know
about works or how to construct something you are familiar with. Do
not name it. Your partner must *guess* what it is from the explanation.

146

12.2 Flowcharts

A 📼 You'll hear an editor explaining the stages of the book production process. Look at the flowchart and decide in which boxes the operations in the list below should be placed.

- Artwork and illustrations are commissioned to fit in spaces
- Books go to publisher's warehouse
- Designer designs layout and chooses typeface
- Designer produces paste-up/Authors & editor correct galley proofs
- Editors and authors discuss completed typescript
- Orders are shipped to wholesalers
- Sheets are folded, cut and bound and cover is put on
- Typesetter corrects galley proofs and makes them into pages

The Stages of Book Production: From Writing to Bookshop

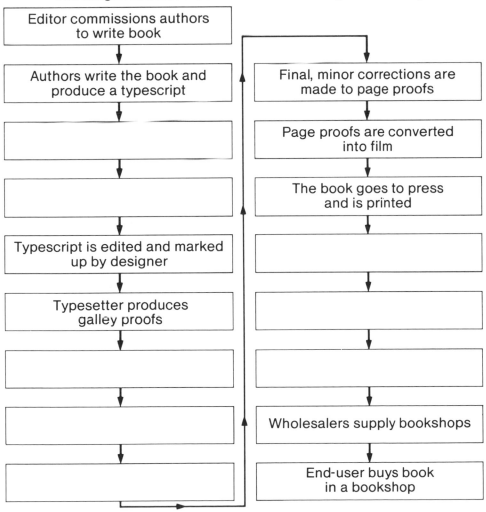

B Compare your answers with those of your partner. Decide which points you would concentrate on when explaining the process to a foreign visitor.

C Work in pairs. Look at this flowchart of another operation – in this case that of booking a ticket for a flight. Work out together how the process takes place. Number the boxes in the order in which the operations would be done. Notice that at several points decisions have to be taken.

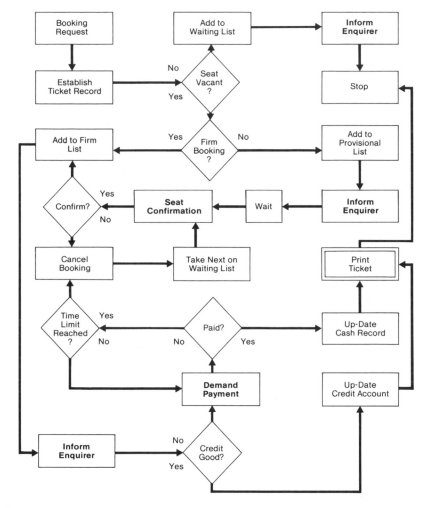

D Work in pairs. Draft a short set of explanations of the process of booking a flight which you could use to instruct a new employee in your company.

E Work in groups. Show your draft to another pair and look at theirs. If you were unfamiliar with the procedure, how helpful would you find the explanation?

148

12.3 Explaining, giving instructions   *Functions*

If somebody asks you to show them how a machine or something
works, these are some of the expressions you will find useful:

1 To explain the order in which certain things are done, you can say:

> First of all...
> The first thing you have to do is...

2 If you want to add a further point, you can say:

> Make sure you...
> Oh, and by the way, don't forget to...
> Oh, and be careful not to...

3 If you want to check that the other person is following you, you
  can say:

> That's clear, is it?
> ..., if you see what I mean?
> Does that seem to make sense?

4 You will need expressions such as the following, when you ask
  someone to help you:

> Excuse me, could you show me how to...?
> Can you help me please?
> Do you by any chance know how the... works?
> I wonder if you could show me / tell me...

5 Here are some expressions to use if you've not understood the
  explanation, or if you can't follow the instructions, or if you want
  to check that you've understood so far:

> These buttons / levers all look the same, don't they?
> I'm sorry, what did you say that thing was called?
> I'm sorry, could you repeat that bit about the... again?

6 When you think you've understood, you can say:

> If I've understood right...
> So is the basic idea that...?
> You mean...

A You'll hear two people explaining things. As you listen try to work out what it is they are explaining. How well do you think the people know each other?

B Work in pairs. Number what you think is the correct order of these figures showing how to use a coffee machine. Then one of you should look at File 94 and the other at 36.

C Work in pairs.
1. Choose one of the following ideas and explain to your partner what to do.
   - Your friend has bought a new camera: explain how to put the film in.
   - Explain to a visitor how to use the automatic ticket machine on the underground/tram/bus/train system of your town or a town in your country.
   - Explain to a visitor to your country how to play a typical card game or chess.
   - How to operate a compact disc player or video-recorder. How to operate a record player.
   Take it in turns to explain.
2. Write down the main points that can't be left out of the instructions.
3. Work in groups. Find another pair who have dealt with the same things. Compare the notes you've just made.

12.4 Modal verbs
Grammar

Look at the different uses of these modal verbs.

Possibility

1. When you say something **may** or **might** happen or be true, it will possibly happen or be true in the future, but is not certain:
   Carol may finish it by tonight.
   Things change, I might even lose my job.

150

2. **Can** is used to indicate that it is possible for someone to do something or for something to happen:
    Anybody can learn how to use a word processor.

3. You use **could** to indicate that you think that something is possibly true or is a possible explanation for something:
    That could be one reason why it broke.

4. **Could** is also used with 'I' and 'we' to indicate that something is possible and that you are considering doing it:
    I could ask him to help, I suppose.
    We could send the part on Friday.

5. You also use **might** when you give advice or suggest something:
    There are a few things we might compare notes on.

6. **Could** is also used (usually with 'you') to make a suggestion:
    Couldn't you just employ more staff to finish the order?

7. **Can** is also used to say that something is allowed:
    What are the rules for when you can and can't go on holiday?

8. **May** is used in questions to ask for permission:
    May I look around the plant now?

Obligation

9. If you say that someone **must** or **must not** do something, you think it is very important for them to do it or not to do it:
    You must learn to remain calm under pressure.
    You must not use the machine until the green light is on.

10. You tell someone that they **have to** do something when you are giving them an instruction or telling them how to act:
    You have to watch the control lamp, before using the machine.
    He'll have to spend a lot of money, if he wants the new model.

11. **Have got to** is an informal way of saying 'must' or 'have to':
    If you want to finish early, you've got to concentrate very hard now.
    We've all got to work together on this project.

12. You use **should** or **ought to** to say that you think it is a good idea and important for something to be done, and that it would be slightly wrong of you or them not to do it:
    Shouldn't you switch that off first?
    Oughtn't we to phone for the police?
    We ought to order a replacement, oughtn't we?

13. You use **ought to** or **should** to say that you think that an action or someone else's behaviour is morally right:
    They ought to earn more money for all their effort.
    Somebody ought to do something about it.

⟫→

14. When you say something **need not** happen, you mean that it might happen but that it is not necessary that it will happen:

> Such tax cuts need not be inflationary.
> It needn't cost very much to produce.

15. If you tell someone they **must** do something, you may be suggesting that they should do it or inviting them to do it:

> You must call on me at the office, when you're here.
> You must come round for a meal some time.

A Work in pairs. Rewrite each sentence using a modal verb. The first one is done for you as an example.

1. It is vital we get that order. We *have got to get that order.*
2. We're not able to help you this time. We ....
3. If you want the job, it's important to apply soon. You ....
4. Wouldn't it be possible to pay promptly this time?
5. If you have problems after the guarantee runs out, the supplier is not obliged to help.
6. It is not right for that company to get the order.
7. If a machine breaks down under guarantee, it is necessary for the company to repair it without extra charge.
8. Perhaps we'll be able to find the fault, if we look. We ....
9. It is possible for them to sell the shares. They ....
10. Experience is essential for this job. You ....
11. Perhaps the switch is broken. The switch ....
12. After the guarantee period it's only right that they don't charge the full price.

B Work in pairs. Look at these signs. Using a modal verb, take it in turns to explain what you think they mean to your partner.

C Work in pairs. Imagine you are talking to a group of people who have just moved to your country to work or have just come to your firm to work. What would you tell them about the rules of behaviour at work or in public places? Make a list of DOs and DON'Ts. Report your results to another group.

12.5 Producing the goods

Manufacturers often streamline production in order to adapt to new developments in the market.

A Work in pairs. Look at this description of a plant for producing potato crisps. What reasons are given for rationalization of the operations of the company?

B As you read the introductory passage mark whether the following statements are true [√] or false [×]:

1. Production facilities were adequate.
2. Sophisticated machinery was expensive.
3. It was a good time to create a specially built plant.
4. Priority was given to creating a larger work environment.
5. Systematic arrangement of machinery would make production more economic.
6. The welfare of the employees was taken care of.
7. The local community protected their environment.

It was during the 1970's that the need for additional production facilities became evident. Walkers Crisps had become so popular that demand often outstripped production capacity. At the same time, technology was changing and more sophisticated machinery was beginning to become available.

It was an ideal opportunity to take a clean sheet, to create a purpose designed factory on a green field site. Here was the chance to build a facility which would encourage greater efficiency, in a better working environment.

Operating efficiency was to be a prime consideration. The latest technology was to be incorporated in a logical sequence to ensure economy of operation. The 450 employees were to be well catered for, with 1500m² of offices, laboratories, locker and laundry rooms, and canteen facilities available for all. Protection was also to be given to the local community with careful control of emissions and waste disposal.

The four lines now operating represent a carefully scheduled combination of human skill and experience with high technology and automation.

C Work in pairs. Look at the diagram which explains how potato crisps are produced and the various operations involved in their manufacture.

Read through the descriptions and number the order in which the various processes take place. Which of the names of the different stages go with which paragraph?

Decide at which points you would use ... then ... , ... next ... , after that ... , finally ... .

COOKING
FLAVOURING
GRADING
PACKING
PEELING
SLICING
WASHING
WEIGHING

1 POTATO HANDLING

Every day, up to 20 lorry loads of potatoes – each of 20 tonnes – arrive.

The potatoes are unloaded by conveyor and transferred gently by bucket lift into four 50 tonne capacity holding hoppers. Great care is taken in this transfer, for these potatoes are living organisms and are easily bruised and damaged.

Released from the hopper, they pass through a 'spring cleaner' which removes mud and other surface matter, before floating through an agitated bath, which removes stones from the load.

A

Walkers utilise sophisticated weighing machines which automatically request crisps from the high level 'stages' along which they pass after flavouring.

The crisps drop onto one of ten automatic weighing trays, and the machine with extraordinary accuracy selects the best combination to give the required weight.

B

The washed slices are now ready for cooking in the 4500 litre cookers, at a temperature of 360 F. To heat the vegetable oil Walkers

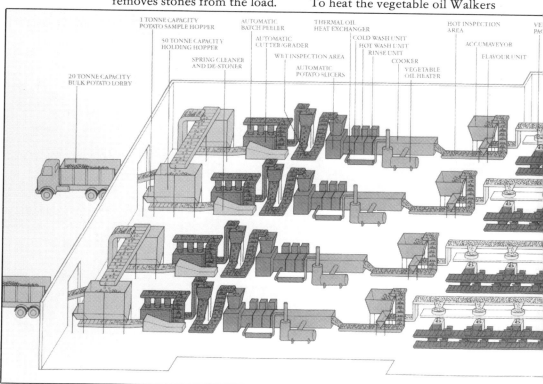

use a direct heating system. The entire cooking process is hooded and designed in such a way that only clean steam is emitted to the atmosphere.

C

The potato slice thickness for a Walkers Crisp is very important. Walkers use slicers, with blades reset electronically at intervals of between 5 and 40 minutes, depending on the potato batch. Each line has eight such machines, with four in operation at any one time.

D

The next stage is the cutting and grading, which is carried out in machines designed by Walkers.

Larger potatoes are automatically cut down to rejoin the line, and smaller ones are rejected.

E

As they emerge into the Hot Inspection area, the crisps are

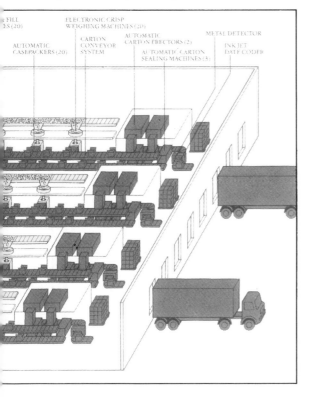

evaluated carefully for colour and crispness. Some characteristics will only become apparent at this stage.

If they pass the tests, they are flavoured – using powdered flavourings sprinkled from above, and then held in a hopper or 'accumaveyor' which hold 20 minutes production.

F

The dispensed crisps then pass into a vertical form and fill packing machine, which removes packaging film from a roll, forms it into a tube, and catches the crisps as they fall through the weigher. The bags are then sealed and separated, emerging as the familiar packet of Walkers Crisps.

G

The clean potatoes are carried by bucket lift into automatic batch peelers (a kind of revolving, abrasive drum). Skilled operators judge the precise timing necessary.

H

The sliced potatoes are then cold washed to remove the starch.

A quick rinse, and they pass under an 'air knife' blower to remove any excess water.

10 CARTON PACKING

Even this stage is now automated, with the packs being placed in cartons by Bishopbarn Auto Casepackers. Empty cartons are erected at high level, and then travel along the Torvale conveying system to the casepackers, which fill them. The cartons then move on a lower level to the Padlocker machines which seal them with adhesive tape.

Finally, the cartons pass through a metal detector, a jet-sprayed date code is imprinted and they are stacked manually on pallets for loading on the 40' trucks which transport them to the warehouse, taking over 100,000 crisp packs per journey.

155

12.6 When things go wrong . . . What do we do?

YOUR ROLE: You work for an American manufacturing company at one of its European plants. You are the personal assistants of the Chief Executive Officer. There have been a number of delays and breakdowns in production recently which have been reported in the press. Work in pairs.

17 May 19—

Breakdown leads to bottleneck

Delta tools were yesterday unable to meet their daily deadline.

On account of a sudden, inexplicable breakdown at their Southford site the main assembly line was put out of action.

Components from supplying firms continued to be delivered, but despite determined attempts to utilize all the available space the plant was soon brought to a halt. The late shift had t~ be sent home an~ ~~ ~~ ~~ ~'

A You have been asked to consider what steps can be taken to prevent the same problem happening again and to report to head office in Europe. Study the following information. See if you can find out what happened.

Industrial Research Consultants Inc.
Buffalo Grove Il 60090 USA

Consultant's Report
April 5. 19—

You have a wide range of equipment on the site at this point, as you can see from the attached drawing. All available space has to be utilized. So we must restrict the number of materials which are actually present at any given time. Clearly if a particular component is not available when it is required on the assembly line that might lead to a hold-up. In most production units you will, of course, have bottlenecks. But we should not allow any gaps to occur, if possible. The latest conveyor technology is clearly required.

A further point concerns production time. The machines do not operate night and day at the moment and the operators work a two-shift system at present. We are hoping to put forward a plan to streamline production in the coming months. Once we have solved the technical problems — and our designers are currently working on a project to modernize your handling equipment — all the facilities in the plant will be coordinated to enable you to step up production of the new range of machines.

Unfortunately, as you know, there has been a major problem with reorganizing the maintenance schedule. In the past two years standby crews were on duty around the clock. But this has proved to be the p~~~~ ~~ ~~

Memo

To: Production Director
From: Chief Executive
Date: April 10, 19—

This is a great idea, Ralph! Please investigate fully
automated handling equipment and the possibility of
installing new robots for finishing and assembly shops.
Also make sure the recommendations of the consultant are
put into practice.

INTERNAL MEMO

FROM: Production Director
TO: Personnel Director   April 15, 19—

John: As you know we're working under great pressure
in all departments at the moment to keep up the output
for the export and US orders. The new jobs are needed
badly. All our maintenance staff are extremely
overworked.

Can you please re-advertise the vacant jobs for the
additional maintenance engineers and the five new
technicians. Things cannot go on as they are doing.
We're badly understaffed. One day the new robots are
going to break down, when the line is not covered by
the service department. You know how much we need
people with all-round electronic and mechanical
qualifications so that the wide range of machines we
operate are fully supervised at all times.

We must introduce a 3-shift system for the maintenance
people. They never have time to put the faults right
at the moment. You should emphasize the large bonus
payments for working unsocial hours and nights and

B   Take notes and draft a letter to your European regional director
explaining what happened.

C   Work in groups of four with another pair to compare notes.
Read the letter they have drafted.

12.7 Production and operations  *Vocabulary*

Fill in the gaps with words from the list.

apprentices   by-product   cutback   dismantle   know-how
manpower   output   setbacks   slowdown   utilization

1. Increase in industrial .... in some countries is connected to the low wages which are paid there.
2. But cheap .... alone is no guarantee of high productivity. Investment in technology is also needed.
3. For example, the new technology needed to produce synthetic textiles requires increased inputs of capital and ....
4. This means that the trend is towards a gradual .... in manufacturing in other countries.
5. In Europe, for example, steel production has been .... because demand has fallen.
6. So steel manufacturing facilities are being .... all over the world because of over-capacity.
7. One result is that in traditional industries, jobs for blue-collar workers and training posts for .... are having to be scaled down.
8. With the introduction of fully automated factories in the electronics industry, there is a demand for full-capacity, round-the-clock .... of production facilities.
9. Despite .... slow progress is being made in cutting industrial pollution in some areas.
10. But it is currently impossible to eliminate waste as a .... of nuclear energy.

"Here's your problem – the batteries are in upside-down."

SCHWADRON

12.8 Robots and automation: the factory of the future

A Work in pairs. Imagine that you are preparing a report on the ways in which robots **may, might, can, should** or **ought to** be utilized. **Should** they be installed in a new plant or used more generally in industry? What do advertisements claim that robots can do? How widely are they being used in North America, Western Europe and Japan? Make notes.

B As you read this advert, find out how the robot is programmed:

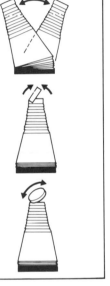

Megacraft will assist from conception to fully operative system

advance path control
Megacraft has a control system which makes programming the robot's movements simple

Unlimited possibilites
The secret lies in calculating the path to be taken by the robot while it is in operation

Uncomplicated programming
If you want to teach your robot new tasks, all you need to do is to program it. The actual programming is simple and can be performed by the user. The 'Job and Log' teaching method may be used. This means that you position the robot to the points on a path where it is to carry out a function. The robot's function button is used to direct the robot to stop or carry out a task, and it may be also used to select path type, etc. The program may be stored for further use. Programming couldn't be easier.

Transmission of data
By transferring data from other systems, such as a CAD computer, programming may be made even easier

C Read this article from a news magazine. Find the expressions which are used to describe what the authors see as similarities to what human workers used to do.
What do the following numbers refer to in the article:

1961	6 per 10,000	80,000
20,000	36 per 10,000	$1 billion
28,000		

March of the iron men

Iron men have been on the march for more than a quarter of a century now. Since the first industrial robot joined the production line at General Motors in 1961, American manufacturers have recruited 20,000 steel-collar workers, replacing many times that number of blue-collar equivalents. In Western Europe, the robot population has increased even more – to an estimated 28,000 units today. But where western manufacturers seem to prefer their robots to be spread thinly through their workforces (around six per 10,000 industrial workers), Japanese firms have embraced them (36 robots per 10,000 industrial workers). In modern Japan, more than 80,000 industrial robots are working around the clock.

Building robots has become a $1 billion business. Until recently, the biggest customers for them were the motor manufacturers, who used robots mainly for spot-welding and spraying paint. Now the electrical and electronics industries, espec-ially in Japan, are the biggest buyers. In the process, the way robots are being used is becoming more complex. Electronics firms want robots to be able to pick up very small objects (like microchips and circuit boards) and join them together. They need to be much cleverer than earlier robots. The second-generation robots now join-ing production lines are being equipped with such senses as touch and sight. Their sensors let them pick up misplaced parts or make adjustments for inaccuracies in the objects they handle. For the first time they can start doing basic inspection jobs.

D 📼 You will hear a radio programme in which someone talks about training people in the skills of using computers and robots. Mark whether the following statements are true [√] or false [×]:

1. The robot discussed at the beginning is a toy.
2. The microcomputer the people are discussing is used for a variety of purposes.
3. The computer trainer says any individual can learn to programme a computer on the course.
4. The computer trainer says that the machine can simulate a robot.
5. The training programme uses particular methods for 15- and 16-years-olds.
6. Young people on the programme work in engineering factories.
7. The training programme believes in the usefulness of learning to use your hands.
8. According to the person interviewed, training in computing provides an alternative to practical skills.

E 📼 Listen to the interview again. What is the relevance of the training discussed in your opinion?
What is the point of the training programme according to the man interviewed? Take notes.

F Form larger groups and compare your notes. What advantages and disadvantages do you see with the introduction of more industrial robots? Can you agree on areas where you think it is a good idea to use them? What will industrial workers then do? What do you think about training people to work with robots? Who decides what robots make? What is your opinion of this? Could or should robots be used to make more socially useful products or to make even more profits? Who will pay for our pensions if robots replace even more workers? The robots?

12.9   Business with a fairer face   *Read and discuss*

A   Work in pairs. List some of the reasons you can think of for running a factory or business. Why do people do it?

B   Join another pair. Compare your lists. Can you agree on the main purposes behind industry, trade and commerce?

C   Work in pairs. Now read the following article carefully and mark whether the statements which follow it are true [√] or false [×]:

Business with a fairer face

Martyn Halsall on a company where altruism is the motivating force

TRAIDCRAFT is at the heart of the unemployment crisis. Its headquarters are on Tyneside, where pockets of unemployment reach 60 per cent. Its head offices are at Gateshead, where employment has shrunk from 23,000 to 7,000. Through its fair trade import policy it supports 6,000 jobs in the Third World.

Because of the excellence of its commercial business practices, its success is a parable of alternative economics. The company deals directly with some 140 producers, ranging from two private companies to many cooperatives, examining each for acceptable wages and work practices, before agreeing to handle their products. Sales are organised through a catalogue, four shops and a national network of volunteer representatives. At the busiest time of the year, in late autumn, the 130 staff are handling up to 800 orders a day.

In his small managing director's office, 39-year-old Richard Adams, wearing corduroys and open-neck shirt, outlines business progress which would be the envy of many non-altruistic companies. Growth marches on at 30 per cent a year; worth £1 million of new business this year. The company has now outgrown the 63,000 square foot former carton factory it bought in almost derelict condition for £108,000 and is now acquiring another 45,000 square feet nearby. It expects to need further space in three years' time.

Mr Adams expects the growth rate to be maintained for the next five years. Expansion on his projections would add another 100 to the Gateshead workforce and possibly double the number of people employed abroad.

The company is also switching the balance of its products, from the primarily craft and gift image which still occupies the majority of its catalogue, to more utilitarian products and foodstuffs. Stock levels are monitored by computer and recently installed conveyor belts help to move the orders.

Traidcraft tries to mirror a just society in its own wage structure, which starts at £4,700 for an 18-year-old packer and rises only 2.7 times for the highest paid. "Yet the money that people earn here is probably equal to all the wages coming from those other 6,000 jobs," said Mr Adams. "The average income of our partners is about £80 or £90 a year. It's absolutely desperate but that has to be set in the local context."

The company seeks to balance commerce with education; helping the rich world to understand and respond to the needs of the less fortunate, and encouraging Third World producers towards economic self-sufficiency. Company activity is "part of the global commitment of Christians to bring about peace, reconciliation, justice and wholeness in the world". It inevitably re-opens the debate about Christians and politics.

The Nicaraguan coffee the company sells is marketed to beat the Ameri- ⟫→

can economic boycott. Other products have needed to be packaged for demanding Western standards, widening potential markets. Mr Adams said the postbag included some very strong letters asking why the company was "so political". "We say we feel we've got to be political if we are involved in justice and trade." He also points out the efforts the company is making to help people stand on their own feet and encourage local enterprise.

Traidcraft acknowledges its limitations; both in encouraging technology and influencing patterns of international trade. "It's only by changing people's conscience in the long term that we will have any major effect on international trade," said Mr Adams. "We can't do that ourselves; we can only have any effect in certain small areas."

In July the company issued a prospectus inviting public subscription for one million non-voting shares, to provide additional working capital for further growth in sales and capital expenditure. With almost three months remaining, 700,000 shares have been sought. "People will respond to organisations putting people before profit," said Mr Adams.

Traidcraft would like to expand beyond its established South-east Asian and Central and South American trade bases.

Mr Paul Miller, lecturer in business policy at the University of Newcastle, said: "There is a tendency for an organisation of this type to be rather romantic; this place isn't romantic – it actually makes money." He is impressed equally by the open information policy, which circulates details of all meetings to employees, and the rapid growth. In its crusade for economic justice in the developing world, Traidcraft has good news for both rich and poor.

1. According to the article, the company is situated where it is because of the unemployment.
2. Traidcraft provides a good example of a non-profit-orientated company.
3. According to the article, the company accepts the wages and conditions of firms it deals with.
4. The operations of Traidcraft will require further factory space in the future.
5. According to the managing director, the workforce will be double the number it was.
6. According to the article, the company is switching its sales to include computers.
7. The company wants to raise the wages of its employees.
8. Traidcraft thinks that education and commerce help the rich more than the Third World.
9. According to the article, for Traidcraft trade and politics cannot be separated.
10. The company believes it can make steps towards change in trade patterns.
11. Many people are investing in Traidcraft because its shares are selling successfully.
12. According to a lecturer, Traidcraft is making money because it is not run in a commercial manner.

D   Do you know of any companies in your country which are run in a similar fashion to Traidcraft? Can you imagine that this way of running a business can/will spread? Give your reasons why/why not. Do you think companies should be run for profit or to supply people with what they need to live?

13 A new job

Applying for a new job and seeking promotion.
Interviewing and being interviewed.
Relative clauses. Reading advertisements aloud.

13.1 Your career history

A CV ('curriculum vitae' or 'resumé') is essential if you're applying
for a new job or for promotion within your own company, or even to
register as a delegate at a conference. Some information might be
given in your CV, some in your letter of application – and perhaps
some on a Supplementary Information sheet (giving information
relevant to the particular job you're applying for). There are no fixed
international rules about this: different countries have different
practices.

A   Work in pairs. Decide where *you* in your country and in your line
of business, would normally give this information:

1. Your name, address and telephone number.
2. The title and reference number of the job.
3. Your date of birth.
4. Your marital status.
5. The name and address of present (or last) employer.
6. Your hobbies and leisure interests.
7. The sports you play.
8. Details of all the jobs you have had.
9. The languages you speak, read or write.
10. Details of the examinations you passed at school.
11. Details of the professional diplomas or degrees you have gained.
12. Details of training courses you have attended.
13. Details of your achievements and responsibilities in your working career.
14. Your suitability for the job advertised.
15. Your reasons for applying for this job.
16. When you are available for interview.
17. Details of your present (or last) job.
18. Your current (or last) salary.
19. The salary you would expect to receive.
20. The names and addresses of two or three referees.

in your CV or resumé?   on a Supplementary Information sheet?
in your Letter of Application?   – or on an Application Form?   ⟫→

What *other* information would you provide and where would this be given?
Which of the information would you *not* give at all?

B   Work in groups of four. Two of you should look at File 107, the other two at 111. Each pair will have a different person's CV or resumé to look at.

1. Study the CV together. What 'picture' does it give you of the person?
2. Tell the other pair about the person whose CV you've been studying. Ask them about the person they've been studying.
3. Finally, read the CV that the other pair were studying.

C   Now it's your turn to produce your own career history in English. Work in pairs.

1. Discuss what your own CVs or resumés will include. Make notes.
   - What information will it include?
   - What elements of the two CVs in Files 107 and 111 will it include? What further details would *you* include in yours?
   - How much space will you allow for your education and training, and how much for your work experience?
   - How long will your CV be – can you fit everything onto a single side?
2. Draft your CV and give it to your teacher to be checked.
3. Rewrite your draft CV and, if possible, have it typed or word-processed.

13.2   Classified advertisements   *Reading aloud*

If you're reading aloud, it's not only the pronunciation of words that's important, but also the way you read. Look at this ad:

JOIN OUR PR TEAM – TOP SALARY!

We need someone to join our team who can manage to do ten things at once, while remaining cool and calm in a crisis!

We are a leading PR Company and we can offer you a fulfilling and challenging role working with our Director of Travel.

You will need to be hard-working, flexible, well-organised and energetic. You'll be attending presentations, arranging meetings, travel and lunches, and liaising with executives of major international companies.

This is a superb opportunity for the right kind of person and we'll pay you a top salary with bonuses.

Call or write today and tell us about yourself!

Jim Brown, Anglo-European PR, 99B Baker Street, London, W1J 9PQ
tel. 01 670 8071

A  Listen to the first reading: what's wrong with it?
Now listen to the second reading. How is this better?

B Read the text aloud yourself, but first make sure you understand
and know how to pronounce all the words. Use a dictionary if
necessary. In this version of the text, the words that are joined up
together when pronounced are marked like this: ‿

Join our PR team – top salary!
We need someone to join our team
who can manage to do ten things at once
while remaining cool and calm in a crisis!
We are a leading PR Company
and we can offer you a fulfilling and challenging role
working with our Director of Travel.
You will need to be hard-working, flexible,
well-organized and energetic.
You'll be attending presentations,
arranging meetings, travel and lunches,
and liaising with executives of major international companies.
This is a superb opportunity for the right kind of person
and we'll pay you a top salary with bonuses.
Call or write today and tell us about yourself!
Jim Brown, Anglo-European PR,
99B Baker Street, London, W1J 9PQ
telephone 01 670 8071

C Work in groups of three. One of you should look at File 35,
another at 63 and another at 75. You will each have a Help Wanted
ad from an American newspaper to read aloud.

*"Six thousand a year may not sound much,
but look at it this way."*

13.3 Applying for a job

A Work in groups. Imagine that you have received a lot of applications for a job in your firm. Sort them into three piles:

A: These look promising! B: These are possibles.
C: Thanks, but no thanks! (hopeless cases)

1. As you will see from my enclosed CV, I have been working for my present company for three years. I joined them as assistant works manager and was promoted to production manager last year. Before that I had spent two years taking a full-time diploma course

2. My name's Jim Brown and I can do great things for your company! I'm 29, unmarried, fit and healthy and I've got all the qualifications and experience to make me the ideal.

3. I am sure I would be able to manage the department successfully, as I am good at supervising people and at giving clear instructions. I feel that I would be

4. I wish to apply for the job you have advertised. Please send me further details.

5. I noted with interest your advertisement for a 'Marketing Assistant' in today's Daily Planet.

6. I am writing about the job in your advetisement in todays Evening post. I am having five years experiance in the export and import trade as well as the qualificications you . . .

7. I am ambitious and my present job doesn't offer me the chance to expand.

8. If you consider that my experience and qualifications are suitable, I would be available for interview at any time.

9. I enclose a CV, which gives full details of my qualifications and work experience. In support of my application, I should like to mention the following points:

10. Although my present employers are first-rate and our relationship is excellent, I am keen to extend my range and am looking for a more rewarding and challenging post.

11. I would be grateful if I could discuss the post available in person and perhaps go into my background and my suitability for the post in more detail.

B Look again at the ads in Files 35, 63 and 75. Choose one of the jobs advertised there – *or* choose a job advertised in a recent newspaper that you might *really* apply for.

1. Decide with your partner what information you will give in your letter of application and/or in a supplementary information sheet. Make notes.
2. Draft your letter (and information sheet). Show your work to a partner and ask for comments. Then give it to your teacher for checking.
3. Write (or type) the final version(s).
4. Compare your letter with the letter in File 87.

13.4 Equal opportunities?   *Read and discuss*

A Look at these ads and discuss the questions below:

equal opportunity employer

Applicants are considered on the basis of their suitability for the post, with equal opportunities for women, black/ethnic minorities, lesbians and gay men and people with disabilities, and regardless of marital status, age, creed/religion and unrelated criminal conviction. All posts are open for job-sharing.

SOUTHAMPTON CITY

Your application will be judged solely on its merits irrespective of race, marital status, sex, sexual orientation, age, religion or disability.

An equal opportunity employer

1. Do ads in your country often contain similar statements?
2. How does the law in your country make sure that minorities are not discriminated against in employment?
3. Find out your partners' views on this practice.
4. What are your views on job-sharing? What seem to be the advantages and disadvantages of this? Would you encourage or discourage job-sharing if you were an employer?

B Read the text and answer the questions on the next page:

Too old at 30

I'M CONTEMPLATING applying for my fifty-first job. It's been a long time since I wasted stamp money this way. In fact, when I reached the fiftieth without success I decided to abandon job-hunting and got out my pen to scratch a living instead.

But there's another wildly exciting job in the paper today,

"salary £9,500–£11,250 according to age and experience." The good news is the pay, the bad news is that damning little phrase "according to age and experience" which means I won't get the job.

It's not that I have more age than experience – I've led an incident-packed existence. Unfortunately it's not all related to a single-strand career structure. Journalist, temp, company

>>>→

director, wife and mother, market researcher, and now, at thirty-something, I'm trying to use my Cambridge degree in criminology.

I'm a victim of the sliding pay-scale. Employers can obtain a fresh 22-year-old graduate to train a lot cheaper than me. Yet I'm the ideal employee; stable, good-humoured, child-bearing behind me, looking for 25-plus years of steady pensionable employment.

Ageism is everywhere. It's much more prevalent than sexism in the job market, or that's how it seems from where I'm standing. Even the BBC is a culprit. Their appointments brochure says in part: "The BBC's personnel policies are based on equal opportunities for all ... This applies to ... opportunity for training and promotion, irrespective of sex, marital status, creed, colour, race, or ethnic origin and the BBC is committed to the development and promotion of such equality of opportunity." "Traineeships ... are available to suitably qualified candidates under the age of 25."

Ageism's lagging behind sexism, racism, and handicappism because even the oppressed seem to accept the discrimination. The public and private sectors are obsessed with attracting young high-fliers. Yet there are many professions that would benefit from the maturity and stability the older entrant can bring. This is recognised by the Probation Service, for example, who welcome experienced adults looking for a second career.

The armed services and police, perhaps, could think about strenuous aptitude and fitness tests rather than imposing a blanket upper limit on entrants which is arbitrarily and variously fixed between 28 and 33.

The administrative grade of the Civil Service, assumes the rot sets in at 32.

My own pressing concern is to alleviate my guilt. I loved every minute of my university education, and I'm desperately grateful to the Government for financing me through this at a cost of over £10,000. But unless someone gives me a job how can I pay them back in income tax?

Jenny Ward

Work in pairs. Decide whether statements 1–10 are true [√] or false [×], according to the article. Then discuss questions 11–15.

1. The writer is over forty years old.
2. She gave up applying for jobs some time ago.
3. She has not had much experience of working for a living.
4. Employers think that someone of her age is too expensive to employ.
5. She needs a job so that she can support her family.
6. People get as angry about ageism as about other forms of discrimination.
7. Employers are looking for bright, ambitious people of any age.
8. More mature employees would be valuable assets to many professions.
9. People in their thirties can't get jobs in government departments.
10. She wants to 'repay' the State for her university education.

11. What would you do if you were in the same position as the writer?
12. Do you know any people who are unlucky or unsuccessful in getting jobs?
13. Can you explain the reasons for their lack of success?
14. What could they do to improve their chances of success?
15. Do you know any people who are particularly good (or lucky) in getting jobs? Why are they successful?

There are two types of relative clause in English:

IDENTIFYING RELATIVE CLAUSES These identify a person or thing in the same sentence. Notice the lack of commas:

You seem a bit upset – why is that?
   Well, you see, I applied for a job *that I saw advertised last month*. But you didn't get it?
      No, I phoned first and then I wrote a long letter. And the letter *that I got back* was just a photocopy! It said that the job *that I wanted* had already been given to someone inside the company.
But you thought that it was still vacant?
      Yes, the person *who spoke to me on the phone told me* the post was vacant.
How annoying!

Instead of **that** we can use **which**; instead of **who** we can use **that**. If, and only if, the subordinate clause (in italics in the examples) has a subject within it, we can omit **who** or **that**:

Is everything OK with our order?
   No, the documents (**that/which**) *you mailed to us last week* haven't arrived.
Can I discuss the matter with someone else, please?
   No, I'm afraid the person **who/that** *knows about this* is not available right now.

■ **Whom** is more common in formal writing than in conversation. We might write: but we'd say:

The person to whom you spoke was	The person you spoke to was ....
The people with whom I am working	The people I'm working with ....
The man from whom I received the letter	The man I got the letter from ....

NON-IDENTIFYING RELATIVE CLAUSES These are used to give more information about a known person or thing. They are more common in writing than in speech – again, notice the use of commas:

Alex Brown, **who** *wrote to you about this*, is no longer with our firm.
Getting a good job, **which** *everyone has a right to*, is not easy.
The application form, **which** *is enclosed with this letter*, must be returned to us by April 24.
Please telephone Ms Kurtz, **whose** *extension number is 666*.
Mr Gay, **to whom** *you spoke yesterday*, is our Personnel Manager.

A   Work in pairs. Decide where you will put any commas that are necessary in each of these sentences. Then complete each sentence, using your own ideas.

1. The qualifications   that are mentioned in a job advertisement   ....
2. An interviewer   who tries to frighten the candidate   ....
3. On the other hand, an interview   which is too relaxed and friendly   ....
4. My friend Nick   who feels very nervous at interviews   ....
5. A handwritten letter   which many companies prefer to a typed one   ....
6. A CV   which gives too much information   ....
7. Your curriculum vitae   which you should always send a copy of   ....
8. Your application for the post   which was mailed on 4 May   ....
9. Unfortunately, the envelope   in which your documents were sent   ....
10. Mrs Mary O'Farrell   with whom you have been corresponding   ....

B   Work in pairs. Imagine that you've just joined the Personnel Department of Acme Industries. Many of the people in the firm have similar names! Look at the information below and on the next page and work out who's who.
Make up a sentence about each person, following this pattern:

Tim Smith, who works in the Export Department, is 24 and enjoys golf.
or Tim Smith, who is 24 and enjoys golf, works in the Export Department.

Export Department:
Tim Smith, Carlo Mendez, Maria Schneider, Allan Gallini

Marketing Services:
Carlos Mendoza, Tom Schmidt, Mary Schindler, Alice Galtieri

Office Services:
Alan Gallagher, Carol Mendel, Mario Schnabel, Thomas Smythe

Tim, 24, enjoys golf	Tom 61, plays the violin
Thomas, 29, married to a Mexican	Alan, 36, has four children
Alice, 17, started in May	Allan, 55, used to work in France
Carol, 37, likes gardening	Carlos, 23, likes dogs
Carlo, 44, was born in Brazil	Maria, 19, speaks Spanish
Mario, 34, has red hair	Mary, 21, lives near the airport

13.6 Questions, questions!

 A skilful interviewer avoids asking questions like these:

> Have you written many reports and letters in English?
> Are you an aggressive person?

Yes.
No

but instead asks questions like these:

> Can you tell me about your experience in writing English?
> What kind of person would you say you were?

If a candidate has more chance to speak, the interviewer has more time to listen to what he or she says and can form a better impression.

If you want a question to sound more friendly and less aggressive – or if you want to play for time while you think of another good question to ask – you can use expressions like these:

> Could you tell me...?
> I wonder if you could tell me...
> Would you mind telling me...?
>
> I'd also like to know...
> I'd like to know...
> Do you happen to know...?

You can give yourself a little time to think before you answer a difficult question by using these expressions:

> Let me see, ...
> I'm not sure about that.
> I've no idea, I'm afraid.
>
> That's a very good question!
> Oh, let me think, ...
> I'm afraid I don't know.

Which of the expressions would also be useful if a colleague was asking you for information?

 Some interviewers like to give candidates a hard time by asking them difficult questions. Here are some typical questions that an interviewer might ask:

1. Tell me about yourself.
2. What do you think are your strengths and weaknesses?
3. We have a lot of applicants for this job, why should we appoint you?
4. What has been your most valuable experience?
5. How would you describe your personality?
6. When did you last lose your temper? Describe what happened.
7. Which is more important to you: status or money?

≫→

8. How long do you think you'd stay with us if you were appointed?
9. Why do you want to leave your present job?
10. What makes you think you'd enjoy working for us?
11. Are you an ambitious person?
12. What would you like to be doing ten years from now?
13. What are you most proud of having done in your present job?
14. What was the worst problem you have had in your present job and how did you solve it?
15. What is the best idea you've had in the past month?
16. What is your worst fault and what is your best quality?
17. Don't you think you're a little young/old for this job?
18. What are your long-range goals?
19. Describe your present job – what do you find rewarding about it?
20. What do you do in your spare time?
21. What excites you about the job you're doing now?
22. What worries you about the job you're doing now?
23. Describe your ideal boss.
24. How would you rate your present boss?

A Work in pairs. Think of two more difficult questions you have really been asked or might be asked at an interview. Add these to the list above.

B What would your own *answers* to each of the 24 questions be? Discuss this with your partner and make notes.

C 🖾 Find a different partner and take it in turns to ask each other the 24 questions. Perhaps try to give each other a hard time by asking supplementary questions like these:

Why do you think that?
In what way exactly?
Could you explain why you think that?
What do you mean exactly?
Can you give me an example of that?
Are you quite sure you mean that?

13.7 A good interview?

Listen and discuss

A 🔲 You'll hear part of two interviews. Answer these questions:
1. Which of the candidates performed better?
2. Which interviewer did the better job, do you think?

B 🔲 Listen to the interviews again. Decide what answer *you* would give to each of the questions the interviewer asks.
(There's a pause after each question for you to suggest your answer and then you'll hear the candidate's reply.)

C Work in small groups. Here is some advice that might be given to an inexperienced interviewer. Which of the points do you agree with entirely – or partly? Give your reasons.

- Make sure you are not interrupted or phoned during the interview.
- Read the candidate's CV and application letter before the interview begins.
- Ask the candidate to explain why he or she keeps changing jobs.
- Make sure you have a clear picture of the scope of the job.
- Ask each candidate the same questions.
- Decide on a maximum of four key qualities required for the job.
- Make sure the candidate has an uncomfortable, low chair.
- Ask the candidate about his political and religious beliefs.
- Only trust a candidate who looks you straight in the face.
- Trust your first impressions.
- Never let the candidate feel relaxed.
- Avoid talking too much yourself.
- Avoid open questions that can be answered with Yes or No.
- Find out the candidate's opinions on a variety of topics.
- Encourage the candidate to ask you about fringe benefits, the pension scheme and promotion prospects.
- Tell the candidate about the status of the job and its terms and conditions.
- Interview groups of candidates, rather than one by one.
- Tell the candidate when he or she may expect to hear your decision.

D Imagine that a young friend of yours is about to attend an interview. Note down at least ten pieces of advice that you would give to him or her. Here are a few suggestions:

Wear smart, formal clothes.   Sit up straight.
Don't smoke.   Arrive on time.
....
....

13.8　A progress interview

Employees are often given a 'progress interview' some months into a
new job, so that they can get (and give) feedback on their
performance so far. Participants on training courses often take part in
similar mid-course/mid-term interviews too.

A　Work in pairs. Make a list of ten questions that might be asked at
such an interview in *your* firm OR during the course you're doing
now. Here are some examples:

> What have been your most valuable experiences with us so far?
> Which parts of the course have been least valuable to you?
> What particular difficulties have you had?
> How well do you get on with the other members of staff/participants?

B　[▓]　Work in groups of three. You will be taking part in three
interviews – as interviewer, as interviewee and as 'observer'.
The observer's role is to make notes and give advice to the other two
on their performance in the interview.
When it's your turn to be the boss / course organizer, look at File 81,
when you're the employee/trainee look at 53 and when you're the
observer look at 71.

1. Student A plays the role of boss / course organizer, B is the employee/trainee and
   C is the observer.
2. The observer gives feedback to A and B.
3. Student A plays the role of employee/trainee, B is the observer and C is the boss /
   course organizer.
4. The observer gives feedback to A and C.
5. Student A plays the role of observer, B is the boss / course organizer and C is the
   employee/trainee.
6. The observer gives feedback to B and C.

*"We're a parent company,
Wolper – not to be confused
with your real parents."*

13.9 The Real Thing

A   Work in two groups. Each group should decide on one job that would be attractive and realistic for most of the members of the class to apply for. Perhaps this could be your 'ideal job' – the one you'd immediately apply for if you saw it advertised.
Write a classified ad for the job and, if possible, make copies for the other group to see. Alternatively, put it on the noticeboard or stick it to the board.

B   [▓▓] In this simulation half the class will be playing the role of interviewers and the other half the role of candidates. Each panel of interviewers are members of a firm of consultants, and they will interview several candidates for both jobs advertised. Decide which members of the class are going to play the roles of candidates, and which are going to be the interviewers. Follow the instructions on the left or on the right below, according to your role.

1   INTERVIEWERS: Work with the other member(s) of your panel. Decide what questions you are going to ask each candidate.
What personal qualities are you looking for? Are you going to be kind to the candidates or give them a hard time?

CANDIDATES: Choose one of the jobs advertised. Write a letter of application for it (and maybe also a Supplementary Information sheet) to accompany your CV. If possible, make copies of your letter and your CV so that each panel has a copy of each to study before the interview.

2   INTERVIEWERS: Read the letters of application and the CVs you receive. Decide which candidates look promising and what special questions you'll ask each one.

CANDIDATES: Work with another candidate and decide what impression you'll try to give. Look again at the difficult questions in 13.7 and make sure you know how to answer them.

3   Now it's time for the interviews to take place.
Each interview panel should have its 'office' in a different part of the room. Candidates go to a different 'office' for each interview. Your teacher will tell you how long is available for each interview and work out a timetable that allows time for panels to see at least three candidates. Each panel must stick to this schedule, so that other panels are not kept waiting.

≫→

INTERVIEWERS: Look at the checklist in File 89.

CANDIDATES: Between interviews you should wait in a separate area – preferably in another room or in the corridor.

4 When the interviews have finished, all the interviewers and all the candidates should meet in separate areas.

INTERVIEWERS: Tell the other panels about the candidates you have interviewed.
You can recommend up to three people for both posts. Decide which candidates will be short-listed.

CANDIDATES: Imagine that you're meeting in a local café or bar.
Tell the other candidates how you got on in your interviews. What mistakes did you make?
Which of the panels conducted the best interviews? What advice would you give them about their interviewing techniques?
Decide which panels were the best.

5 Now meet again as a class.

INTERVIEWERS: Announce your short lists of successful candidates.

CANDIDATES: Announce which panels you voted 'top interviewers'.

NOTE: If everyone wants to have the experience of playing both roles, you will need to do the simulation twice. However, most people feel much more confident about being interviewed after they have played the role of interviewer a few times, so this may not be necessary.

14 Working together

Asking for and giving advice. Talking about and dealing with problems at work. Discussing changing work conditions for women. Describing office working conditions. Consulting and reporting to superiors. Order of Adverbs.

14.1 Asking for and giving advice

Functions

If you want help or advice, you can use the following expressions:

> What ought I to...? I'd like your advice on...
> Do you think I should...? What would you do if you were me?

If you are talking to a person you don't know so well, you can say:

> I would appreciate your advice on... I should like to ask...
> Could I ask for some advice on...?

If you don't want to sound too bossy, you can say:

> Might it be an idea to...? Have you ever thought of...?

Some more direct ways of making suggestions or advising are:

> If I were you I'd... Why don't you...?
> You'd better...

To advise a stranger or a business client, you can say:

> My advice would be to... I would recommend...
> If I were in your position, I would... I would advise...

If you wish to accept the advice someone is giving you, you can say:

> That's a good idea. Good idea, let's try that.
> That sounds great, I'll try it.

>>>→

But, if you don't wish to accept the advice, you can say:

> No, I don't think I could do that.   Well, perhaps another time.
> I'm not sure that's such a good idea.

A 📼 Work in pairs. You'll hear three short conversations. How well do the people know each other? In which cases does the person accept the advice given?

B 📼 Now you will hear three conversations in which people ask for advice. Suggest what advice you would give before you hear the answer given. Say whether you agree or disagree with the advice given and why. How well do the people know each other?

C 🎭 Work in groups of four. You will each be offering advice to different people on the problems they have working together with other people. Student A should look at File 34, student B at 29, student C at 72 and student D at 27.

14.2 What next . . .?

A Work in pairs. Read the extract from a company handbook on its policy about employee involvement. What is the most important point, in your opinion? What words are used to describe the procedure discussed?

It is Shell companies' policy to promote a management style of direct involvement of employees in decisions affecting their jobs. Staff are encouraged to discuss the objectives of the unit in which they work before these are finally established. Through the staff reporting system, staff are also encouraged to take part in setting their work targets for the coming year, to identify their own training needs and to develop their own ambitions so that these may be taken into account in career planning. This approach which Group companies believe to be beneficial to the business and to give recognition to the legitimate expectations of employees is the core of its employee relations philosophy.

Many companies like to involve their staff in helping to set targets and find out which employees may be promoted or could benefit from further training. One of the ways they do this is by means of a counselling or progress interview (i.e. a planned discussion between manager and employee to review how the employee has done his/her job since the last progress report).

B   Read the list of comments on progress interviews from the point of view of the manager and the employee. Put them in order of importance.

- **For employees, it's necessary:**

1. to know how they are getting on in their jobs
2. to have the opportunity to discuss their work in detail with the boss
3. to discover their own weaknesses
4. to find out what view the boss has of them
5. to know how to work more effectively
6. to discuss their future within the organization
7. to see how their careers are developing

- **From the point of view of managers and the company:**

8. managers can profit from closer contact with individual employees
9. managers can find out what their employees do well or could do better
10. managers can review the performance of their staff by interviewing them
11. the company can profit from interviews, because they create closer working relationships
12. interviews help the company to find out which people can be promoted
13. interviews can help make people believe in the company more
14. interviews can help to find out which employees can benefit most from further training

C   You'll hear part of an interview in which a manager talks to an employee. When the recording stops you have to continue the interview.

One of you should look at File 84, and the other at 54. Before you begin, decide which department you're working in: accounts, orders, sales, production control etc.

D   Work in pairs. Draft a report of the interview from the perspective of the manager. Decide whether you would recommend the employee for promotion. Give reasons for your decision.

E   Work in groups. Look at another pair's report. Now discuss the interview you have had in a larger group. Ask another group what they discussed. What decisions did they come to? What experience do any of you have of such interviews? What is your opinion of them? How is progress watched in your country/company?

14.3 Women at Work! *Discussion*

A Work in pairs. Think about jobs in your country. Make two lists:
one of jobs which women now do and which their mothers did not do
in the past. The other list is of jobs which their mothers' generation
used to do. What differences do you find? Find three reasons why you
think the changes have taken place.

B Work in groups. Compare your lists with another pair. What sort
of changes have taken place in the relationships between men and
women at work? Do you agree on the reasons why the changes have
taken place? What further changes do you expect and would you like
to see?

C Work in pairs. Now consider these pieces of information
referring to various aspects of the working life of women:
  How many of the points discussed apply to your country?
  Which of the ideas presented do you agree with or disagree with?
Draw up a list of important areas in which, in your opinion, the
working conditions of women have been improved recently or need
to be improved still further. Which points would you like to add
which have not been mentioned here?

> The profile of a well-known British bank illustrates
> the fact that women do not and never did have
> equal access to the career path which men took
> advantage of. The presence of women in the large
> number of routine but essential jobs in fact allowed
> the career path of men to be maintained.
>
> **Of the total of 67,500 employees in 1983, two-
> thirds were women. More than three-fifths of
> these were in the bottom two salary grades.**

*"That's an excellent suggestion,
Miss Triggs. Perhaps one of the
men here would like to make it."*

180

Membership of the Banking, Insurance and Finance Union in Britain

Year	Women	Men	Total	% Women
1925	1,639	22,749	24,388	6
1945	6,532	20,625	27,257	24
1965	21,409	37,035	58,444	37
1985	81,819	75,469	157,468	52

Before you read the next extract, list the things you pay out of your salary, if you work (if you don't work, put down what your parents have to pay), in taxes, health insurance or social security contributions. What other deductions are there? For what? Now read the text. What is the most important message in your opinion? What do you understand by the word *benefits* and by *covered earnings*?

A WOMAN'S GUIDE TO SOCIAL SECURITY

If you interrupt your career

For you or your dependants to get any Social Security benefits, you need credit for a certain amount of work. The amount of credit you need depends on when you reach 62, become disabled, or die. If you stop working before you earn enough Social Security credits, no benefits will be payable. But credits you have already earned remain on your work record, and you can always go back to work and earn any additional credits you need to get benefits.

This rule applies to both women and men. But it's particularly significant to a woman because she may prefer to stay home while she's raising children.

One thing to keep in mind, though, is that the amount of any monthly benefit payable on your record could be affected by years of no earnings. The amount of your benefit – and your family's benefit – is based on your covered earnings over a period of years. If several years of no earnings (or low earnings) have to be counted, then your benefit may be lower than it would have been if you worked throughout your life.

D   What connections do you see between the points mentioned above and the cartoon on the next page? Imagine what it would be like:

if your bosses were all women . . .
if your clerks and typists were all men . . .
if your manual workers were all women . . .
if your receptionists were all men . . .

E   Work in groups. Compare the list of items you made in pairs (in C). What similarities or differences do you find? Can you agree on a new list of priorities?
How does the situation of women presented here compare with their working status in your country or in firms with which you're familiar? What changes do you see / would you like to see?

≫→

182

14.4 Getting on together

A Work in pairs. Look at this list of 'problems'. Which ones do you think your boss or supervisor would be able to help you with? Who could help you with the other problems?

- the artificial light affects your eyesight
- you need time off to go to a funeral
- it's your birthday today: you want to go out with your family
- there is no room for your car in the company car park
- the union membership fees have been increased
- you think the canteen food is making you fat

B 📼 You'll hear four conversations in which people are talking to their superiors. What problems are being discussed? Which speakers are friendly or unfriendly, which are helpful or unhelpful? How do you think the situations will turn out?

How would you deal with similar situations?
Write notes and compare them with another pair.
What sort of experience have you had in dealing either with superiors or with juniors in your working life?

C Work in pairs to discuss this problem:
Imagine that you have been working in the department for several years. The old department head dies suddenly and a new manager comes in from another firm. You were expecting to be promoted but the new manager promotes a younger person instead of you.

Draft a letter to your divisional manager about the actions of the new departmental head. In the letter, explain the situation from your point of view, express how you feel about what has happened and demand some action.

14.5   Flexible working hours   *Case Study*

A   Work in groups. Imagine that you are personal assistants to the
personnel manager of a large international company.
Your task is to work out an acceptable and suitable compromise with
limits to flexitime for all staff *or* for certain staff members.
A system of flexible working hours has been proposed, among other
things because of the problems with rush hour traffic.

The facts
The office opens at the moment from 9 am to 5 pm with a lunch hour
from 1 to 2 pm. Three quarters of the staff work a 35 hour week. The
rest are part-time. During office hours telephones have to be
answered and visitors need to be received.

Further factors which need to be considered:

Management proposals
Only certain days in the week should be designated 'flexidays'. There
should be a period of 'core time' which is non-negotiable except for
normal exceptions (unavoidable visits to the dentist etc).

Staff suggestions
Some secretaries would like to leave earlier on days other than
Thursdays as the shops do not stay open later and so are fuller.
Clerical staff are prepared to work during the present lunch hour.
An extension of working hours is acceptable if they are credited
later.
One department has proposed a 'pairing' system, where you always
have someone else to cover for you in your absence.

Staff requests
There are a number of part-time workers, all women, about 25% of
the office staff, who would prefer to work the majority of their 17½
hours in the mornings.
Several people have requested time to take their children to pre-
school and school and also to fetch them in the afternoon. They
would prefer to start at 10 on certain days.
The canteen must stay open longer at lunch time, if necessary.

B   Draft a report in which you summarize the results of your group.
Write your proposals and your recommendations to the Personnel
Manager in the form of a memorandum. Present your reports to
another group for their comments.

14.6 Order of adverbs *Grammar*

A 🔲 Look at these examples, which show where you can place different adverbs in a sentence. The examples show the 'comfortable' places, though other, more emphatic, places can be used sometimes.

BEFORE	MID	AFTER

Unexpectedly, the firm increased its profits.
   The firm unexpectedly increased its profits.
      The firm increased its profits unexpectedly.

Last year the firm increased its profits.
      The firm increased its profits last year.

Recently the firm has increased its profits.
   The firm has recently increased its profits.
      The firm has increased its profits recently.

      The firm increased its profits in Japan.
   The firm certainly increased its profits.
   The firm never increased its profits.
      The firm increased its profits really well.

   The firm surely won't increase its profits.
   The firm can really increase its profits.

B Move the adverbs into the most 'comfortable' place in the sentence.

1. The corporate headquarters moved from Houston to Charlotte.   **recently**
2. The company realized that it was a profit-making area.   **very quickly**
3. Our staff worked the whole year.   **hard**
4. The machine was serviced by the engineer.   **carefully**
5. The production schedule will be achieved.   **probably**
6. We are modifying our early retirement scheme.   **currently**
7. They check their inventory.   **weekly**
8. I'm sorry to say there is little we can do.   **immediately**
9. The customer delivered the cargo.   **punctually**
10. We have sufficient material in stock.   **luckily**

C Mid-position adverbs

Adverbs like the ones below often go in mid-position. Look at the examples and notice what is meant by 'mid-position'.

never   always   often   usually   once   rarely   hardly ever
frequently   ever   obviously   probably   certainly   apparently
almost   nearly   completely   just   hardly

We have always rewarded good work.　　We can always reward good work.
We always reward good work.　　Good work will always be rewarded.

D Put the adverbs on the right in the correct position in each sentence.

1. There have been disputes in our company.
2. Last year there were go-slows in the production plant.
3. The company went bankrupt as a result.
4. Now our firm is going to open a European factory.
5. We would have accepted the offer.
6. Workers can expect the facts.
7. You don't know what we're talking about.
8. Our subsidiaries achieve essential production targets.
9. Their operating expenses remained low.
10. The supervisor forgot to carry out an inspection.

rarely
frequently
nearly
probably
certainly
hardly
obviously
never
apparently
completely

14.7   Information helps everyone

A Work in pairs. Read these two extracts. What advice is given in the first one? What does the writer of the second one wish to find out more about?

A firm which advises companies how to produce reports writes:

> Employees are likely to achieve greater job satisfaction and to perform better if they identify their interests with those of their company. The provision of regular information in finance, production and marketing contributes materially to this sense of identity.

Dear Sir,

Like many employees at Labrco International I am very interested to know as much as possible about the activities and plans of the company.
A number of reports in the press recently have suggested that Labrco is intending to encourage more participation on the part of the workforce. I for one would warmly welcome more information about any such scheme.

B 📼 You'll hear the training manager of a large international company discussing the company's policy on information.

1. Which of the following points and procedures does he mention?
   - [ ] use of the noticeboard
   - [ ] one-way communication
   - [ ] employees' right to have facts about the company

□ informal information system
□ profit and marketing objectives of the company
□ information programme
□ training for consultative committees
□ employees' desire to express their opinions
□ two-way communication
□ the importance of the company newsletter

2. What is his opinion of communication with the workforce?

C Work in groups. Answer the following questions:

1. How effective do you think such programmes are?
2. Compare the situation with that at your own place of work.
3. What sort of procedures are possible/necessary in your opinion?
4. What projected changes or improvements would you like to see in communications between employees and superiors?

14.8 Working together in a company   *Vocabulary*

Fill in the gaps with words from the list

arbitrate   drawbacks   force   industrial action   lay-offs   lump sum
mutual   negotiable   overtime   reject   redundant   sack

1. Many employers are prepared to talk to their workforces about wages, but say that things like the reduction of the working week are not ....
2. Many workers still gladly accept the opportunity to work .... if the foreman asks them.
3. The union members .... the company's offer and decided to take strike action.
4. Before the present strike there had been a long period without any .... in the company.
5. The courts were called upon to .... the dispute.
6. They arrived at a solution which was to the .... satisfaction of both sides.
7. In some countries, if the proprietor of a company .... a worker without notice, he can be fined.
8. In times of recession the threat of .... of workers increases.
9. In most West European countries legal protection is provided for workers. This means that employees cannot be .... to take early retirement.
10. But often younger workers are attracted by the offer of a .... payment.
11. Everyone hopes that they will not remain .... for long once they have lost their job.
12. Such people do not see the .... until it is too late.

14.9   Life in the office   *Listen and discuss*

A   Work in pairs. Office life is different from country to country.
What would you tell a foreign visitor about office routines in your
country?

☐ working hours   ☐ provision of crèches
☐ flexitime   ☐ canteen food
☐ working contracts   ☐ union recognition
☐ relationship to 'boss' ☐ wage negotiation
☐ . . .

B   🔲 You'll hear about office routines in the USA. Which aspects
are discussed which were included above? Decide which statements
are true [✓] or false [✗]:

1. The start to the official working day is 8.30.
2. People tend only to work when the boss can see them.
3. People are not paid for what they do but their time.
4. Employees are expected to work through the lunch hour.
5. Flexitime is very common in the USA.

188

6. It is difficult to get a job contract.
7. Working in an office is like being in a big family.
8. The atmosphere is usually very formal.
9. The staff are not allowed to talk to one another.
10. Coffee is available the whole day.

C   Work in groups. List the differences and the points of contact
with your own country. Which aspects would you like to see copied
and which are you glad do not exist in your country?

D   Make notes of the points you would emphasize if an American
enquired about working routines and relations among the workforce
and office staff in your country or company.

14.10   A consultative meeting

A   🎭 Work in groups of four. You are taking part in a
consultative meeting between managers and worker representatives.
Decide who will be A, B, C or D.

Read the agenda to see what the meeting is about. Then A looks at
File 95, B at 49, C at 82 and D at 110.

```
Quarterly Consultative Meeting

Room A 15. Administrative Block

9.15 a.m. Tuesday 12 December 19—

    AGENDA

1   Minutes of previous meeting

2   Matters arising

3   Introduction of new production system

4   Proposed new work routines

5   Re-training programme

6   Any other business
```

B   Work in pairs. Draft a report or minutes of the meeting.

C   Work in groups. Show your report or minutes to another pair
and check what they have written. Compare what important
differences or similarities you find in each group's report or minutes.

15 A special project

It's Been Said There Are Three Important Things To Consider When Choosing A Business Site.

Location, Location, Location.

IF YOU'RE WORRIED ABOUT MOVING YOUR COMPANY A FEW MILES THINK HOW THE GERMANS, AMERICANS AND JAPANESE FELT.

JANUARY

Your firm produces a range of delicious, high-quality main courses and desserts that are a speciality of your region, selling in supermarkets and to the catering trade. The products are ready to cook in a microwave or conventional oven.

1. 📼 You'll hear a description of a similar product. What are its main features and why is it successful? Make notes.

2. Work in small groups. Design a new product for the export market. This will be a range of fresh (not frozen), ready-to-cook specialities of your region or country.
3. Think of a good brand name and design a package.
4. Describe your product to the other groups.
5. Decide which of the products will be most likely to succeed in the British and in the American markets. From now on, *this* will be the product you will manufacture and market.

Two special project teams will be responsible for finding a new location where the product will be manufactured and marketed in the UK and the USA: team A in the UK and team B in the USA. When the factory comes on line, the team will manage it during the first year – or, if you wish, permanently.

6. Decide on your criteria for choosing a location by grading these points in order of importance:

low cost of premises	low taxes for new businesses
availability of supplies	good road communications
good, cheap housing	closeness to principal markets
language	availability of cheap skilled workers
nearby airport	quality of life: convenience, facilities etc living
city or country	development area or large city

What other factors are important, do you think?

7. Look at these maps of possible sites: which seem to be more suitable, according to the criteria you have just established?

FEBRUARY

1. Read this memo from the Board:

TO: Special project teams
FROM: Board of directors

- Both plants will be semi-automated. Provisional orders
  have been placed for the special ovens and packaging
  machines.
- There will be approximately 50 production staff in each
  plant at start-up, rising to 100 in 2–3 years.
- Plant and offices will be on the same site. Marketing,
  sales and production will be working in close cooperation to adapt the product to local customers'
  requirements: supermarket chains may require 'own
  label' brands, ingredients may have to be changed to
  suite local tastes, etc.
- Available buildings will be used.

---

2. The controller will tell you which team you're in and which country you're
   being sent to. You will then be given copies of documents to study, including
   descriptions of the sites you will have to choose between.
   When you have studied the documents, find out what your colleagues'
   impressions and reactions are.

3. [cassette icon] You'll hear a report from a colleague who has visited the sites. Make notes
   and amend your documents accordingly.

4. Decide on the best location for your premises. Remember that you will be living
   there yourself for a year or longer!
   Report your decision to your counterparts in the other country by fax, phone or
   in person.

5. Decide what DEPARTMENTS you will need to establish (transport, maintenance,
   financial services, etc).
   Decide how many staff, supervisors, managers, sales reps, etc you will need.
   The members of your team will fill many of the top managerial positions: what
   posts will they take? What experts will you need to recruit locally for your
   management team?
   [telephone icon] Inform your counterparts in the other country by phone.

6. Draft a brief outline showing how your branch will be organized: explain how
   you will make sure that your staff work happily and efficiently.
   Fax a copy of this to your counterparts in the other country.

7. Finally, both teams should meet to exchange experiences and discuss what has
   been done this month.

MARCH

This month each team will be planning the move.

■ If there are too many tasks for you all to deal with in the time available, the team should be split into *smaller groups*, each dealing with a *different* task, but liaising with the other groups.

1. Decide what you'll need to do to prepare for the opening of the new location. Rearrange the events in this list into a more logical order and add any important events that are missing.
   Then draw a flow diagram.

> Plans approved by head office
> Sign contract with owners of premises / development corporation
> Begin rebuilding/redecoration of premises
> Finish rebuilding/redecoration of premises
> Confirm orders for production and packaging machinery
> First delivery of production & packaging machinery
> Final delivery of production and packaging machinery
> Install production and packaging machinery
> Order office equipment
> First delivery of office equipment
> Final delivery of office equipment
> Install office equipment
> Advertise for office staff
> Interview office staff
> Appoint office staff
> Advertise for production staff
> Interview production staff
> Appoint production staff
> Advertise for warehouse and dispatch staff
> Interview warehouse and dispatch staff
> Appoint warehouse and dispatch staff
> Begin setting up factory equipment
> Finish setting up factory equipment
> Factory staff begin training
> Factory staff begin first full-scale production run
> Marketing and sales staff move into offices and begin training
> Other office staff move into offices and begin training
> Begin marketing campaign
> Begin sales drive
> First shipment of the product leaves the warehouse
> Product available to the catering trade
> Product available in the shops

   Fax a copy of your flow diagram to your counterparts in the other country. *Make it clear what you have added to the list.*

2. Draft a short press release to be sent to local papers, radio and TV to inform them of your plans to set up a new plant. Fax a copy to your counterparts in the other country.

≫→

3. You'll have to recruit office and factory staff. Will you set up and staff your own recruitment office or use a local agency?
Draft an advertisement to find local people (staff and managers) who may be interested in working for you.
Fax a copy to your counterparts in the other country.

4. Finally, both teams should hold a meeting to discuss what has been done this month – and to decide what still remains to be done by both teams.

APRIL

This month, the members of each team are divided into two smaller groups. Each group will have to deal with a different part of the project.

1. The controller will give you the relevant documents for the month. One group will be discussing MATERIALS, SUPPLIES AND DISTRIBUTION, the other MARKETING AND SALES.

    ☎ At least twice during the month, phone your counterparts in the other country and get a progress report from them. Make notes during the call and then relay the information back to your partners.

2. Towards the end of the month, rejoin the other members of your own team and hold an informal meeting to find out what they have been doing this month.

3. Finally, both teams should meet to discuss what has been decided so far.

MAY

By now, both teams' final plans have been submitted to the board of directors for approval.

1. The controller will give each team a copy of a fax: find out your colleagues' reactions to the information it contains.

2. Draft an agenda for the proposed meeting. Decide which member of your own team should chair the meeting. Decide where the meeting should be held.

3. ☎ Phone (or send a fax to) your counterparts in the other country to get their agreement on the agenda and venue.

4. Prepare your team's contribution to the meeting. Each member of your team should speak about a different aspect.

5. THE MEETING: The final meeting is held, with both teams putting forward their arguments.

Files

1

YOU ARE IN THE A TEAM
Please make sure everyone in your team chooses a different name and
position for this role play activity.
Use your own real first name and title (*Mr, Ms, Dr* etc). Write your
new identity on a badge or label, so that others can see who you are.

NAMES:
Rossi   Macpherson   Jabbari   Schmidt   Martin   da Silva
Gomez   Foster   Kobayashi   O'Neill   Lefèvre   Cartier   Bellini
(*or invent another surname*)

POSITIONS:

personal assistant	secretary	managing director
training officer	production manager	vice-chairman
purchasing manager	personnel manager	export sales manager
chief designer	safety officer	office manager
warehouse manager	transport manager	chief accountant
sales director	works manager	company secretary

(*or invent another position*)

Imagine that you are all **colleagues** or fellow-workers in the same firm: ACME
Industries. You're going to meet some **visitors** (members of Team B) who you must
introduce to your colleagues.

1. A visitor from Team B will introduce him- or herself to you.
   Talk to this person until your teacher gives you a signal.
2. Find a colleague to introduce your visitor to. At the same time you will be
   introduced to another visitor. Say goodbye to your first visitor and then start a
   conversation with the second visitor. Your teacher will tell you when to begin
   the next step.
3. Repeat step 2 with a different colleague.
4. Continue until your teacher asks you to stop.
5. Look at File 7, choose a new identity and play the role of a visitor this time.

2

Listen to your partners' phone call and then comment on it. Then,
after you have given them your comments, look at 31. (In a group of
four, Student C should look at 31 and D at 91.)

3

1. Dr Hamish MacPherson, Rannoch Enterprises p.l.c., 45–55 Sauchiehall St., Glasgow, GL1 8PG, Scotland
2. Señor Vicente Araixa Llorens, Calle Naranjo 50 – 5° G, 46011 VALENCIA, Spain
3. Mr Hidetoshi Mayagi, Crown Products Ltd, 40–5 Chajiri-cho, Arashiyama, Nishikyo, Kyoto-shi, Japan
4. M. René Floquet, Auvergne-Moteurs S. A., 33–39 av. Union-Soviétique, 63000 Clermont-Ferrand, France

4

First help your partners to solve their problems. Then play this role:

You are the head of the orders department in accounts. You have been helping to train two order clerks. Both are very capable people and they fit in well with the work in the department. Your boss tells you that rationalization and re-organization in the company mean that only one clerk will be needed when their training programme has finished.
You have been asked to recommend one for the job. You cannot sleep properly at night. What should you do?

When your partners have advised you, discuss what you did with the rest of the class.

5

You are temporarily sharing an office with your partner. Read this list of your 'problems' *before* you begin the conversation. See if your partner can help, and offer to help solve your partner's problems.

You think the office is overheated.   You have lost your diary.
You want to have lunch in the canteen.   You have a headache.
You are going to get some coffee from the machine.
You can't understand some technical terms.
You want to leave early but you're expecting a call from Paris.
You can't find the file for the Hong Kong clients.

6

Use your own name.
Call the Hotel Cambridge to confirm your reservations for tomorrow night for 3 nights. One double and one single room. The person staying in the single room (Mr Greenwood) will require the room for an extra night – is this all right? You will be arriving at 11 pm, so make sure the rooms are kept for you till then. You will be paying by Diner's Club card (#777 4580 2132 9). Will you be able to get a meal in the hotel when you arrive?

When the call is over, ask the student(s) who was/were listening to comment on your 'performance'. That is the end of this activity.

7

YOU ARE IN THE B TEAM
Please make sure everyone chooses a different name and nationality for this role play activity. Use your own real first name and title (*Mr, Ms, Dr* etc).

Legrand	Geneva, Switzerland	Harris	Plymouth, England
Gabrielli	Milan, Italy	Müller	Munich, Germany
Yip	Singapore	Rockford	Detroit, USA
Beaumont	Lille, France	Martens	Brussels, Belgium
Vlachou	Salonika, Greece	Carreras	Barcelona, Spain
Oliveira	Sao Paulo, Brazil	Fukuda	Osaka, Japan
Wallnöfer	Vienna, Austria	MacPherson	Edinburgh, Scotland

(*or invent your own surname and place of origin*)

Imagine that you are all **visitors** to ACME Industries. You're each going to meet someone who works for ACME (members of the A Team). They will introduce you to a colleague.

1. Introduce yourself to someone who works at ACME Industries.
   Talk to this person until your teacher gives you a signal.
2. Your host will introduce you to one of his or her colleagues.
   Say goodbye to your host and then talk to this new person.
   Your teacher will tell you when to begin the next step.
3. Step 2 will be repeated with a different ACME employee.
4. Continue until your teacher asks you to stop.
5. Look at File 1, choose a new identity and play the role of a member of ACME Industries' staff this time.

8

You are the chief buyer for a mail order company or chain store. You know this salesperson well. Find out:

- the wholesale price of the product
- the recommended retail price of the product
- how quickly the goods could be shipped
- what kinds of customers the product would appeal to
- why your customers might find the product attractive
- how each item is packed and how many there are in a carton
- if the product is supplied complete and ready to use
- where the product is manufactured

9

The estimated costs of some of the proposals are:
- Replacing typing chairs £85; armchairs £105
- New coffee machine: £27 per week rental
- Crockery for canteen (with company logo): £245
- Extension to car park: £3500

10

1. Mr Hugh O'Shea, Gloucester Products Ltd, 114 North Shields Road, Newcastle NE5 47G
2. Mrs Leena Suominnen, Koivisto Kirja Kauppa OY, Kirkkokatu 28, 20100 TURKU, Finland
3. Mlle. Annick Hautefeuille, S.E.B.A.R.A., 123 rue Drouet-d'Erlon, 5100 Reims, France
4. Señora Begoña Iraola Echebarria, Paseo Nervión 120 – 14 F, 48020 BILBAO, Spain

11

You are temporarily sharing an office with your partner. Read this list of your 'problems' *before* you begin the conversation. See if your partner can help, and offer to help solve your partner's problems.

You think the office is very hot and stuffy.
You have to buy someone a birthday card.
You don't want to talk shop over lunch.
You want to call home.
You are thirsty.
You need some photocopies made.
You want to know the times of trains to the main station.
You won't have time to phone Toronto before lunch.

12

Look at this price list for hi-fi equipment. As you can see, some of the prices have been increased or reduced.
Ask your partner about the prices on his or her list and find out which prices have been changed. Alter your own list accordingly.

LXI 15-inch Speakers	$169.95	
LXI 10-inch Speakers	~~$ 79.95~~	$ 84.99
Stereo Headphones	$ 69.95	
Cassette Deck – Dolby controls	$169.95	
LXI Cassette Deck	~~$149.95~~	$144.99
Direct-drive Turntable	$149.95	
Belt-drive Turntable	$119.95	
AM/FM Stereo Tuner	~~$499.95~~	$389.99
Mini "Go-Anywhere" Phones	~~$ 29.95~~	$ 32.50
Stereo Cassette Player/Recorder	$279.95	
Mini Compact Stereo System	$129.95	
Stereo Cassette Tape Deck	~~$169.95~~	$175.96

13 Imagine that you are a firm of package designers and specialist printers. You are the ones who sent the *message* on page 25.

REPLY to 1: Request shipment by airmail. Offer to pay for this yourself.
MESSAGE 2: OK to sub-contract printing of stick-on labels?
REPLY to 3: Offer to get your local agent to discuss this.
MESSAGE 4: OK to deliver order in two batches: first on 1st May, second on 1st June?

14 These are your department's suggestions:
– more staff parties and picnics
– better toilets and showers
– open roof garden to staff
– more comfortable tables and chairs in staff canteen
Add your own ideas . . .

15

ORDERS	Customer: CHIMERA GMBH			No.087
Date	Order		Invoice	Date pd
21 Jan	1500 mtr fabric		Gr 286	28.2.XX
16 June	855 mtr cttn		hj 004	19.8.XX
29 Sept	2000 mtr spec. cttn fabric		ln 985	

You work for Brimo SpA. Your company sell their fabric to garment manufacturers and have had a large one-off order to supply Chimera GmbH. You have not yet received an outstanding payment for invoice/order LN 985 for 2000 metres special cotton fabrics. The payment is 30 days overdue – today's date 15 December 19xx. (Now turn back to page 80.)

16 You are Mr/Ms Tanaka, a supplier.
You met Mr/Ms Suarez at a trade fair last year.
He/she may be interested in placing an order for some of your products. Call him/her and invite him/her to be your guest for lunch next Thursday when you'll be in town.
Ask him/her to suggest a nice restaurant near his/her office.
Find out what sort of restaurant it is and how you can get there on foot from the central railway station. Ask what time you should book a table.

When the call is over, ask the student(s) who was/were listening to your conversation to comment on your 'performance'. Then, if you are in a group of three, look at File 91. (If you are in a group of four, look at 109.)

17 Your partner has the other half of this price list. Ask polite questions to find out the missing information.

Code no.	Description	Prices in $ & £		Delivery
4478	green 58 × 72 cm PVC	$33.85	£25.75	3 w⌐·
4478A	white 58 × 72 cm PVC	$32.65	£24.85	
4479	pink 44 × 72 cm heavy paper	$22.00	£16.7⌐	
4480	red 88 × 88 cm PVC	$79.75	⌐.6⌐·	
4482	blue 12 × 65 cm polystyrene	⌐⌐⌐		
4483	black 43 × 17 cm PVC			
4487	green 44.5 × 25 c⌐			
4487B	white 44.5 × 2⌐			
4488	clear 7⌐			

18 Use your own name. You work for a subsidiary of Medusa S.A. Call your firm's head office and find out the name, address and phone number of **Mr or Mrs G. Peters**, who lives somewhere in Switzerland. You haven't met the person you're calling.

When the call is finished, look at File 66.

19 Look at the diagram below of the structure of a company. Your partner has the missing information. Ask him or her questions about the company structure.

Who is in charge of . . . ?   Who reports to . . . ?
What does . . . do?   What is the name of the head of . . . ?

EUROCHEMCO ORGANOGRAM

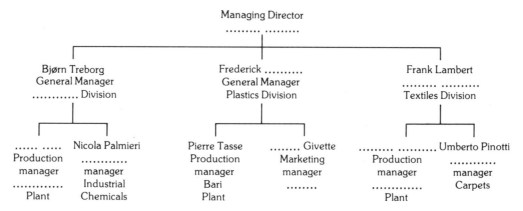

20

Imagine that you are a firm marketing consumer goods.
You are the ones who sent the *reply* on page 25.

MESSAGE 1: *Offer to send product prototype by courier or airmail.*
REPLY to 2: *No, all the printing must be done by yourselves.*
MESSAGE 3: *Request revised quote for 50,000 pcs instead of 35,000*
REPLY to 4: *Agree to 2 deliveries, or insist on single delivery (your decision).*

21

Discuss these ideas with your partner. Your partner has some
additional ideas. Which of these things do you consider to be the most
important?

1. You have a permanent record of what you want to say.
2. Information is available for people who were not present at the time.
3. Written words are less important than speaking; information is more important
   than the person giving it.
4. If the information is complicated it is hard to say in speech.
5. You cannot prove what was spoken in conversation.
6. If you write things down, it's easier to pronounce them correctly.
7. You can impress people much more in writing.

22

You are area sales representative for an importer. The customer is
chief buyer for a mail order company or chain store. You know this
customer well. Give your customer this information:

- Each radio is packed in protective
  foam inside a very attractive,
  illustrated carton (about half the size
  of this page).
- Batteries not supplied: they might
  leak.
- You could supply suitable batteries
  separately @ £47 per 100.
- The product is manufactured in
  Korea.
- You have stock for immediate
  delivery.
  Further shipments take 4 weeks.
- The wholesale price is £134 for a
  carton of 20 (retail price about
  £12.95).

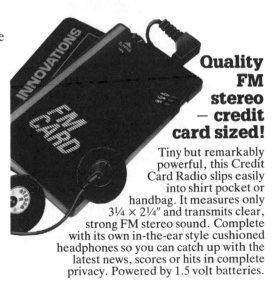

Quality FM stereo – credit card sized!

Tiny but remarkably
powerful, this Credit
Card Radio slips easily
into shirt pocket or
handbag. It measures only
3¼ × 2¼″ and transmits clear,
strong FM stereo sound. Complete
with its own in-the-ear style cushioned
headphones so you can catch up with the
latest news, scores or hits in complete
privacy. Powered by 1.5 volt batteries.

23 As you can see, there is some information missing from the description of the firm below. Read out those parts you have and listen to your partner read out the other parts. Try to answer these questions:

What areas does the firm work in?   Who works with the firm?
What is the firm contributing to?   What products does the firm produce?
How successful has the firm been recently?

Moving in the Same Direction

Lucky-Goldstar is a group of 26 Korean companies working in chemistry, electronics, and services.

Today, Lucky-Goldstar products and services ranging from engineering plastics, home appliances and fiber-optic communication systems to construction, finance and trade

We also operate Korea's largest private research institutes, investing 4.5% of sales into R&D each year.

Overseas subsidiaries like Goldstar of America (in Huntsville, Alabama) are contributing to higher employment, too.

Lucky-Goldstar. A team of 70,000 individuals working together with companies around the globe.

Take time to get to know us better. Contact the *Business Development Dept., Lucky-Goldstar Int'l Corp., Yoido P.O. Box 699, Seoul, Korea. Phone (02) 785-5694, Telex K27266 LGINTL.*

LUCKY-GOLDSTAR

24 Apologize or complain to your colleague because:
- You've forgotten to get last year's sales figures from the Sales Manager. Now she has left the building.
- Your colleague shouldn't have made a long-distance private call on the office phone.
- Your colleague should have telexed New Orleans, not written a letter. A telex is quicker and more reliable than airmail.
- You have made an appointment for your colleague to see the Managing Director in five minutes' time – it was the only time the MD was free this week.
- Your colleague should have contacted the Data Processing Manager before sending in an order for computer software.

25

Use your own name. You work in the head office of Medusa S.A. The caller works in a subsidiary company, but you haven't been in touch before. The address the caller requires may be one of these:

Gudrun Peters
Gesellschaftsstrasse 44 A
CH-3012 Bern
Switzerland
telephone (031) 65 78 16

Gordon Peters
33 avenue de l'Hôpital
CH-2017 Neuchâtel
Switzerland
telephone (038) 77 19 90

When the call is finished, look at File 51.

26

Look at the diagram below of the structure of a company. Your partner has the missing information. Ask him or her questions about the company structure.

Who is in charge of . . . ?   Who reports to . . . ?
What does . . . do?   What is the name of the head of . . . ?

EUROCHEMCO ORGANOGRAM

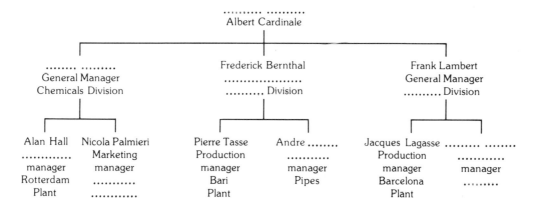

27

(You are student **D.**) Advise your partners how to solve **their** problems. Then tell your partners your own problem:

You work in the accounts department with a colleague. Your colleague has been responsible for credit control and you have been responsible for writing the invoices. You find the work boring and would like to do both activities. Your colleague appears to have much more interesting work to do.

Ask your partners' advice. When your problem has been discussed, look at File 4.

28

Design a questionnaire to find out the importance of various factors in choosing a holiday destination.
The people you ask should decide how important these factors are on a scale 1 to 10 (or 1 to 5 – if you prefer) for a main holiday *and* for a second holiday:

different way of life	night life	good food
historic places	beautiful scenery	meeting people
learn new things	bargain prices	gifts & souvenirs
summer sports	winter sports	relaxation
outdoor activities	visiting friends & relations	
part of longer trip	no language problems	

29

(You are student **B**). Advise **A** how to solve his or her problem. Then tell your partners your own problem:

You are sharing an office with a colleague who constantly comes late. You have to make excuses for their not being in the office when people ring up. You also make up stories to hide the fact from your boss. You like your colleague and get on well otherwise. But the situation is beginning to make you ill.

Ask your partners for advice. When your problem has been discussed, find out about **C**'s problem and advise them what to do. Then **D**'s problem. When all these problems have been discussed, look at File 102.

30

You are area sales representative for an importer. The customer is chief buyer for a mail order company or chain store. You know this customer well. Give your customer this information:

- The stationery kit and pens bar are designed as a matching set.
- They are available separately.
- Each stationery kit and pens bar is wrapped in plastic inside a brown cardboard box.
- Both are complete and ready to use.
- The products are manufactured in Italy.
- You will have stock in two weeks.
- The wholesale price of both products is £159 for a carton of 50 (£5.95 retail?).
- You could supply a real leather version of the stationery kit @ £47 per 20.

Office essentials go miniature

A miniature stationery set measuring only 4¾" × 3½" × 1½" that slips neatly into any brief-case or your pocket. It contains a tiny but effective stapler, scissors, tape measure, knife, sticky tape, water-based glue, ruler, eraser and paper clips. To match, a smart pens bar which doubles as a stand. It holds a black ball point, blue and red rolling ball pens, a mechanical pencil and a bright yellow highlighter. It measures 5" high × 2½" wide.

31

You are Mr/Ms LaRue, a customer.
Call Mr/Ms Peterson to find out whether the goods you have ordered
have been dispatched yet. The order number was RAJ 4581. The date
you placed the order was January 16. If they haven't been sent, try to
get him/her to hurry them up. Get him/her to call you back (023 1550 extension
18) to tell you *exactly* when you can expect the goods to arrive.

When the call is over, ask the student(s) who was/were listening to comment on
your 'performance'. Then look at File 50.

32

Begin by listening to your partner reading the first half of a company
report. Make a note of the figures he or she reads out. Then read out
the second half to your partner. Compare the figures with the text
afterwards.

To make it easier to read, the report is reprinted below in 'breath-sized' pieces with
stressed syllables underlined. When you are reading from this version, stop briefly
at the end of each line to take a breath and only let your voice fall when there is a
full stop.

> Total lending was DM 13.4 billion, of which
> DM 11.9 was earmarked for the German
> economy.
> ■ Assistance to developing countries amoun-
> ted to DM 2.4 billion. Considerable emphasis
> was placed on the environmental protection
> program initiated the previous year, financ-
> ing for small and medium-sized companies,
> and indirect support of the building industry.

Total lending
was thirteen point four billion Deutschmarks,
of which
eleven point nine billion Deutschmarks
was earmarked
for the German economy.
Assistance to developing countries
amounted to
two point four billion Deutschmarks.
Considerable emphasis was placed
on the environmental protection program initiated the previous year,
financing for small and medium-sized companies,
and indirect support of the building industry.

33

```
FROM NAVES LIMON
MERRY CHRISTMAS! WE ARE PLEASED TO TELL YOU THAT BOTH
VESSELS HAVE BEEN DELIVERED TO OUR CUSTOMERS WHO ARE
WELL PLEASED. WE HAVE HAD SEVERAL ENQUIRIES FROM OTHER
PEOPLE IN COSTA RICA AND ELSEWHERE IN CENTRAL AMERICA.
ANOTHER ORDER EXPECTED IN THE NEW YEAR.
WOULD YOU CONSIDER US AS YOUR EXCLUSIVE DISTRIBUTOR IN
CENTRAL AMERICA (NOT INCLUDING MEXICO OR PANAMA)?
WE LOOK FORWARD TO HEARING FROM YOU.
```

34

(You are student A). You begin. Tell your partners *your* problem:

You are sharing an office with someone and you are not happy with the fact that this person smokes. You have tried several times to mention that it is affecting *your* health. You have thought of asking the supervisor if you can change offices, but you are afraid that it may be interpreted as exaggerating.

Ask your partners for advice. When your problem has been discussed, find out about B's problem and advise them what to do. Then C's and D's problems. When all these problems have been discussed, look at File 83.

35

Sales engineer
Rapidly expanding precision
    bearings manufacturer
is looking for an aggressive,
problem-solving,
motivated decision-maker
to cover Imperial and
    San Diego counties.
Our candidate must develop,
with minimum assistance,
the full sales potential of the
    assigned territory,
calling on new and established
    customers . . .

36 Your partner has the other half of these jumbled instructions about how to make coffee with the machine. Work together to number the order in which you would explain what the correct amount of coffee is and how to make it. Don't forget to number the diagrams (figs. 1–7).

COFFEE (fig. 1 and 2):
Put 1 or 2 level measure spoons of (fast filter ground) coffee in the filter.
Fill the cups to the rim since some of the water always evaporates and some water remains in the coffee dregs.

HOW TO MAKE COFFEE
Fill the water reservoir with the required quantity of cold water.
Push the switch downwards. The pilot lamp lights up (fig. 6).
The machine switches off automatically after use. The coffee is not kept warm.

37 The estimated costs of some of the proposals are:
- Plants: £195 per floor + £25 monthly service
- One extra day unpaid leave: £120 in labour costs
- New lighting and heating system: £1250 per floor
- Paintings: £5000; framed posters: £350

38 Recently you met Nicole Boireau from Chaussures Chevalier. She was talking to you about her dealings with Linda Green of Light Leather Products. This is what she said:

'I've known Linda about five years now and we've always had little problems.
She sends the invoices a week after the deliveries.
And she sends the invoices in triplicate!
They only grant us credit for two weeks.
Linda's prices occasionally vary from the ones we have agreed on.
Even if I pay in advance, we never get a discount.
If we have a cash flow problem at our end, I always ring Linda up first.
And she often bothers me for what she calls 'outstanding accounts'.
But I always settle the accounts regularly.
Oh, and she never lets me pay in French currency, which I think is rather mean.'

Report this conversation to your partner, who has been talking to Linda Green.
Begin like this:
    Nicole Boireau told me that . . .

39

In this role play, you play the roles of a series of passengers, who want to fly to some of the following destinations. Choose your destinations and then ask for details of your flight: find out when it departs, when you have to check in, when boarding starts and so on.

Aberdeen	Amsterdam	Antwerp	Belfast
Birmingham	Brussels	Chicago	Copenhagen
Dublin	Dundee	Düsseldorf	Edinburgh
Frankfurt	Geneva	Glasgow	Guernsey
Isle of Man	Jersey	Larnaca	London Heathrow
London Gatwick	Madrid	Milan	Munich
New York	Oslo	Paphos	Paris
Rotterdam	Singapore	Southampton	Tenerife
Toronto	Zürich		

40

As you can see, there is some information missing from the description of the firm below. Read out those parts you have and listen to your partner read out the other parts. Try to answer these questions:

What areas does the firm work in?   Who works with the firm?
What is the firm contributing to?   What products does the firm produce?
How successful has the firm been recently?

Moving in the Same Direction

For each of the last five years, annual growth has averaged 24%, with sales reaching the U$12 billion mark in 1986.

are helping to create a better quality of life both at home and abroad.

But these accomplishments aren't ours alone.

Successful partnerships with such companies as AT&T, Hitachi, Siemens, and Caltex are doing a lot to stimulate mutual growth, while promoting economic development and free market systems in other countries as well as our own.

With management systems that are resulting in greater worker satisfaction, lower absenteeism, and better quality off the production line.

Bringing the world's latest technologies to Korea, and the fruits of Korea's can-do spirit to the world.

Contact the *Business Development Dept., Lucky-Goldstar Int'l Corp., Yoido P.O. Box 699, Seoul, Korea. Phone (02) 785-5694, Telex K27266 LGINTL.*

LUCKY·GOLDSTAR

41

Begin by reading this company report to your partner, who has the
second half of the same report. Then listen to the part your partner
reads out and make a note of the figures which you hear.
Compare the figures with the text afterwards.

To make it easier to read, the report is reprinted below in 'breath-sized' pieces with
stressed syllables underlined. When you are reading from this version, stop
briefly at the end of each line to take a breath and only let your voice fall when
there is a full stop.

KfW records another good year

KfW, one of West Germany's ten largest credit
institutions, had another good year.
■ The balance sheet total rose from DM 78.5
to DM 85.8 billion. Earnings were up some
37% to DM 149 million.

K F double U
records
another good year.
K F double U,
one of West Germany's ten largest credit institutions,
had another good year.
The balance sheet total
rose from
seventy-eight point five billion Deutschmarks
to eighty-five point eight billion Deutschmarks.
Earnings were up
some thirty-seven per cent
to a hundred and forty-nine million Deutschmarks.

42

Your partner has the other half of this price list. Ask polite questions
to find out the missing information.

			.5	3 weeks
				5 weeks
		.6.75		immediate
		$/9.75	£60.75	10 days
	..olystyrene	$12.60	£9.75	4 weeks
	, cm PVC	discontinued: not available		
	..44.5 × 25 cm nylon	$15.00	£11.50	7 days
	white 44.5 × 25 cm nylon	$14.00	£11.00	14 days
4488	clear 78 × 95 cm PVC	$89.50	£68.25	to order only

43 Call the Provence Restaurant (the best in town) to book a private room for a visiting group of clients next Tuesday evening, ideally from 7.30. There will be 10 to 14 in your party. You won't know exactly how many until Tuesday morning. Three of your guests are vegetarians – does this present any problems?

When the call is over, ask the student(s) who was/were listening to comment on your 'performance'. Then look at File 64.

44 You are a guest at the Hotel Miramar. Ask one of the receptionists to help you with each question:

1. What time is breakfast? Where is it served?
2. How can you get to Mendoza in the north?
3. Is there a room for a meeting of 8 people that you can use?
4. You want to have your onward flight to Asunción reconfirmed.
5. Can you book a flight to Rio Verde in the south?
6. How long does it take to get to the airport?
7. Your flight to Miami leaves at midnight. When should you leave the hotel? Where can you leave your luggage till then?
8. What time is dinner served in the hotel?
9. Is there a room you can use as an office in the hotel?
10. You want to book a taxi for 8 am tomorrow to the University.
11. You want to send a fax to your office in your country.
12. You want to change your room to one with a better view.
13. You want to go to Granada in the east. Can you get there by train? Can you book a room in a good hotel there?
14. You want to change $100 into pesos.
15. You need someone to type out some letters in English.
16. How do you get to the airport for your flight to Rio Verde?
17. You've been looking for the swimming pool in the garden.
18. You need to buy a toothbrush.
19. What time do you have to check out?
20. You want to reserve a room for your next visit in a month's time.

45 You are interested in the GR440 Screen Spy product that AntiSpy manufactures.
Call them and find out how much it costs and how quickly you can get one delivered.
Say that you are prepared to pay a cash deposit.
You can collect yourself from their warehouse in California.
There is no problem with getting an import licence.

46 Make a list of five or more regions or countries that are in competition with yours. Design a questionnaire to find out people's attitudes to the *less* attractive features of these regions *and* your own region.

Ask people which of these phrases describe each destination:

bad weather   too far away   too expensive
hard to reach   language problems   unfriendly, gloomy people
too crowded   no beaches   nothing for children to do
too quiet   bad food   no package tours available
other: .... (*please specify*) ....

47 Here are some tips for chairing the meeting:

1. Begin by stating the purpose of the meeting.
2. Give the name of the person you want to speak next.
3. Make sure everyone has a chance to give their views.
4. If someone is taking too long, say *Thank you* and name the next person who wants to speak.
5. If there is disagreement on any point, call for a vote.
6. Make sure one member of the group is keeping minutes: ask them to read out the notes at the end, if there's time.
7. Keep to the time limit: if necessary stop the discussion and summarize the conclusions and decisions you have come to.

48

```
NOTE FROM MR RICHARDSON
Pls send a letter to Naves Limon in C.R.
Find out:
        Are they satisfied with the order?
        Can we provide any after-sales advice?
Encourage repeat order.
```

49 You are the *personnel manager*.
These are some points you should try to raise in the meeting:

- new developments needed because of competition
- company is consulting and communicating with workers as always
- no delay in publishing details of new schemes
- we cannot make any promises about future developments

50 You are the manager of the Provence Restaurant (the best in town). Your menu includes fresh fish and vegetarian dishes.
Accept a booking for your private room for next Tuesday. You require a written confirmation of this by letter or telex (459879). As you already have another party arriving at 7.30, any further parties should arrive at 8 for 8.30. You need to know the *exact* number of places first thing on Tuesday (your early morning phone number is 015 454).

When the call is over, ask the student(s) who was/were listening to comment on your 'performance'. Then look at File 73.

51 You are still working in the head office of Medusa S.A.
Use your own name. Call the person you spoke to before in the subsidiary company.
You require some information about a company who are about to place an order. Make a note of all the details you need:

Company name: Triad International
address: ....
                   ....
                   ....

name of contact: Mr (or Miss?) Jean Barclay
last transaction: last May or June
payment record: ....

52

ORDERS	Customer: ADONIS SA		No: 118
Date	Order	Invoice	Date pd
9 Feb	65 jackets	272/02	5 March
20 May	12 ps gloves	589/05	10 June
1 October	500 ps spec.cttn overalls	365/10	

You work for Chimera GmbH. Your company sells its garments to wholesalers and companies and has had a large one-off order to supply Adonis SA with special cotton overalls. You have not yet received an outstanding payment for invoice 365/10 for the order of 500 pairs of special cotton overalls. The payment is 30 days overdue – today's date 15 December 19xx. (Now turn back to page 80.)

53 You are the EMPLOYEE or COURSE PARTICIPANT.
Imagine that you are being interviewed by your present boss or the course organizer about your progress in your course/work so far. Find out how well you have been doing and let your boss/the organiser know what you think of the work/course so far.

54 First you are the *employee* (later you will change roles).

1. You would like to bring up the subject of wanting to have more responsibility . . .
2. You aren't satisfied with what you have been doing so far . . .
3. You are looking for greater challenges . . .
4. You feel your qualifications and your experience mean that you need less supervision in your job . . .

Now change roles: take up the role of *manager*:

5. Several people in the department are under consideration by the management . . .
6. They are looking for someone who is prepared to show initiative and to work under the supervision of the personal assistant of the vice president / managing director . . .
7. The company is looking for someone who enjoys contact with people outside the company . . .
8. The company is looking for somebody who is prepared to travel a lot – and to be away from home sometimes at the weekends . . .

55
```
FROM: NAVES LIMON

WE ACKNOWLEDGE SAFE ARRIVAL OF TWO CONTAINERS, NOW
UNPACKED. BOTH VESSELS IN PRIME CONDITION. TKS FOR
SPEEDY AND FRIENDLY SERVICE. PLEASE NOTE: WE ASKED
FOR SIX COPIES OF HANDBOOK FOR EACH VESSEL, NOT SIX
ALTOGETHER. PLEASE SEND FURTHER SIX COPIES BY
FASTEST ROUTE.   BEST.
```

56 This is the telex you receive from John Granger:

```
+++
FROM: J. GRANGER

PLS SEND ACKNOWLEDGEMENT RECEIPT OF PAYMENT
FOR ORDER NO. 04276 SOONEST.

REGARDS, J. GRANGER
```

57 Recently you met Linda Green from the Accounts department of Light Leather Products. She was talking to you about her dealings with Nicole Boireau of Chaussures Chevalier. This is what she said:

'I've known Nicole for about a year. We've never had any serious problems till recently.

She sometimes takes a week to settle the account.

I don't like to overdo things so I only send one copy of the invoice.

Just recently I offered to extend credit for 30 days.

And we always maintain our prices once we have signed a contract.

We always allow her company discount if they pay punctually.

I never hear about the reasons for non-payment from her, unless I ring up myself.

If I know there might be difficulties, I delay sending the reminder to give her time.

Some months we have to send two reminders, because Nicole's so slow in paying.

But at least, I don't insist on Nicole paying in sterling. I think that is rather generous of me, because a lot of other suppliers do insist.'

Report this conversation to your partner, who has been talking to Nicole Boireau. Begin like this:
  Linda Green told me that . . .

58 You are on duty at the reception desk at the Hotel Miramar. Answer your guests' queries.

HOTEL MIRAMAR INFORMATION

- Domestic flights depart from National Airport (5 km from here) to other cities: Mendoza: 8.30 14.30 Granada: 10.30 17.30 Rio Verde: 12.00 18.15. (Allow 30 minutes by taxi + 45 minutes to check in.)
- There are no trains to Mendoza or Rio Verde, but there is a comfortable overnight sleeper to Granada, which departs at 11 p.m..
- You can reserve rooms at associate hotels in Granada and Mendoza through the computer.
- International flights depart from Simon Bolivar Airport (25 km from here). Allow 1 hour by taxi + 1 hour to check in.
- To reconfirm a flight, you need to have the ticket in your hand to do this.
- Taxis are normally always available outside the hotel. They cannot be booked in advance.
- breakfast 6.30–10 a.m. in the Atlantic Restaurant on the second floor up the stairs (ie first floor for Europeans);
- lunch in the Gaucho Grill or Atlantic Restaurant 1–3.30 p.m.;
- dinner in the Gaucho Grill, Atlantic

Restaurant (8–11.30 p.m.) or RoofTop Room (20th floor) 10 p.m.–3 a.m. RoofTop Room has a cabaret and dancing.
- There are 3 private office suites/meeting rooms in the hotel for up to 12 people.
- The services of an English-speaking secretary are available on an hourly basis from the Anglo Agency (24 hours notice). The hourly rate is 4000 pesos. Photocopies can be made here in the hotel office. Telexes can be sent and received here, but not fax.
- The swimming pool (open from 6 a.m. to 7 p.m.) is on the roof. Towels available from the attendant (always on duty – press the bell to call him).
- Checking out time is 11 a.m. Luggage can be stored for guests who have checked out.
- Rooms with a sea view are $65, rooms overlooking the garden are $55. You have only one $65 room available now, but several for next month.
- Today's exchange rate is $1 = **595** pesos.

59

You are the proprietor of Agencia Léon of Mexico City.
Make sure AntiSpy answers these questions:

- Are batteries rechargeable on 220 & 110 volt and both 50 & 60
  cycles (Hz)?
- Will it operate directly from mains if batteries are low?
- Can it interfere with other phones in same building?
- Ask DDP price for 10 to be shipped immediately.

When you have finished, look at File 69.

60

You are on duty at the information desk at Manchester Airport one
Friday morning in April. Help the people who enquire about the
flights shown on this timetable:

DESTINATION	flight no.	departs	arrives	DESTINATION	flight no.	departs	arrives
ABERDEEN:	BA5690	08.35	09.35	LARNACA	CY 457	09.50	17.25
	SM 301	09.15	11.00	LONDON Heathrow	BA 4403	06.50	07.40
	BA 5694	12.25	13.50		BA 4413	07.45	08.35
AMSTERDAM	KL 154	08.55	11.00		BA 4423	08.30	09.20
ANTWERP	BRAX 102	08.40	11.55		BA 4443	10.00	10.50
BELFAST	BA 5492	07.45	08.30		BA 4453	12.00	12.50
	LC 255	08.50	09.55		DA 193	12.30	13.20
BIRMINGHAM	BA 5681	09.15	09.45	LONDON Gatwick	BR 982	07.00	07.55
BRUSSELS	SN 618	08.50	11.00		BR 984	08.45	09.40
CHICAGO	AA 55	11.10	13.35		BR 986	11.45	12.40
COPENHAGEN	BA 994	07.30	10.15	MADRID	BA 888	10.45	14.15
DUBLIN	BA 844	08.05	08.50	MILAN	BAAZ 912	10.30	13.35
	EI 205	10.20	11.05	MUNICH	LH 077	10.30	14.55
DUNDEE	SM 301	09.15	10.25	NEW YORK	BA 183	14.00	16.15
DÜSSELDORF	LH 077	10.30	12.50	OSLO	DA 842	10.50	14.30
EDINBURGH	LC 561	07.20	08.30	PAPHOS	CY 457	09.30	15.55
	LC 563	10.25	11.35	PARIS	AF 963	07.30	09.45
FRANKFURT	BA 962	07.45	10.25	ROTTERDAM	BRAX 102	08.40	11.20
GENEVA	BA 942	11.00	13.45	SINGAPORE	SQ 037	13.00	13.30
GLASGOW	BA 5642	07.30	08.20	SOUTHAMPTON	BA 5681	09.15	10.50
	LC 563	10.25	12.10	TENERIFE	BY 708	09.50	14.00
GUERNSEY	GE 727	11.30	13.00	TORONTO	AC 841	12.35	14.50
ISLE OF MAN	JE 322	08.30	09.15	ZURICH	SR 843	08.10	11.05
JERSEY	VF 725	11.30	13.00				

AA	American Airlines Inc	CY	Cyprus Airways	LH	Lufthansa
AC	Air Canada	DA	Dan Air	SM	Air Ecosse
AF	Air France	EI	Aer Lingus	SN	Sabena
BA	British Airways	GE	Guernsey Airlines	SQ	Singapore Airlines
BAAZ	British Airways/Alitalia	JE	Manx Airlines	SR	Swissair
BRAX	British Caledonian/Connectair	KL	KLM-Royal Dutch Airlines	VF	British Air Ferries
BY	Britannia Airways	LC	Loganair VF		

Latest check-in times:
BA ("Super Shuttle") to Heathrow: 10 mins; domestic: 15 mins; Belfast 30 mins;
international 20 mins; intercontinental 45 mins
Boarding times: 15 mins before departure time for all flights

61 Apologize or complain to your colleague because:
- You have forgotten to phone Los Angeles and now it's too late as it's after office hours for them.
- Your colleague should have checked with you before placing the order with the people in Toronto.
- You have left a file at home – it contains the documents your colleague needs to have for a meeting today.
- You didn't send the quote to Garfield International yesterday, and now you may have lost the order.
- Your colleague shouldn't get back to the office late after lunch – you always have to answer the phone for him or her.

62 Make a list of five or more regions or countries that are in competition with yours. Design a questionnaire to find out about people's attitudes to your region *and* to its competitors.
The people you ask should rate each destination for its qualities on a scale 1 to 10 (or 1 to 5 – if you prefer):

good value for money	easy to get to	good facilities
good entertainment	health and sport	peace and quiet
friendliness	hospitality	wilderness
culture	beautiful scenery	uniqueness

Ask them to describe each place in one sentence like this:
'When I think of __, I think of __'
(e.g. 'When I think of S__ I think of cold winds and a flat landscape'.)

63 Sales Professionals only!
Earn thirty-five to fifty thousand dollars first year commission. National Revenue Corporation is seeking highly qualified professional/sales persons to become Executive Consultants and market our urgently needed cash flow management services . . .

64 You are the reception manager at the Hotel Cambridge. Someone will call to confirm his/her reservations. The computer confirms that the caller has a firm reservation for a twin-bedded room and a single room from tomorrow for 3 nights. There is a trade fair this week and all your single rooms are fully booked for the next ten days.

There are one or two doubles available. You will only hold reserved rooms till 9 pm unless you have confirmed reservations by American Express or Diner's Club. Note the caller's name and the name of the person who will occupy the single room. Ask for a contact phone number. The Coffee Shop serves meals till 2 am.

When the call is over, ask the student(s) who was/were listening to comment on your 'performance'. That is the end of this activity.

65 These are your department's suggestions:
— more flowers and plants
— more flexibility about taking time off
— better lighting and heating
— more pictures or posters on the walls
Add your own ideas . . .

66 Use your own name. You are still working for the same subsidiary of Medusa S.A. You'll receive a call. The information the caller requires may be in these files:

Company name:	Triad International ltd
address:	133 Pembroke Way
	Ipswich, UK
	IP4 7GJ
telephone	0473 57830
name of contact:	Miss Jean Barclay
last transaction:	May 31 19—
payment record	excellent: they always pay on time

Company name:	Triad International S.A.
address:	67 boulevard Gramsci
	23098 Bordeaux Cédex
	France
name of contact:	Mr Jean Barclay
last transaction:	June 3 19—
payment record:	Poor: they need 2 reminders and can't be relied on

67

You are Mr/Ms Suarez, in charge of buying supplies for your firm. You met Mr/Ms Tanaka at a trade fair in his/her country last year. He/she supplies a product you may be interested in. You haven't heard from him/her since then.

Next Thursday you are free for lunch but have to be back in the office at 2.30 for a meeting. If you are asked to recommend a restaurant, suggest a place you *really* do like in your own town.

When the call is over, ask the student(s) who was/were listening to comment on your 'performance'. Then look at File 109.

68

You are Clive Bullock (or Carol Thomas) and you're the Reservations Manager at the Stafford (or Ritz) Hotel.
BEFORE YOU START, look at the points below – make sure you cover all of them. Make notes during the call.

1. Answer the phone, say hello and introduce yourself (name of hotel, your name and function). Ask how you can help.
2. Note down the caller's name and use the name during the call.
3. Check if the last date is the leaving date or 'night of' date.
4. Find out what rooms the caller requires.
5. For the week they require you have only 1 single available.
   Point out that a single is much smaller than a double. Doubles for sole occupancy would be more comfortable.
6. Quote your rates per night:
   STAFFORD: £39 single; £69 or £79 double
   (RITZ: £99 single; £149 or £169 double)
7. The top price rooms have a balcony. All double rooms have twin beds, bath and shower, colour TV, direct dialling telephones.
8. Confirm that the rooms requested are available.
9. Explain that the room rate includes full English breakfast.
10. Ask for the caller's name, address and contact phone number.
11. Ask for written confirmation by telex or letter. Explain that you will send your written confirmation. The telex or letter should state time of arrival.
12. Explain that all your rooms are quiet.
13. Explain that only rooms with balcony have a view of the park.
14. Confirm details of booking. Read out the notes you have made to make sure you have understood the details correctly.
15. Say goodbye.

69

You work in the export sales department of AntiSpy Products. Answer the phone and give the caller any information he or she requires. Consult your print-out in File 115.

70

You are Jean Meyer, René van Hoorn's assistant. You'll receive a call from Mr Müller's assistant or colleague.
Use this information:

- May 26th would be the best day for a meeting with Mr Müller – René is free from 11 am to 4 pm that day.
- Find out how long Mr Müller needs with Mr van Hoorn.
- On May 27th René has a meeting from 8.30 am that goes on till 12, but he is free for lunch that day.
- In the afternoon of May 27, René has an appointment with M. Janvier from Azimov S.A. at 3 pm.
- Suggest that Mr Müller has lunch in the office canteen.
- The best restaurants are in the city centre and there wouldn't be time for Mr van Hoorn to get there and back on May 27th.
- Find out if Mr Müller would like to eat at a typical Belgian family restaurant: there is a nice little place round the corner.
- Find out if Mr Müller is likely to change his mind again.

71

You are the OBSERVER.
As you listen to the interview, make notes on these points:

What impression did each person give?
If they were nervous, how did this affect their performance?
Were there too many Yes/No questions?
Which questions did they answer badly?
Which questions did they answer well?
What advice would you give them for their next real interview?

72

(You are student C.) Advise A and B how to solve *their* problems.
Then tell your partners your own problem:

You are working in the orders department with a colleague.
Originally you both shared the orders on a fifty-fifty basis. In the past few weeks you have noticed that you have been responsible for the processing of more than two thirds of the orders dealt with. You feel the workload is unfairly divided.

Ask your partners for advice. When your problem has been discussed, advise D how to solve his or her problem. When all these problems have been discussed, look at File 93.

73

Listen to your partners' phone call and then comment on it. After you've given your comments you'll be at the end of this activity.

74

You are John Granger, chief clerk for Vesta Vehicles. Listen to what the assistant clerk from Universal Utensils asks you. Then mention these points:

1. You have no record of the delivery of the items.
2. Apologize for the non-payment. Explain that the delivery note has not been received by your department yet. You think there may be a simple explanation for this. Perhaps the delivery note has not been passed on at your end, someone might be ill, it may have got lost . . .
3. Mention that for December's order you received 25 gross of switches, but had actually ordered 35 gross. Your accounts department automatically paid the invoice which was sent without checking it against the delivery note. It was only afterwards that you noticed the discrepancy.

75

Clerk typist
A leading manufacturer
of underwater TV
viewing systems
and remote control vehicles
has an opening for a sharp individual
with the ability to learn quickly
and accurately . . .

76

You are calling to book three rooms at the Stafford Hotel (or the Ritz) from 9 to 15 May.
BEFORE YOU START, look at the points below – make sure you cover all of them. Make notes during the call.

1. Introduce yourself (your own real name and company).
2. Find out if any rooms are available from 9 May to 15 May.
3. Explain your requirements: the rooms are for Mr Hall, Ms Castel and Mr and Mrs Holzger, who require twin beds.
4. Find out the cost of single and double rooms.
5. Find out the difference between rooms at different prices.
6. Book two doubles at the lower price and one at the higher price.
7. Find out whether the rates include breakfast.
8. Ask for quiet rooms – not overlooking main road.
9. Ask for rooms with view of park.
10. Decide whether to have all three rooms with balcony + view.
11. Ask them to send you four copies of the hotel brochure.

77

Mr George James
Managing Director
Alan and James Ltd
Quality House
77–81 London Road
Bristol
BL5 9AR
Great Britain

Ms Alison Freeman
Marketing Co-ordinator
United Packaging Inc.
11 East Shore Drive
Green Bay
Wisconsin
WI 53405
USA

Mr R.G. Flinders
Sales Manager
Independent Products Pty
18 Canberra Way
Liverpool
NSW 2170
Australia

Miss J.V. Bernstein
Candex Convention Organizer
Dominion Centre
80 Prince of Wales Drive
Ottawa
Ontario
KT5 1AQ
Canada

78

MEMORANDUM

From:	The Managing Director	*for*	*please*
To:	Personnel Manager	*ACTION*	*DISPLAY*
	Division A	*COMMENT*	*FILE*
Date:	27 April 19—	*INFORMATION*	*RETURN*
		DISCUSSION	*PASS TO:*

....

Subject: Installation of coffee machines

The Board is thinking of installing automatic coffee
machines in the offices of each division. Before we do
this we need to know:

1 how much use our staff will make of them
2 how many we would need
3 whether time now used for making coffee would be saved.

Can you provide us with your views on
– how the staff will react to the idea and
– how we can deal with the union on the matter.

If possible, I would like to receive your report before
the next Board Meeting on 1 June.

Handling Information	AIKASHINKO AWB 121-18107600 OSAKA via NARITA					Keep packets dry. Notify: Kaiji Kentei Kyokai 2-Chome, Hanamitsu-cho Kobe, Japan	
No of Pieces RCP	Gross Weight	kg lb	Rate Class / Commodity Item No.	Chargeable Weight	Rate / Charge	Total	Nature and Quantity of Goods (incl. Dimensions or Volume)
1	15.5	K	N	15.5	2.050	. . . .	Plugs
1	. . .	K	N	23.5	2.050	. . . . . .	Plugs
1	20.8	K	N	. . .	2.050	43.050	Electrical sockets
1	. . . .	K	N	20.0	2.050	. . . . .	Electrical sockets
3	0.2	K	C	. . .	. . . .	0.525	Advertising displays
		K					
		K					
		K					
7	79.2					. . . . . .	

Prepaid / Weight Charge / Collect / Other Charges

80

You are the assistant clerk from Universal Utensils. These are the things you should refer to in your phone call to Mr Granger:

1. A revised price list / increase has come into force since the order was taken (used to be $1.60). As is well known your price lists always say subject to change . . .
2. Ask him if he has received the delivery note. Normally, if you overcharge a customer by mistake you send a credit note. At the end of the month you send each customer a statement which shows all the transactions in that month.
3. As we are dealing with a regular customer you say that credit can be granted. Ask for written confirmation about the overbilling for the outstanding sum.

81

You are the BOSS or the COURSE ORGANIZER.
Imagine that you are interviewing a member of your staff / a course participant about his or her progress in the course/job so far. Give your opinion of his or her performance and find out what he or she thinks of the work/course so far. Perhaps start like this:
'Come in. I'd like to talk to you about your work / the course so far . . .'

You are the *senior worker representative*.
These are some points you should try to raise in the meeting:
  – ask why the news has been given so late
  – fears that further job losses will follow
– women are affected most
– workers are not opposed to new technology – are future-oriented

83

Begin by playing this role and ask your partners to give you advice:

You are the personnel manager of a small company. The holiday plan is normally left to the employees to arrange among themselves. This time a large number of people want to take the same two weeks in August. Some members of staff want you to decide, but you believe in each department deciding democratically. What should you do?

When your partners have discussed your problem, advise them how to solve their problems. When you've all finished, discuss what you did with the rest of the class.

84

First you are the *manager* (later you will change roles).

1 You have the employee in view for promotion . . .
2 There is however a problem . . .
3 In order to comply with your request . . .
4 The management expect the person in line for promotion to go on a training course (with other prospective candidates for promotion) . . .

Now change roles: take up the role of *the employee*:

5 You are prepared to change jobs if necessary . . .
6 You feel you are not working to the full limit of your capacities . . .
7 You take over the job of department deputy head . . .
8 You would like to spend more time with your family, if possible . . .

85

Listen to your partners' phone call and then comment on it. Then, after you have given them your comments, look at 6. (In a group of four, Student A should look at 73 and D at 6.)

86

FROM NAVES LIMON
TKS FOR YOUR QUOTATION NO 0067. WE WISH TO ORDER TWO
PB 5000 AT YOUR QUOTED TOTAL CIF PRICE OF ONE
THOUSAND EIGHT HUNDRED AND SEVEN THOUSAND, EIGHT
HUNDRED AND FIFTY DOLLARS INCLUDING SPECIAL ANCHORS.

ONE CUSTOMER ALREADY WAITING ALREADY HAS PAID US
DEPOSIT. PLEASE SHIP AS SOON AS POSSIBLE. CONFIRM
DEFINITE DELIVERY DATE TO PUERTO LIMON. PLEASE CONFIRM
12 MONTH GUARANTEE, REPLACEMENT PARTS BY AIRFREIGHT,
AS PROMISED BY MR RICHARDSON. AWAITING YOUR REPLY.
BEST,
NAVES LIMON

87

Dear Mr Brown,

I noted with interest your advertisement in today's Guardian.

You will see from the enclosed curriculum vitae that I have five years experience as a PA, three of which have been in the field of marketing and public relations. My responsibilities have included all types of secretarial work, arranging and attending presentations, working with clients and solving problems that arise.

Although I have an excellent relationship with my present employers, I feel that my prospects with them are limited and that there would be more scope for my talents with a larger, more dynamic company.

If you consider that my qualifications and experience are suitable, I should be available for interview at any time.

Yours sincerely,

88

The estimated costs of some of the proposals are:
- Rebuilding toilets and showers: £4500
- New tables and chairs for canteen: £750
- Safety work on roof garden: £950
- Staff parties/picnics: no cost to the company

89

During the interview, make notes on each candidate's experience or potential under these headings:

Working under stress
Dealing with people in English
Travel
Work experience
Health

Working with other people
Administration
Education and training
Personality
Present job

90

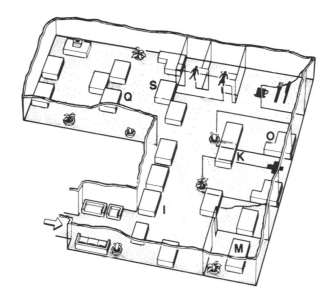

91

You are Mr/Ms Peterson, in charge of shipping customer's orders and answering queries about delayed shipments.

These orders have been held up for the reasons given:
ARG 4581 Delay due to rejection by quality control.
Revised shipment date: 30th of this month
RAJ 4581 Delay due to staff sickness in production dept.
Revised shipment date some time next week. Airfreight at no extra charge.

When the call is over, ask the student(s) who was/were listening to comment on your 'performance'. Then look at File 85.

92

Discuss these ideas with your partner. Your partner has some additional ideas. Which of these things do you consider to be the most important?

1. You can plan things before you write them down.
2. You have more time to take in and understand information if it's written down.
3. People take something that is written more seriously.
4. Many people can read the same information at different times.
5. Writing is safer from a legal point of view.
6. Writing things down allows you to change the facts a little to suit your own purposes.
7. Most people only believe what they have read.

93 Begin by helping **A** and **B** to solve their problems. Then play this role yourself:

You are trainee personal assistant to the accounts manager. You have very good prospects of promotion, as the personal assistant is retiring in three months' time. You have been working for the company for about 6 months, when you get the offer of a job in a rival company for a slightly higher salary than now. The prospects are also quite good. But you get on well with your present boss and your other colleagues. What should you do?

When your problem has been discussed, advise **D** how to solve his or her problem. When you have all finished, discuss what you did with the rest of the class.

94 Your partner has the other half of these jumbled instructions about how to make coffee with the machine. Work together to number the order in which you would explain what the correct amount of coffee is and how to make it. Don't forget to number the diagrams (figs. 1–7).

THE CORRECT QUANTITY OF COFFEE
Put 1 or 2 cups under the water outlet openings (fig. 4 and 5).
NB. If you use a single cup put it in the middle under both water outlet openings.
Too much coffee can affect the working of the filter.
1 spoon of coffee is sufficient for 1 cup (125 ml) of coffee:
2 spoons of coffee are sufficient for 2 cups (250 ml) of coffee.
Spread the coffee evenly in the filter (see fig. 1 and 2).
Never use more than 2 level measure spoonfuls.

WATER (fig. 3):
You can use the cups in which you are going to drink the coffee as a measure.

95 You are the *general manager*. You also chair the meeting (unless there is a fifth member in the group).
These are some points you should try to raise in the meeting:

– changes in product range
– productivity increase is necessary
– re-training possibilities for all workers
– no need to reduce number of workers

96 You are Jim Dale, Sales Manager of Ramco Batteries, Manchester. You are about to announce a new lightweight zinc cadmium battery, the RAMCO Hercules, especially designed for electric vehicles.

• Find out about Broadway's specification. Your new Hercules meets this perfectly.
• Prototypes are available now for testing.
• You are now tooling up for production to begin next week.
• Quote firm shipping date of 4 weeks from today.
• Say that you can deliver at 10% off Arcolite's price.

97 MEMORANDUM

To: All members of staff, Northern Branch
From: K.L.J.
Date: 5 December 19—
Subject: PERSONAL COMPUTERS

The board urgently requires feedback on our
experience with PCs in Northern Branch.
I need to know, for my report:

1. What you personally use your PC for and your
   reasons for doing this. If you are doing work
   that was formerly done by other staff, please
   justify this.
2. What software you use. Please name the programs.
3. How many hours per day you spend actually using
   it.
4. How your PC has not come up to your expectations.
5. What unanticipated uses you have found for your
   PC, that others may want to share.

Please FAX this information directly to me by 5p.m.
on WEDNESDAY 7 December.

If you have any queries, please contact my
assistant, Jane Simmonds, who will be visiting you
on Tuesday, 6 December. Thank you for your help.

98

Most Credits are fairly similar in appearance and contain the
following details (numbers correspond to those in the example):

1. The type of Credit (Revocable or Irrevocable).
2. The name and address of the exporter (beneficiary).
3. The name and address of the importer (accreditor).
4. The amount of the Credit, in sterling or a foreign currency.
5. The name of the party on whom the bills of exchange are to be drawn, and
   whether they are to be at sight or of a particular tenor.
6. The terms of contract and shipment (i.e. whether 'ex-works', 'FOB', 'CIF',
   etc).
7. Precise instructions as to the documents against which payment is to be made.
8. A brief description of the goods covered by the Credit (too much detail should
   be avoided as it may give rise to errors which can cause delay).
9. Shipping details, including whether transhipments are allowed. Also recorded
   should be the latest date for shipment and the names of the ports of shipment
   and discharge. (It may be in the best interest of the exporter for shipment to be
   allowed 'from any UK port' so that he has a choice if, for example, some ports
   are affected by strikes. The same applies for the port of discharge.)
10. Whether the Credit is available for one or several shipments.
11. The expiry date.

99 This telex has arrived from Uniplex s.r.l. in Pisa:

```
+++
THANK YOU VERY MUCH FOR THE ORDER FOR 45 (FORTY-FIVE) X 100
METRE REELS OF 40 (FORTY) MILLIMETRE OF OUR MCL 88 CABLE.
I CONFIRM THAT THIS IS AVAILABLE EX-STOCK AND THAT WE CAN SHIP
THIS AT THE END OF THIS MONTH. WE SHALL BEGIN PACKING TOMORROW.
I AM CONFIDENT THAT YOU WILL BE IMPRESSED WITH THE QUALITY OF
THIS PRODUCT. WE ARE PLEASED TO BE DOING BUSINESS WITH YOU AND
LOOK FORWARD TO CONTINUING CO-OPERATION IN THE FUTURE.
OUR INVOICE FOLLOWS BY AIRMAIL.
BEST WISHES.
PIERO CONTI, EXPORT MANAGER, UNIPLEX, PISA.
```

These are your records on the computer about the two firms:

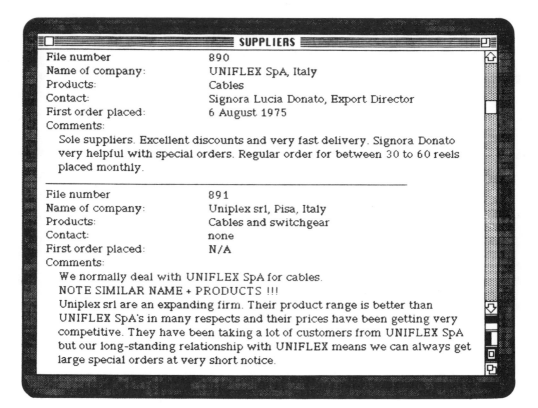

SUPPLIERS

File number — 890
Name of company: — UNIFLEX SpA, Italy
Products: — Cables
Contact: — Signora Lucia Donato, Export Director
First order placed: — 6 August 1975
Comments:
Sole suppliers. Excellent discounts and very fast delivery. Signora Donato very helpful with special orders. Regular order for between 30 to 60 reels placed monthly.

File number — 891
Name of company: — Uniplex srl, Pisa, Italy
Products: — Cables and switchgear
Contact: — none
First order placed: — N/A
Comments:
We normally deal with UNIFLEX SpA for cables.
NOTE SIMILAR NAME + PRODUCTS !!!
Uniplex srl are an expanding firm. Their product range is better than UNIFLEX SpA's in many respects and their prices have been getting very competitive. They have been taking a lot of customers from UNIFLEX SpA but our long-standing relationship with UNIFLEX means we can always get large special orders at very short notice.

100 These are your department's suggestions:
- more comfortable chairs
- a better coffee machine
- proper plates in the canteen instead of plastic
- more car parking spaces
Add your own ideas . . . .

101

102

Begin by listening to **A**'s problem. Help to solve it by giving
advice. Then play this role yourself:

You are the personal secretary to the managing director. He keeps
asking you to have dinner with him, but he is married and you do
not want to get personally involved. If you reject him, this may affect your chances
of promotion. What should you do?

When your partners have solved your problem, advise **C** and **D** how to deal with
their problems. When you have all finished, discuss what you did with the rest of
the class.

103

```
FROM ALPHA MARINE
THE GOODS YOU REQUIRE ARE NOW AVAILABLE FROM STOCK. WE
WILL DELIVER IN OUR OWN TRANSPORT ON 19 AUGUST. PLEASE
ADVISE IF GOODS REQUIRED MORE URGENTLY. YOU COULD
ARRANGE COLLECTION EX-WORKS BY YOUR OWN CARRIER IF
DESIRED. REGARDS.

FROM LYSANDER FREIGHT AND SHIPPING
WE HAVE ARRANGED FOR TWO FORTY-FOOT OPEN TOP CONTAINERS
TO BE DELIVERED TO YOUR FACTORY TO ARRIVE AT 9 AM ON
16 AUGUST. THEY WILL BE COLLECTED FOR ONWARD SHIPMENT
TO DOCKS ON 23 AUGUST IN TIME FOR BOOKED PASSAGE ON 30
AUGUST ON M/V CARIBBEAN STAR TO PUERTO LIMON. ARRIVING
PUERTO LIMON 10 OR 11 SEPTEMBER. PLEASE CONFIRM THAT
THIS ARRANGEMENT IS AGREEABLE. BEST REGARDS.
```

Handling Information	AIKASHINKO AWB 121-...					Keep packets dry.　　　Notify: Kaiji Kentei Kyokai 1-4, 2-Chome, Hanamitsu-cho Kobe, Japan	
No of Pieces RCP	Gross Weight	kg lb	Rate Class / Commodity Item No.	Chargeable Weight	Rate / Charge	Total	Nature and Quantity of Goods (incl. Dimensions or Volume)
1	...	K	N	15.5	2.050	31.775	Plugs
1	23.2	K	N	....	....	48.175	Plugs
1	...	K	N	21.0	2.050	......	Electrical sockets
1	19.5	K	N	....	2.050	41.000	Electrical sockets
3	0.2	K	C	0.5	1.050	......	Advertising displays
		K					
		K					
		K					
7	..					164.525	

Prepaid / Weight Charge / Collect / Other Charges

105

Call Agencia Léon in Mexico. Reassure them that you have consulted your technical department and they confirm that:

Batteries are rechargeable on all voltages.
A universal plug is fitted for mains operation and recharging. It can interfere with FM radio in the same room but *not* with any other phones. Consult your print-out in File 115 to quote price and delivery.

When you have finished, look at File 45.

106

Look at this price list for hi-fi equipment. As you can see, some of the prices have been increased or reduced.
Ask your partner about prices on his or her list and find out which prices have been changed. Alter your own list accordingly.

LXI 15-inch Speakers	~~$169.95~~	**$174.99**
LXI 10-inch Speakers	$ 79.95	
Stereo Headphones	~~$ 69.95~~	**$ 59.99**
Cassette Deck – Dolby controls	~~$169.95~~	**$152.50**
LXI Cassette Deck	$149.95	
Direct-drive Turntable	~~$149.95~~	**$135.50**
Belt-drive Turntable	$119.95	
AM/FM Stereo Tuner	$499.95	
Mini "Go-Anywhere" Phones	$ 29.95	
Stereo Cassette Player/Recorder	$279.95	
Mini Compact Stereo System	~~$129.95~~	**$119.99**
Stereo Cassette Tape Deck	$169.95	

107

CURRICULUM VITAE

Name:	MARY BRENDA SCOTT
Address:	44 London Road, Winchester SO16 7HJ
Telephone:	0962 8890 (home) 0703 77877 (work)
Date of Birth:	30 August 1967
Marital status:	single

EDUCATION

Churchill Comprehensive School, Basingstoke	1978–1983
Winchester Technical College	1983–1985

QUALIFICATIONS

C.S.E.	Maths, English French, Geography, History, Chemistry	1983
G.C.E.	'O' Level Commerce, Economics, Spanish	1984
BTEC National	Secretarial Practice, Office Practice	1985

EXPERIENCE

Office assistant	Totton Engineering, Totton	1984–1985
Secretary to Sales Director	Totton Engineering, Totton	1985–1986
Personal Assistant to Export Manager	Millbank Foods, Southampton	1986 to date

My work with Millbank Foods has involved responsibility for giving instructions to junior staff and dealing with clients and suppliers in person and on the telephone. I have accompanied the Export Manager to Food Trade fairs in Germany, France and the USA.

OTHER INFORMATION

I speak and write French and Spanish quite well (intermediate level). I am now taking an evening course in German conversation.

OTHER ACTIVITIES AND INTERESTS

I play club basketball regularly and I sing and play guitar with a local country and western band.

REFERENCES

Mr S.J. Grant, Personnel Manager, Millbank Foods, 34–42 South Dock Drive, Southampton SO8 9QT

Mr John Robinson, Sales Director, Totton Engineering, Cadnam Street, Totton SO23 4GT

Miss P.L. MacPherson, Head Teacher, Churchill Comprehensive School, Independence Way, Basingstoke BA8 9UJ

108

```
+++
ATTENTION: JACQUELINE LARUE

THANK YOU FOR YOUR TELEX. WE WOULD LIKE 3 ROOMS ON THE EXECUTIVE
FLOOR AT 139 CANADIAN DOLLARS FOR THE NIGHTS OF 12, 13, 14 JUNE.
WE WILL BE CHECKING OUT ON 15 JUNE. OUR ARRIVAL TIME AT VANCOUVER
INTERNATIONAL AIRPORT IS 22.15 AND THE FLIGHT NUMBER IS LH 086.
PLEASE ARRANGE FOR US TO BE PICKED UP BY LIMOUSINE. THE DINERS
CLUB CARD NUMBER IS 334 0098 1245 AND THE EXPIRY DATE IS 23
NOVEMBER 19--. PLEASE CONFIRM THIS RESERVATION.
REGARDS
FRED MEIER
+++
```

Same message using common abbreviations:

```
+++
ATTN: JACQUELINE LARUE

TKS FOR YR TLX. WE WD LIKE 3 ROOMS ON THE EXECUTIVE FLOOR AT 139
CANADIAN DOLLARS FOR THE NIGHTS OF 12, 13, 14 JUNE. WE WILL BE
CHECKING OUT ON 15 JUNE. OUR ARR TIME AT VANCOUVER INTERNATIONAL
AIRPORT IS 22.15 AND THE FLT NO IS LH 086. PLEASE ARRANGE FOR US
TO BE PICKED UP BY LIMOUSINE. THE DINERS CLUB CARD NO IS 334 0098
1245 AND THE EXPIRY DATE IS 23 NOV 19--. PLS CFM THIS
RESERVATION.
RGDS
FRED MEIER
+++
```

109

Listen to your partners' phone call and then comment on it. Then, after you have given them your comments, look at 43. (In a group of four, Student B should look at 43 and A at 85.)

110

You are the *worker representative for health and safety.*
These are some points you should try to raise in the meeting:

- ask whether work will become more stressful than before
- office staff fear their work may also become more boring
- introduction of computers and VDUs can bring difficulties
- guarantee needed that working conditions will not be negatively affected

111

CAREER HISTORY

NAME IN FULL	George Guy Michaelides
PRESENT ADDRESS	45 Richmond Road, Colchester, Essex CO4 2JK
TELEPHONE NUMBER	0453 25982 (home) 0453 8/96/ (daytime)
DATE OF BIRTH	7th April 1950
NATIONALITY	British
MARITAL STATUS	Married, 2 children (7 and 4 yrs.)

EDUCATION AND QUALIFICATIONS

1961–70	Northgate Grammar School, Ipswich, GCE 8 'O' levels; 4 'A' levels (French, Maths, Chemistry, Physics)
1970–74	University of London BSc Mechanical Engineering
Professional	Member of the Institute of Mechanical Engineers

EXPERIENCE AND ACHIEVEMENTS

1984– to date: Neptune Engineering Ltd, Quay Road, Poole (manufacturers of marine engines and equipment)
Export Sales Manager responsible to Managing Director for sales of engines to over 40 countries in Europe and overseas. Staff of 35 representatives and 15 office staff. Also responsible for budgeting, recruitment and training of staff. Built up sales from £13M to over £45M. Set up and trained sales teams to cover markets outside EEC.

1977–84: Poseidon Shipping S.A., Piraeus, Greece (manufacturers and repairers of cargo vessels)
Sales Manager responsible to owners for contracts with shipowners in all countries outside Greece. Staff of 4 representatives and 4 office staff. Built up sales by over 250%. Researched and established new markets in Britain, Japan and over 20 other countries.

1974–77: Trident Engines, Manchester Road, Salford (manufacturers of heavy-duty diesel engines and transmissions)
Trainee sales engineer/Assistant Export Sales Manager responsible to Sales Manager for sales to France, Germany and Greece.

OTHER INFORMATION

1985– to date: Presentations at trade exhibitions in EEC countries
Technical articles in journals and conference papers
Fluent French and Greek (both spoken and written); good spoken German; reasonable spoken Italian and Spanish

112 **table assembly instructions**

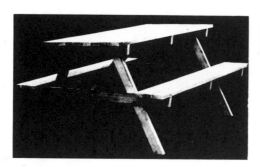

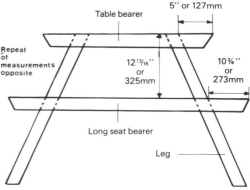

Table bearer

5″ or 127mm

Repeat
of
measurements
opposite

12¹³⁄₁₆″
or
325mm

10¾″
or
273mm

Long seat bearer

Leg

113

ORDERS	Customer: BRIMO SPA		No: 287
Date	Order	Invoice	Date pd
15 March	15 bales	AC 96	17 April
25 July	20 bales	BR 87	pd
25 Oct	100 bales	UN 42	

You work for Adonis SA. Your company produces yarn to sell to fabric manufacturers and has had a large one-off order to supply Brimo SpA. You have not yet received an outstanding payment for invoice/order UN 42 for 100 bales of first-class cotton yarn. The payment is 30 days overdue – today's date 15 December 19xx. (Now turn back to page 80.)

114

You are Mr Müller's assistant or colleague. When Mr Müller returns and sees the letter, he tells you that he is now no longer free on the 24th. He asks you to phone René or Jean to change the appointment.

- Give your name and say you're ringing on behalf of Mr Müller.
- Apologize and explain the situation: Mr Müller has had to delay his arrival in Belgium. He won't be there till the 27th.
- Ask if the appointment can be changed to May 27.
- Let Jean know that Mr Müller will need at least an hour in the office, plus time over lunch if possible.
- If OK, invite both René *and Jean* to lunch with Mr Müller.
- Ask Jean to book a table for three at very good restaurant, as he or she knows better which are good.
- Say that you will send a telex to confirm this arrangement, but that the agreed time and date are now 'definite'.

115

<u>AntiSpy Products Inc</u>

STOCK POSITION AND PRICES   APRIL 7, 19--

CJ 4000 P BUG DETECTOR
STOCK NOW: 45
NEXT DELIVERY TO WAREHOUSE: JUN 15 QUANTITY: 100
LIST PRICE: $359 CIF
DISCOUNTS: 5+ 20%   10+ 25%

LR 44 "OCTOPUS" TELEPHONE SCRAMBLER
STOCK NOW: 9
NEXT DELIVERY TO WAREHOUSE: AUG 15 QUANTITY: 300
LIST PRICE: $299 CIF
DISCOUNTS: 5+ 20%   10+ 25%
NOTES: CUSTOMER MUST ACQUIRE IMPORT LICENSE FOR THIS
PRODUCT (CCCN 0303 8100)

SP 700 SCREEN PROTECTOR
STOCK NOW: 75
NEXT DELIVERY TO WAREHOUSE: MAY 30 QUANTITY: 500
LIST PRICE: $299 CIF
OFFER PRICES TO MAY 1ST: $199 OR $499 FOR SIX
NOTES: CUSTOMER MUST SPECIFY SIZE AND MAKE OF SCREENS TO
BE FITTED
NORMAL DISCOUNTS DO NOT APPLY BEFORE MAY 1ST

GR 440 SCREEN SPY
LIST PRICE: $2950 FOB AIRPORT
AVAILABLE TO SPECIAL ORDER ONLY, CASH WITH ORDER.
CUSTOMER MUST PROVIDE IMPORT LICENSE (CCCN 4102 2000).
READY FOR SHIPMENT DATE: 12 MONTHS FROM DATE OF ORDER

116 This telex has just arrived from Mr Reynard:

THANK YOU FOR YOUR LETTER OF MAY 20. I WAS VERY SORRY TO HEAR ABOUT
YOUR PROBLEMS WITH OUR SERVICE AGENTS. I HAD NO IDEA THAT YOU WERE
IN ANY WAY DISSATISFIED.
IF YOU HAD LET ME KNOW EARLIER, I COULD HAVE INVESTIGATED THIS
IMMEDIATELY. OUR SERVICE AGENTS IN YOUR COUNTRY ARE NORMALLY MOST
RELIABLE AND I CAN ONLY ASSUME THAT THE PARTICULAR ENGINEER
RESPONSIBLE FOR YOUR AREA IS AT FAULT.
LET ME ASSURE YOU THAT OUR AFTER-SALES SERVICE TO YOU IN FUTURE
WILL BE EXCELLENT. IN FUTURE YOU WILL RECEIVE ATTENTION WITHIN 24
HOURS OF CALLING THE ENGINEER.
IF YOU EXPERIENCE ANY OTHER DIFFICULTIES, PLEASE CALL ME OR TELEX
ME AT ONCE AND I WILL TAKE IMMEDIATE ACTION.
AGAIN, LET ME SAY HOW SORRY I AM. WHEN I HAVE INVESTIGATED THE
CAUSES OF YOUR DIFFICULTIES, I WILL LET YOU KNOW THE OUTCOME.
BEST WISHES,
HENRY REYNARD

Draft another letter or telex – or notes for a phone call to Fox.

Acknowledgements

The authors and publishers are grateful to the authors, publishers and others who have given permission for the use of copyright material identified in the text. In the cases where it has not been possible to identify the source of material used the publishers would welcome information from copyright owners.

Page 48 Saab-Scania AB; page 52 left-hand column – Philipp Holzmann AG, right-hand column – Siemens (Munchen); page 73 invoice form © Simplification of International Trade Procedures Board (SITPRO); page 75 Credit document. This document which appears by kind permission of Barclay's Bank is an illustrative example only and the details appearing on it represent a purely fictitious transaction; the signatures are also fictitious. In the same way any rate used is not intended to be accurate or an indication of current trends. Page 82 GKN Group Services Ltd; David Wickers for *On the money-go-round* which first appeared in the *Guardian*; page 98 The product enclosure is reproduced by the kind permission of Dove Computer Corporation, Wilmington, NC; page 111 advertisements for the Stafford and The Ritz hotels are reproduced by kind permission of Cunard Hotels Ltd; page 113 menu by courtesy of the King's Head Hotel, Wimborne; page 114 the illustration is of the Hotel Seiler au Lac reproduced by with kind permission of the Proprietor; page 120 The items in the collage are reproduced with thanks to The Cambridge Exhibition Company, The Cambridge Theatre Company, Cambridge Newspapers Ltd, Cambridge Computer Store, Cambridge Personnel, Cambridge Symphony Orchestra, Cambridge Arts Theatre; page 127 collage prepared with the kind permission of The Swedish Tourist Board, Iceland Tourist Information Bureau, Finnish Tourist Board, States of Jersey Tourism, Cornwall Tourist Board, the French Tourist Bureau, Wigan Metropolitan Borough Council; page 131 top advertisement S.A. Spa Monopole N.V. of Belgium, bottom left British Rail (this is a Young Persons Railcard 1987 Press Advertisement), bottom right Hutchison Whampoa Limited, Hong Kong (with special acknowledgement to Ogilvy and Mather, Hong Kong, creators of the Hutchison Whampoa print campaign); page 133 Nimslo Cameras Ltd; page 148 reproduced from the Ladybird title *How it Works – The Computer* by David Carey with the permission of the publishers, Ladybird Books Limited, Loughborough; page 150 illustrations based on a series of diagrams produced for a Philips product; page 153, 154, 155 Walkers Crisps; page 161 Martyn Halsall for *Business with a Fairer Face* which originally appeared as an article in the *Guardian*; page 167 London Borough of Camden Council and Southampton City Council; page 167 *Too old at 30* condensed and amended version of an article by Jenny Ward which originally appeared in the *Guardian*; page 178 extract from a section on Personnel in the Shell *Information Handbook* reproduced by kind permission of Shell; page 182 cartoon by Posy Simmonds which first appeared in the *Guardian* (text slightly amended) reprinted by kind permission of A D Peters and Co Ltd; page 190 collage compiled with the kind help and permission of Livingstone Development Corporation, Telford Development Corporation, New Jersey Division of International Trade, Wigan Metropolitan Borough Council; page 201 and 204 Innovations Ltd; page 202 and 208 Lucky-Goldstar International Corporation; page 206 NMB Corporation; page 220 Hydro Products, San Diego.

The cartoons on pages 19, 29, 30, 45, 67, 79, 95, 107, 158, 165, 174 and 180 are all reproduced by kind permission of *Punch*.
Photographs by Jeremy Pembrey.
Photograph on page 188 by Marc Anderson.
Drawings by Clyde Pearson.
Artwork by Ace Art, Peter Ducker, Hard Lines and Wenham Arts.
Book designed by Peter Ducker MSTD.